Horse Preacher

ELWELL CRISSEY

To

PAUL HOLSINGER,

*An
Enthusiastic Historian
and Superb Teacher.*

With Sincere Appreciation,

*February, 1990
Bloomington, Illinois*

Horse Preacher

A Methodist Circuit Rider
Travels the Prodigious
Tallgrass Prairies
of Illinois
During the 1830s

ELWELL CRISSEY

Blue Water Publishing
Tigard, Oregon
1989

Library of Congress Cataloging-in-Publication Data

Crissey, Elwell,
    Horse Preacher:
    Bibliography: p. 205.
    Includes index.
       1. Crissey, William Stoddart, 1811-1888. 2. Methodist Church -- Illinois -
Clergy -- Biography. 3. Circuit Riders -- Illinois -- Biography. 4. Illinois --
Biography. I. Title
BX8495.C75 1989 287'.6'092 [B] 89-1004

ISBN 0-926524-10-0

ABOUT THIS BOOK
Horse Preacher was entirely designed, typeset, assembled, proofed and readied for the printer on Apple Macintosh® computers and printed at 300 dots per inch on Apple LaserWriter printers. Completed camera-ready pages with all type and proof illustrations precisely in place were generated using Microsoft Word® and Aldus Page-Maker®. Original illustrations were scanned on a DEST® 1200 scanner and four illustrations were created using conventional 150-line halftone screens. The typeface selected is Allied Corporation's Times Roman, converted by Adobe Systems to PostScript for the Apple LaserWriter® and set at 12 points with auto leading. Original pages were printed using Boise Cascade Laser Paper. The mass storage system employed was a Rodime Systems® 45 Plus hard disk. The pages of the book are printed by Chehalem Printing of Newberg, Oregon, on 50-pound Weyerhaeuser DynaWhite Cougar Opaque vellum paper, while the cover is printed on 12-point Springhill Coated Blanks and bound by the Northwest Book Binding Company of Portland, Oregon. The OTA-bind process used on this book allows it to lie flat on the desk without snapping shut or cracking the spine.

Horse Preacher: A Methodist Circuit Rider Travels the Prodigious Tallgrass Prairies of Illinois During the 1830s

Library of Congress Catalog Card Number 89-1004
First Edition: 1989.

In

reverent gratitude

to the

METHODIST CIRCUIT RIDERS

of Illinois

Commemorating the labors and achievements of the Ministers of the Gospel who, as circuit riders, became the friends, counselors and evangels to the pioneers on every American frontier.

This heroic-sized bronze equestrian statue (opposite), surmounting the granite pedestal bearing the above inscription, was erected on the lawn of the Oregon State Capitol at Salem in 1924. Saturday, April 19 that year, the statue was donated to the State of Oregon by Robert A. Booth of Eugene, Oregon, and dedicated as a memorial to his grandfather, the Reverend Robert Booth who, during the 1870s rode Methodist preaching circuits ministering Christ's Word to pioneer families on the Oregon frontier. The sculptor was the distinguished Canadian artist, Alexander Phimister Proctor of Ontario, internationally renowned for his animal paintings and sculptures.

COMMEMORATING THE LABORS AND ACHIEVEMENTS OF THE MINISTERS
OF THE GOSPEL WHO AS CIRCUIT RIDERS BECAME THE FRIENDS COUNSELORS
AND EVANGELS TO THE PIONEERS ON EVERY AMERICAN FRONTIER

THE
CIRCUIT
RIDER

A description of the
Methodist circuit riders
of the 1830s quoted in
1879 by Charles
Chapman in his history of
Tazewell County, Illinois:

The ministers of the Gospel of the Saviour of the World hunted us up and preached to what few there were; therefore, we did not degenerate and turn heathen, as any community will where the sound of the Gospel is never heard.

I shall not give their names, though sacred in memory, for they were not after the fleece, but after the flock. They had but little to say about science and philosophy; they spoke of purer things.

President Theodore Roosevelt, in a speech delivered at New York City in 1903, entitled "John Wesley and American Methodism," paid this tribute to the Methodist circuit riders:

In the hard and cruel life of the border, with its grim struggle against the forbidding forces of wild nature and wilder men, there was much to pull the frontiersman down. If left to himself, without moral guidance, without any of the influences that tend toward the uplifting of man and the subduing of the brute within him, sad would have been his, and therefore our, fate. From this fate we have been largely rescued by the fact that together with the rest of the pioneers, went the pioneer preachers; and all honor be given to the Methodists for the great proportion of these pioneer preachers whom they furnished.

HOW THIS BOOK CAME TO BE WRITTEN

The inception of any book — that precise moment or event when something happened that eventually caused the book to be written — usually is too elusive to be remembered. With this book the moment when the earliest seed was planted, out of which it grew, can be pinpointed. For if the eminent English-born Methodist historian, James Leaton, had not been appointed pastor of the First Methodist Episcopal Church at Decatur, Illinois, in September 1878, this book could not have been written.

Almost as soon as Dr. Leaton settled into his parsonage at Decatur, he encountered "Father Crissey," the venerable and long-time member of his Decatur congregation, because the Reverend William Stoddart Crissey was the acknowledged patriarch of Macon County Methodism. Forty years earlier Crissey had ridden three Methodist preaching circuits on the Illinois frontier. Later he had been pastor of five prominent churches in the Illinois Conference.

Severe illness compelled Crissey's retirement from the ministry in 1848. The ensuing 15 years, however, completely restored his health, and during the Civil War he was appointed by Illinois Governor Yates as Army Chaplain to Macon County's home-town regiment, with which he served under General Sherman. His men loved Chaplain Crissey, and after the war Decatur people for years honored him as a war hero. Until his death in 1888, old Father Crissey was esteemed by everybody, not only as a Civil War hero, but also as a far-sighted civic leader, a tireless crusader for better education and an eloquent orator and preacher.

When Leaton came to Decatur in 1878 as a pastor of Crissey's church, he soon realized that it had been Crissey himself more than anybody else who had fathered the strong Methodist congregation of which he was then assuming leadership. As fellow clergymen, the two had known each other for many years. Crissey was 67 years old when Leaton arrived; Leaton was six years his junior. Inasmuch as Crissey was constantly and vigorously active in everything pertaining to Decatur's First Methodist Episcopal Church, inevitably, he and Leaton gravitated toward each other.

In 1878 Leaton already was compiling notes for his forthcoming *History of Methodism in Illinois* (the first volume of which would be published at Cincinnati in 1883). Crissey he found to be a brilliantly articulate raconteur and possessed of an accurate memory richly stored with recollections from the early circuits on the Illinois frontier — plus stirring mental pictures of Civil War battles in Tennessee, Georgia and Alabama.

Frequently, during his three years' residence at Decatur, Leaton visited in the Crissey family's little white frame cottage at 429 West Prairie Avenue, which Crissey had built in 1848, and in which he continued to live until his death, 40 years later. It is easy to imagine the two old preachers talking together there for hours, Leaton occasionally penciling notes. Obviously, something about Crissey's memories of the first preaching circuit he had ridden in Illinois ignited Leaton's enthusiasm as he subsequently wrote a detailed "travelogue" of the three-week-long Tazewell Circuit, describing each of Crissey's 25 preaching places and naming the names of many pioneer Methodist families then living in the five counties traversed during the Conference year 1831-1832.

Leaton at some point apparently said to himself: "Here is a first-hand eyewitness portrait in depth — an authentic living remnant — of the Illinois frontier in the early 1830s as actually encountered by one of Methodism's young horse preachers. Crissey's memories of his experiences are unique. I must preserve them for future generations by writing them out and setting the narrative in type." He did just that. Leaton's text, when set in 2 1/4-inch columns of eight-point type, filled 48 inches.

Being resurrected from memory after more than 40 years, its fabric of exact details is remarkable. It seems quite likely that Leaton wrote out his travelogue of Grandfather's year on the Tazewell Circuit at Decatur between 1878 and 1880 while Leaton was pastor of Crissey's church. If so, almost certainly Leaton showed his manuscript to Crissey for approval before taking it to the job printer in Decatur to be set in type and printed.

For many years the item survived unnoticed and forgotten among a bulk of papers safeguarded within the Illinois Methodist Conference Historical Archives near the campus of Illinois Wesleyan University at Bloomington. In 1949, Dr. George H. Thorpe, Conference Treasurer and Acting Historian, aware that my grandfather had ridden the Tazewell Circuit in 1831-1832, exhumed Leaton's unique description, and placed it before me.

A Gold Mine!

It proved a gold mine! For Leaton's (Crissey's) travelogue was so meticulously accurate, so detailed, so coherent that I found it possible, when I laid an Illinois map beside Leaton's text, to retrace exactly Grandfather Crissey's itinerary around the old Tazewell Circuit. That exciting discovery germinated my desire to flesh out Leaton's narrative by additional research. From that came my earliest writings, then expanded manuscripts, and finally this book.

The journey from my first discovery of Leaton's old text to the final publication of this volume that you now hold in your hand has been inordinately long. However, it must be explained that work on it was far from continuous. Across the years were periods of intense concentration on Grandfather Crissey's story, all of them repeatedly interspersed by numerous fund-raising canvasses, promotional campaigns and letter-writing seminars, plus the researching, writing and publication of two books. I do not regret the long lapse, for I feel sure that the interval between start and finish has substantially benefited this book by sharpening my critical faculties. At least, of this I am certain: this end result turns out to be a far different volume from the book I first envisioned. I trust it is also better for the wait.

Capricious and long was the pathway that finally led me into the orbit of William Stoddart Crissey's old Tazewell Circuit. Ever since my boyhood in Missouri I had known vaguely that my father had been born at Decatur, Illinois, and that his father lay buried there, and also that Grandfather Crissey once upon a time had ridden a Methodist preaching circuit. However, to my parochial ears "Decatur, Illinois" sounded so far away that I never imagined myself actually visiting the place. My father died when I was only two years old. If he had lived (and if I had had the gumption to question him) undoubtedly my father could have told me many enlightening details about his father's career in Illinois. Unfortunately, my mother knew little beyond the basic facts above mentioned.

Many years elapsed before I set foot in Macon County's seat. And by the time I arrived there in 1948, I was too tardy to find any members of Grandfather Crissey's family still alive. One lone elderly banker in Decatur confessed to me that he remembered my Aunt Margaret Crissey, "because she was a dedicated crusader against saloons and drunkenness." Clippings in the library of the *Decatur Herald* soon confirmed Aunt Margaret's zeal. But she had died in 1922, and by 1948 even the little white cottage on 429 West Prairie Avenue, where the Crisseys had lived so long, was gone.

On the other hand, I found that Macon County histories were liberally sprinkled with data about my grandfather, who, obviously, had been a Macon County civic leader and a man of some importance. Old Civil War Army records at Springfield verified for me that Grandfather Crissey in 1863 had come out of retirement as a superannuated Methodist clergyman, and had been commissioned Chaplain of the 115th Regiment of Illinois Volunteers. Other official military records showed that he saw battle action in Tennessee, Georgia and Alabama. When Grandfather returned to Decatur after the war, he agitated ceaselessly for improved schools and almost started a new college. A promontory in Decatur called College Hill commemorates to this day Grandfather's once-vigorous but abortive campaign to establish a Methodist college in Decatur.

The county histories told that in May 1856, Grandfather had been chosen by Macon County Republicans their "favorite son" candidate for Illinois State Superintendent of Public Instruction, to be nominated, they hoped, at the Bloomington Anti-Nebraska Convention. On May 29, Grandfather Crissey had listened to Abraham Lincoln's famous "Lost Speech" — the oration that retrieved Lincoln's career and pointed him toward the Presidency. Grandfather had ridden on the train, May 28, carrying the Macon County delegation to Bloomington. Abraham Lincoln rode that same train that day. I'm sure that Grandfather and Lincoln enjoyed at least a "Howdy" handshake introduction to one another; for Lincoln, always the politician, was an eager shaker of hands wherever he found himself amid a crowd of people. Undoubtedly, Lincoln shook the hand of every passenger aboard his train en route to Bloomington that day.

However, the germ of this book sprouted from things that had happened to Grandfather more than 30 years before he met Abraham Lincoln. When my family and I moved to Bloomington, Illinois, in 1948, it was not long before I realized that Illinois' long-ago chimerical city of Decatur was very much a real city of 100,000 or more people, and that it lay southward down U.S. Highway 51, less than 50 miles away. I then remembered, too, that Mother had often described Grandfather Crissey as "a Methodist circuit rider," and that he was buried at Decatur, Illinois, where my father had been born. I determined to visit the place.

Happily, at Bloomington I found Illinois Wesleyan University housing the historic library and archives of the Central

Illinois Methodist Conference. With the gracious guidance of Dr. Thorpe's research within that collection, I soon roused up Grandfather Crissey's revenant, and — incredibly! — a genuinely unique segment of Illinois history surfaced.

This History of the Illinois Tazewell Circuit Apparently is Unique

It may well be the only day-by-day detailed travelogue of a Methodist circuit rider in all American history. Journals by and books about both the great Francis Asbury and the picturesque Peter Cartwright are well known. But the records of neither Asbury nor Cartwright preserve a meticulous, day-after-day travelogue around a frontier Methodist circuit such as was preserved by Dr. James Leaton's description of young William Stoddart Crissey's ministry on the Illinois frontier in 1831 and 1832.

The historian who first perceived the unique value of Crissey's experiences on the Tazewell Circuit had been born in Crowland Parish, Lincolnshire, England, in 1817, and was educated in England. As a young man, Leaton emigrated to the American Middle West. Soon his natural religious instincts led him to gravitate toward that American denomination nearest his native Anglican Catholic theology in Lincolnshire — the American Methodist Episcopal Church. Eventually, Leaton chose to enter the Methodist ministry full time, and was admitted into the Illinois Conference on trial in 1843. His work proved satisfactory, and he rode the Jacksonville Circuit, and later pastored congregations at Sangamon, Jerseyville, Winchester, Alton, Griggsville and Quincy.

In 1850 Leaton became Professor of Natural Science in the Methodist-controlled McKendree College at Lebanon, Illinois. Because McKendree College was situated in the Southern Illinois Methodist Conference, Leaton transferred his membership there, where he remained until 1858. From 1854 through

1857, he was Superintendent of Mount Vernon Academy at Mount Vernon, Illinois.

In 1858 Leaton moved his membership back to the Illinois Conference, in which thereafter he served a long and important ministry, terminating in 1888. Leaton's roster of Methodist appointments in Central Illinois comprised pastorates at Springfield, Quincy, Jacksonville West, Danville, Bloomington, Carlinville, Decatur First Church, Clinton, Paris, Rushville, Jacksonville, Brooklyn and Griggsville. He served as Presiding Elder to the Districts at Quincy and Pana and in 1884 he was made Conference Centennial Agent.

Leaton was appointed Secretary of both the Conferences to which he belonged. In 1887 he was named Illinois Conference Historian. He took that duty very seriously. His brilliant research gifts survive in the three-volume *Methodism in Illinois*, covering the years 1793 through 1852. Only volume one was published; the manuscripts of two later volumes are preserved in the archives of the Illinois Historical Society adjacent to the Illinois Wesleyan University campus at Bloomington. Leaton was awarded honorary degrees by both Illinois Wesleyan University and McKendree College. He died September 10, 1891.

Retracing young William Stoddart Crissey's travels around the Tazewell preaching circuit traversing five Central Illinois counties derives its accuracy wholly from the detailed day-by-day travelogue, written and printed by Dr. Leaton. Interestingly, nowhere else in Leaton's writings did he ever trace precisely day after day the travels of one of Methodism's horse preachers. Why he minutely described young Crissey's Tazewell Circuit between November 1831 and September 1832, Leaton never explained, and neither did William Stoddart Crissey, for he left no journals, papers or diaries. It is a small mystery why Leaton minutely described Crissey's three-weeks circuit, but in doing so he contributed to American religious literature something of considerable importance. This book focuses upon a chapter of frontier experience in the American Middle West, described by an eyewitness. Apparently, it is the only item of its kind.

How It May Have Happened

Let us speculate about it. During the late 1870s Leaton was beginning to delve into the history of early Illinois Methodism. During those same years, at Decatur, sharing a modest little white frame cottage with his children, lived old William Stoddart Crissey, a patriarch of Macon County, universally venerated for his sterling Christian moral character, his statesmanlike leadership in Republican politics, his achievements as a city and county civic leader, his Chaplaincy in the Union Army during the Civil War, and his many years' eloquent preaching and ministering to Methodist Churches throughout Central Illinois.

It does not strain one's imagination to conceive Dr. Leaton as he pursued his historical researches, finding himself being referred repeatedly to "old Father Crissey who knows more about Illinois Methodism than anybody now alive." Then let us imagine Dr. Leaton while he was pastor of Decatur's First Methodist Episcopal Church visiting with the old preacher in his cottage on West Prairie Avenue, often talking together for hours while Leaton busily penciled notes. Assuredly, during those interviews the white-haired Methodist pioneer would have reminisced about that very first preaching circuit he rode in Illinois. The seeds of this book are Leaton's unique little travelogue, dredged up out of old Father Crissey's memories of the Tazewell Circuit.

Admittedly, the above is only speculative, but something of the kind is needed to explain Leaton's remarkable narrative. It is hard to believe that Leaton could have compiled such a quantity of accurate details about names, places and circumstances of the itinerary in any other way than through personal observation. But personal observation by Leaton was never a possibility. There simply was no other way Leaton could have acquired his copious notes about the Tazewell Circuit than by listening to Crissey.

Old Father Crissey's Powerful Memory
Preserved Every Detail

Conceivably, Leaton's meticulous reporting of details describing Crissey's circuit might have been compiled by Leaton if he himself had ridden horseback around the whole three-weeks' 250-mile journey with Crissey, stopping at every "preaching place" visited by young Crissey in 1831 and 1832, and taking down notes at each point while he asked Crissey questions. But Leaton was not ordained in the Methodist ministry until 1843. As a fellow clergyman, he certainly met Crissey at some of the Annual Conferences. But in the 1840s neither he nor Crissey could have spared the time to have retraced together Crissey's old Tazewell Circuit. Furthermore, there was no reason then for them to wish to do so. And by the late 1870s both Leaton and Crissey were too advanced in years to have undertaken such a punishing ordeal.

Undoubtedly, Leaton's unique travelogue of the old Tazewell Circuit derived from copious notes written down by Leaton while old Father Crissey's tenacious memory retrieved with amazing accuracy all those innumerable details about the Tazewell Circuit later recounted by Leaton. Among the liveliest aspects of Leaton's verbal trip around the circuit were his rather blunt criticisms of half a dozen religious leaders encountered along the way in 1831 and 1832. Leaton himself could not have known those people; what Leaton wrote about them could have come only from the old circuit rider himself.

Admittedly, concerning topography I have made some assumptions in describing occasional details. However, I studied early maps of the area delineating its prairie and forested regions, as well as its topographical features and drainage systems. I checked United States Geological Survey maps. I studied closely all histories of McLean, Tazewell, DeWitt, Logan and Woodford Counties. Collectively, these data have made it possible for me to reconstruct within the following pages a reasonably accurate description of the terrain and times traversed by young William Stoddart Crissey, and also some of his experiences as he rode horseback several thousands of miles across those prodigious Illinois prairies of the early 19th Century. Names and descriptions of places and all family names are transcribed from county histories. They can be considered accurate.

E.C.

Contents

How This Book Came to be Written   viii

I. "Merveilleux! Les Grandes Prairies d'Illinois"   1

II. The Circuit Riders Reach Toward Illinois Territory 29

III. How It Was on the Central Illinois Frontier
        in the 1830s   46

IV. The Circuit Rider's Life on the Illinois Frontier
        in the 1830s   66

McLean County, Illinois
        Forested Areas and the Prairies in 1830   83

DAY BY DAY AROUND THE TAZEWELL CIRCUIT

V. Beginning Week:The Long Trail Beckons Again   86

VI. Middle Week: The Loop Farthest Out   98

VII. Final Week: The Way Back to Bloomington   117

VIII. "'Tis Mercy all, immense and free,
        For, O my God, it found out me."   133

IX. William Stoddart Crissey, 1811-1888   148

Sources and Research   205

Acknowledgments   213

Index   217

I

"MERVEILLEUX! LES GRANDES PRAIRIES D'ILLINOIS!"

—ROBERT CAVELIEUR, SIEUR DE
LA SALLE, UPON FIRST VIEWING
THE ILLINOIS PRAIRIES, IN 1679

Wednesday, October 5th, in the year 1831, settlers in Western Indiana, peering out of their log cabins along the old Indian trail which a few years before had been broadened into what they called boastfully the "Fort Clark-Indianapolis Road," saw a young man riding his horse westward through the big timber. They might have noticed that his saddle bags bulged with square-cornered objects that looked like books.

The lone rider that day was 20-year-old William Stoddart Crissey, an ordained clergyman of the Methodist Episcopal Church, on his way back to the Illinois frontier whither he had been dispatched only a couple of days before by his Annual Conference at Indianapolis.

He and his horse forded the shallow Wabash River about seven miles east of the Indiana-Illinois border. Soon afterward young Crissey began noticing again the same phenomenon that had startled him two years previously when he first encountered the unique Illinois countryside. He had been then on his way to the little village of Paris, Illinois, less than 10 miles west of the state line. His year's residence there had somewhat accustomed him to the amazing Illinois prairies, but the spectacular wonder of the vast grasslands continued to impress him deeply.

What the young Reverend Crissey was experiencing that October day was release from the everlasting, never-ceasing canopy of trees that had shaded his out-of-doors life constantly as far back as he could remember. For he was a child of the great forest primeval of North America. That ever-present forest was

1

part of the life environment William Stoddart Crissey had been born into. He sensed it first as an infant in Connecticut.

When he moved with his parents to Cincinnati in 1815, the omnipresent shadowing trees followed him, and they followed him on to Kentucky, where he moved as a boy of 12. Not until he arrived at Paris, Illinois, in 1829 did young Crissey see a spacious countryside where strong, clear sunshine fell unimpeded upon natural meadows and prairies. For one who had lived his life under the perpetual shade of immense and ancient trees, these Illinois prairies were, indeed, wondrous to behold. These were grasses unlike anything young Crissey could have imagined.

It is regrettable that he did not write a book, as did his more famous Presiding Elder, Peter Cartwright. No diaries, journals or notes written by William Stoddart Crissey have survived. However, discriminating research, mixed with some creative imagination, makes possible a reasonably accurate reconstruction of the Central Illinois frontier as young Reverend Crissey experienced it in 1831.

Back in Indiana, the region served by the Paoli Preaching Circuit — young Crissey's first appointment after ordination — was country conspicuously different from that traversed by the Tazewell Circuit in Illinois. Indiana was the westernmost state (north of the Ohio River and south of Lake Michigan, that is) encompassed within the great primeval forest — that vast canopy of trees that once shaded almost all of the North American continent south of the Great Lakes and east of the Wabash River.

"This is the forest primeval"
—Longfellow's *Evangeline*

This gigantic stand of hardwoods exerted profound influence upon early American history, literature and folkways. No more eloquent description of this North American phenomenon has been written than that by Theodore Roosevelt in volume one of his *Winning of the West:*

2

Clearings lay far apart from one another in the wilderness. Up to the door-sills of the log huts stretched the solemn and mysterious forest. There were no openings to break its continuity; nothing but endless leagues on leagues of shadowy, wolf-haunted woodland. The great trees towered aloft til their separate heads were lost in the mass of foliage above, and the rank underbrush choked the spaces between the trunks.

On the higher peaks and ridge-crests of the mountains there were straggling birches and pines, hemlocks and balsam firs; elsewhere, oaks, chestnuts, hickories, maples, beeches, walnuts, and great tulip-trees grew side by side with many other kinds. . . .

All the land was shrouded in one vast forest. It covered the mountains from crest to river-bed, filled the plains, and stretched in sombre and melancholy wastes toward the Mississippi. All that it contained, all that lay within it and beyond it, none could tell; men only knew that their boldest hunters, however deeply they had penetrated, had not yet gone through it.

Another moving description of the North American primeval forest, and an evaluation of its effects upon the people who explored it, is that written by Nathaniel Wright Stephenson:[1]

Of first importance in the making of the American people is that great forest which once extended its mysterious labyrinth from tidewater to the prairies. When the earliest colonists entered warily its sea-worn edges, a portion of the European race came again under a spell of that untamed nature which created primitive man.

All the dim memories that lay deep in subconsciousness; all the vague shadows hovering at the back of

---

[1]From his *Lincoln*, Bobbs-Merrill, Indianapolis, 1922

the civilized mind; the sense of encompassing natural power and the need to struggle singlehanded against it; the danger lurking in the darkness of the forest; the brilliant treachery of the forest sunshine glinting through leafy secrecies; the strange voices in its illimitable murmur; the ghostly shimmer of its glades at night; the lovely beauty of its great gold moon; all the thousand wondering dreams that evolved the elder gods, Pan, Cybele, Thor: all these waked again in the soul of the Anglo-Saxon penetrating the great [North American] forest.

And it was intensified by the way he came,—singly, or with but wife and child, or at best in a very small company, a mere handful.

As late as the 1830s, these feelings still dominated pioneers in some areas west of the Alleghenies. Indiana was then an outer fringe of the great forest. But, in Illinois, pioneers pushing westward encountered open sunshine for the first time after a thousand miles of forest shade. Here was the beginning of the prairies. The encounter shocked them.

Something of young Crissey's astonishment can be discerned in the words written early in the 19th Century by the Englishman, George Flower, and published by the Fergus Printing Company of Chicago in 1882, *History of the English Settlement in Edwards County, Illinois, founded in 1817 and 1818.*

George Flower, born in 1787 in Hertfordshire, England, was a gentleman of wealth and education. After touring Europe, he came to the United States in 1816. Thomas Jefferson invited him to spend the winter as his guest at Monticello. The following spring, Flower organized a small group of his countrymen, and piloted them on horseback across Ohio, Kentucky and Indiana, reaching for the fertile prairies of Illinois, where Flower intended to establish his colony.

In his book, Flower remembered that his earliest excitement about Illinois had been awakened in England when he read

4

Gilbert Imlay's 12 long letters written from Kentucky, and published in America in the year 1797, *Topographical Description of the Western Territory of North America.*

Imlay confined his letters to meticulous descriptions of Kentucky only (as he had agreed on accepting the assignment), but one time Imlay pushed on westward across the Illinois country as far as the Mississippi River. About Illinois he wrote:

> We encamped on the southeastern side of the Illinois River, opposite to a large savanna called the Demi-Quian swamp.[2]
>
> The lands on the southeastern side are high and thinly timbered; but at the place of our encampment are fine meadows, extending further than the eye can reach, and affording a delightful prospect. . . . The Illinois country is in general of a superior soil to any part of North America that I have seen.

Flower admitted that Imlay's description of the faraway Illinois country "struck me forcibly." It was to be somewhere amid those fertile Illinois prairies that Flower was determined to plant his little English colony.

Flower's party had reached the Indiana shore of the Wabash River, still

> . . . determined to find these ever-receding prairies. But even here we could not learn anything of the prairies. Crossing a ferry, we entered the Territory of Illinois.
>
> By side of the road we were following, was a small log-house, our last chance for information or direction. Our informant, stepping from his hut, indicated with his arm the direction we were to take, across the forest without road or path of any kind.

---

[2]The Spoon River, joining the Illinois River opposite Havana.

"Keep a wagon-track in your eye if you can, and you will find the prairie." A wagon-track, or two ruts on the open ground made by wagon wheels, can be followed with some degree of certainty. But this was quite a different affair. A light-loaded wagon had passed a fortnight before through the woods and high underbrush, leaving no mark on the hard ground, and only here and there a bruised leaf or broken stem to indicate its passage. For seven mortal hours did we ride and toil in doubt and difficulty.

Bruised by the brushwood and exhausted by the extreme heat we almost despaired, when a small cabin and a low fence greeted our eyes. A few steps more, and a beautiful prairie suddenly opened to our view.

At first, we only received the impressions of its general beauty. With longer gaze, all its distinctive features were revealed, lying in profound repose under the warm light of an afternoon's summer sun. Its indented and irregular outline of wood, its varied surface interspersed with clumps of oaks of centuries' growth, its tall grass, with seed stalks from six to ten feet high, like tall and slender reeds waving in a gentle breeze, the whole presenting a magnificence of park-scenery, complete from the hand of Nature, and unrivalled by the same sort of scenery by European art.

For once, the reality came up to the picture of imagination. Our station was in the wood, on rising ground; from it, a descent of about a hundred yards to the valley of the prairie, about a quarter of a mile wide, extending to the base of a majestic slope, rising upward for a full half-mile, crowned by groves of noble oaks. A little to the left, the eye wandered up a long stretch of prairie for three miles, into which projected hills and slopes, covered with rich grass and decorated with compact clumps of full-grown trees, from four to eight in each clump.

From beneath the broken shade of the wood, with our arms raised above our brows, we gazed long and steadily, drinking in the beauties of the scene which had been so long the object of our search.

After traveling from the Atlantic shore to the Wabash River, a thousand miles of gloomy forest, or running the length of the Ohio and Mississippi rivers, with a prospect ever bounded by impenetrable foliage, the entrance into one of these beautiful and light expanses of verdure is most enchanting, the beautifully indented outlines of woods and the undulating surface of the prairie affording innumerable sites for tasteful dwellings, the ornamental clumps of full grown oaks scattered by the hand of nature so that they defy imitation by art, the bright verdure, rich herbage, affording food for innumerable flocks and herds, the beautiful flowers, the transparent atmosphere, the soft zephyrs wafted from the South in bland and rich volume, all combine to impress the enchanted beholder with pleasing feelings, even to delusion.

"Les Grandes Prairies d'Illinois!"

After weeks of toilsome, dangerous and seemingly interminable travel beneath the somber shade of the vast North American forest, European pioneers suddenly broke out from under the trees and saw before them the grasslands of Illinois. Within moments they felt their bodies bathed in mellow sunshine pouring down upon them from a spacious sky overhead. But what brought them up stock still, silenced by astonishment, was the green carpet of incredibly tall grasses, stretching away as far as eye could see. Theirs was a unique experience, never seen before by white men anywhere on earth, soon to vanish and nevermore to be repeated.

7

Considering the spectacular experience, the historian, researching that era, would expect that some explorer, eloquent of pen, would have recorded for posterity a panegyric of those magnificent tallgrass prairies of Illinois as witnessed through the eyes of a European suddenly exposed to the sight of them — say, about the year 1831 when the young Reverend Crissey first began riding his Methodist preaching circuit across those very grasslands. Alas, no such chronicle exists.

A contemporary description, wholly satisfactory — definitive and comprehensive — of the prodigious tallgrass prairies of 19th Century Illinois cannot be found. At least my exhaustive research spanning a number of years has not yet discovered it.

The nearest thing to it seems to be the 5,900-word chapter in Frederick Gerhard's book about the Prairie State, published in 1857.[3] Gerhard, living in New York City during the 1850s, was the scholarly editor of *Gerhard's German Reporter*, a publication of modest circulation devoted to assisting European immigrants to locate successfully in the Western American states. Early in his work, Gerhard found himself persuaded that Illinois, in every particular, was superior to any other of the Western territories. To promote its development, Gerhard determined to write an authoritative book about it.

During the fall of 1855, Gerhard journeyed out to Illinois, where he completed a remarkably thorough firsthand investigation. He began by interviewing at Springfield Governor Joel A. Matteson, Lieutenant Governor Dr. Gustav Phillip Korner, and Frances A. Hoffman of Chicago. The two latter were distinguished German-Americans, with whom Gerhard enjoyed an immediate and warm national affinity.

He traveled widely, interviewing "many other persons, such as farmers, merchants, physicians, clergymen, etc., who

---

[3]Illinois As It Is: Its History, Geography, . . . Climate, Soil, Plants, Animals, . . . *Prairies, Agriculture*, . . . *Geology*, . . . , published at Chicago by Keen and Lee, and simultaneously at Philadelphia by Charles Desilver.

have been long residents of the State, and whose personal experience is of much weight." He also compiled 119 letters and written statements from knowledgeable men throughout Illinois. Each man is mentioned personally in Gerhard's acknowledgements.

Gerhard's remarkable work, ever since its publication, has been considered by Illinois historians the indispensable source book of its era. Significantly, nothing in Gerhard's comprehensive evaluation of Illinois impressed him as profoundly as the magnificent tallgrass prairies — to which he devoted one of his longest chapters.

Gerhard, near the beginning of his definitive chapter, "The Prairies," quoted briefly from Captain Basil Hall of London, because Hall had described the Illinois prairies as he saw them in 1828. Hall, after years of service in his King's Royal Navy, during which he visited most of the world's inhabited seacoasts, came to North America. Somehow, he found his way to Illinois. Of course, he was much impressed by that state's prodigious grasses. Captain Hall wrote prolifically, and in one of his books he said this about Illinois' prairies:

> The charm of [the Illinois] prairie consists in its extension, its green flowery carpet, its undulating surface, and the skirt of forest whereby it is surrounded; the latter feature being of all others the most significant and expressive, since it characterizes the landscape, and defines the form and boundary of the plain.
>
> If the prairie is little, its greatest beauty consists in the vicinity of the encompassing edge of the forests, which may be compared to the shore of a lake, being intersected with many deep, inward bends, as so many inlets, and at intervals projecting very far, not unlike a promontory or protruding arm of land. These projections sometimes so closely approach each other that the traveler passing through between them, may be said to walk in the midst of

an alley overshadowed by the forest, before he enters again upon another broad prairie.

Where the plain is extensive, the delineations of the forest in the distant background appear as would a misty coast at some distance upon the ocean. The eye sometimes surveys the green prairie without discovering on the illimitable plain a tree or bush, or any other object, save the wilderness of flowers and grass; while on other occasions the view is enlivened by the groves dispersed like islands over the plain, or by a solitary tree rising above the wilderness. The resemblance to the sea which some of these prairies exhibit is really most striking.

Captain Hall's concluding paragraph is especially noteworthy, inasmuch as Hall himself had served many years on the high seas as mariner in the Royal Navy of Britain. The resemblance of certain aspects of the Illinois prairies to ships at sea, Hall wrote of in these words:

I had heard of this before, but always supposed the account exaggerated. There is one spot in particular, near the middle of the Grand Prairie, if I recollect rightly, when the ground happened to be of the rolling character above alluded to, and where, excepting in the article of color, and that was not widely different from the tinge of some seas, the similarity was so striking, that I almost forgot where I was. This deception was heightened by a circumstance which I had often heard mentioned, but the force of which perhaps none but a seaman could fully estimate; I mean the appearance of the distant insulated trees as they gradually rose above the horizon, or receded from our view. They were so exactly like strange sails bearing in sight, that I am sure, if two or three sailors had been present, they would almost have agreed as to what canvas those magical vessels were carrying. Of one they would all have said, "Oh! she is going nearly before the wind, with top-gallant studding-sails set." Of another, "she has got her canvas hauled up, and is going by the wind." And of a third they might say, "she is certainly standing toward us, but what sail she has set is not quite clear."

Gerhard Describes at Length Illinois' Unique Tallgrass Prairies

Frederick Gerhard began his long essay about the Illinois prairies, thus:

The most remarkable and striking feature, distinguishing the State of Illinois from the other States of the Union, consists in her extensive prairies, which are covered with a luxuriant growth of grass, and forming excellent natural meadows, by reason of which circumstance they received their present name from the earlier French settlers, commence in comparatively small scale, near Lake Erie, and occupy the chief part of the land about Lake Michigan, the upper Wabash, and the Illinois, predominating in the vicinity of the Mississippi; so that this vast prairie, intersected by strips of woods, chiefly confined to the banks and the valleys of the rivers. The prairies are characterized by the absence of timber; they present, in other respects, the same varieties of soil and surface that are found elsewhere; some extend in immense level plains, others as rolling, others again broken by hills, while nearly all of them possess an inexhaustible fertility, and but few are sterile.

Gerhard, while a knowledgeable botanist-naturalist and an astute observer, was also something of a poet. More than once, aspects of Illinois' giant grasses and luxuriant trees elevated his literary style into almost rhapsodic prose. Excerpts from Gerhard's invaluable essay (their sequence in places slightly rearranged to improve coherence), now follow:

Prairie-fowls, either in entire tribes, like our own domestic fowls, or in couples, cover the surface; the males rambling, and like turkeys or peacocks, inflating their plumage, make the air resound with a drawled, loud and melancholy cry, resembling the cooing of a wood-pigeon, or still more, the sound produced by rapidly rubbing a tambourine with the finger.

The multitude of these birds is so surprisingly great, as to have occasioned the proverbial phrase, that "if a settler on the prairie expresses a desire for a dish of omelets, his wife will walk out at night and place her bonnet on the open ground, to find it full of eggs on her return next morning." The plain is literally covered with them in every direction, and if a heavy fall of snow had driven them from the ground, I could see myriads of them clustered around the tops of the trees skirting the prairie. They do not migrate, even after the prairie is already settled, but remain in the high grass, near the newly-established farms; and I often saw them at no great distance from human habitations, familiarly mingle with the poultry of the settlers. They can be easily captured and fed, and I doubt not but they can be easily tamed.

[In the spring] the grass is interspersed with little flowers, — the violet, the strawberry-blossom, and others of the most delicate structure. When the grass grows higher these disappear, and taller flowers, displaying more lively colors, take their place; and still later a series of still higher but less delicately formed flowers appear on the surface. While the grass is green these beautiful plains are adorned with every imaginable variety of color. It is

12

impossible to conceive of a greater diversity, or discover a predominating color, save the green, which forms a beautiful dead color, relieving the splendor of the others.

In the summer the prairie is covered with tall grass, which is coarse in appearance, and soon assumes a yellow color, waving in the wind like a ripe crop of corn. In its early stages of its growth it resembles young wheat . . . .

In the autumn another generation of flowers arises which possesses less clearness and variety of color and less fragrancy.

In the winter the prairie presents a melancholy aspect. Often the fire which the hunters annually send over the prairies in order to dislodge the game, will destroy the entire vegetation, giving to the soil a uniform black appearance, like that of a vast plain of charcoal. Then the wind sweeping over the prairie will find nothing it might put in motion, no leaves which it might disperse, no haulms which it might shake. No sooner does the snow commence to fall than the animals, unless already frightened away by the fire, retire into the forests, when the most dreary, oppressive solitude will reign on the burnt prairies, which often occupy many square miles of territory.

On the lower, humid prairies, where the clayey stratum rises close to the surface, the middle or principal stalk of the grass, bearing the seed, grows very thick, having long and coarse leaves, and attaining a height of nine feet, so that a traveler on horseback will frequently find it higher than his head. Although the plants are very numerous, and stand alone by each other, they seem to grow up each one by itself, the whole effort of vegetation tending upward.

On the undulating prairies the grass is finer, and exhibits more leaves, its roots are interlaced so as to form a compact mass, and its leaves spread in a dense sod,

13

which rarely exceeds the height of eighteen inches, until late in the season, when the seed-stalk shoots up. . . .

The traveller on horseback then looks down upon a sea of flowers, over which float thousands of the most sumptuously colored papilios and scarabees, with the many variegated buzzing insects, while he is nearly overpowered by the penetrating, delicious perfume, with which the immense multitude of blossoms impregnate the air.

In the north the prairies widen, and frequently extend from six to twelve miles in width, intersected in every direction by groups of forests and woods, alternately advancing into and receding from the prairies toward the water courses, the banks of which are usually to be found lined with timber, principally of magnificent growth.

Between these rivers, [the Wabash and the Illinois,] in many instances, are groves of timber containing from 100 to 2,000 acres, in the midst of the prairie, like islands in the sea, this being a common feature of the country between Lake Michigan and the Sangamon River, and the northern parts of the State. . . .

Prairie Fire!

Toward the end of his essay, Gerhard quoted, with obvious enjoyment, the eyewitness description of one of these great prairies ablaze at night. The chronicler was Daniel S. Curtiss, author of a volume of travel experiences, *Western Portraiture*. "Our traveller," wrote Gerhard, "on an evening in the autumn of 1849, had the opportunity of witnessing, in almost a rapture of amaze and delight, the waving prairies on fire, for many miles around." Curtiss continued:

14

I was driving in a buggy, from Platteville to Mineral Point, and reached Belmont mound[4] just at the coming in of twilight. The evening was one of those bland, mellow seasons, usual in the time of Indian summer; and on reaching the centre mound, which lay rolled up and shrouded in smoke, handsome as an apple dumpling all steaming from the kettle, as I felt strongly tempted to know and see farther, I drove nearly to its summit, to take a leisure survey of the vast, flame-lighted, and enchanting panorama, flung out so profusely by artist nature; the moon and stars peered but dimly through the hazy air, adding mystic force to the scenes in the passing twilight.

Soon the fires began to kindle wider and rise higher from the long grass; the gentle breeze increased to stronger currents, and soon fanned the small, flickering blaze, into fierce torrent-flames, which curled up and leaped along in resistless splendor; and like quickly raising the dark curtain from the luminous stage, the scenes before me were suddenly changed, as if by the magician's wand, into one boundless amphitheatre, blazing from earth to heaven and sweeping the horizon round—columns of lurid flames sportively mounting up to the zenith, and dark clouds of crimson smoke curling away and aloft till they nearly obscured stars and moon, while the rushing, crashing sounds, like roaring cataracts mingled with distant thunders, were almost deafening; danger, death, glared all around; it screamed for victims, yet, notwithstanding the imminent peril of prairie-fires, one is loath, irresolute, almost unable to withdraw, or seek refuge. . . .

Next morning I again visited this mound, rode over the charred grass stubble to its top, the scene of so

---

[4] This eminence from which Curtiss observed the prairie fire was in the extreme southwestern corner of Wisconsin, 10 miles north of the Illinois-Wisconsin border and approximately 25 miles northeast of Galena, Illinois (then an important lead-mining region).

much terrific brilliance but a few hours before! Now all that was changed, the green-brown carpet was displaced by the black spread. The ravaging flames had consumed everything, black destruction sickened the heart in sadness — the keenest, darkest emblem of desolation that can be imagined.

Frederick Gerhard then concluded:

Wherever extensive prairies are, one-half of them is burnt in spring, the other half in autumn, in order to produce more rapid growth of exuberant grass, destroying at the same time the tall and thick weed-stalks, together with their seeds. . . .

Language cannot convey, words cannot express the faintest idea of the splendor and grandeur of such a conflagration of prairie, during the night. . . . If you know that the conflagration can cause no damage, you do not cease to gaze with admiration upon the magnificent spectacle.

"Red Buffalo": Friendly Protector of the Prairies

Surprisingly, while fire is the deadliest enemy menacing a forest, fire was a friend to the prairie grasses. Indeed, it is scarcely exaggeration to say that without the help of the annual prairie fires, there might have been no tall grasses surviving in Illinois at all! Written in his characteristic folksy, conversational style, an excellent explanation of this phenomenon is that by the well-known writer, John Madson of Godfrey, Illinois, in his *Where The Sky Began: Land of the Tallgrass Prairie* (Houghton Mifflin, Boston, 1981):

The grasslands had a powerful ally — a ravaging force against which most trees could not hold their prairie gains. Some of the plains Indians called it "Red Buffalo." The white man called it many things. It was wildfire.

Fires in tall prairie could be terrible, spanning the horizons with walls of flame forty feet high and roaring across the grasslands as fast as the winds. That wind was often a prevailing westerly that drove the flames against the most vulnerable front of tree growth — that tentative, insecure, west-facing beach-head where the trees were directly confronted by sweeps of upland grass. . . .

A grassland holocaust, by and large, is easily endured by native prairie. Grasses are highly fire-tolerant. Like their associate forbs, the herbaceous prairie plants, grasses are pre-adapted to fire. Their life processes are largely underground, out of reach of flames, and the fiercest blaze of early spring and autumn were fed by dead, dry plant parts during times when the vital processes of the prairie were safely dormant in roots, rhizomes, and underground parts that are shielded by a heavy sod. Temperatures in a prairie fire may reach 400 F three feet above the ground, but an inch or two beneath the soil's surface the temperature may rise only a few degrees.

Grasses and prairie forbs carry their winter buds safely underground. But woody shrubs and seedling trees, which bear their buds for next year's growth above the ground, are easily killed by fire.

Charles Dickens, although living in faraway London, heard about the amazing Illinois prairies. He made it a point, therefore, during his American tour of 1842, to include a side trip to view the Illinois prairies. Unfortunately, Dickens came to Illinois in the early spring, and therefore saw the prairies in their most dismal aspect; roads and trails at that season were quagmires of mud, while spring flowers and grasses had attained little growth. His report, understandably, was dismal and melancholy. If Dickens had come to Illinois in summer, doubtless his descriptions would have been happier. These are excerpts from the famous English novelist's impressions:

The track of today had the same features as the track of yesterday. There was the swamp, the bush, and the perpetual chorus of frogs, the rank unseemly growth, the unwholesome steaming earth. . . . We again pushed forward, and came upon the prairie at sunset.

It would be difficult to say why, or how — though it was possible from having heard and read so much about it—but the effect on me was disappointment. Looking toward the setting sun, there lay, stretched out before my view, a vast expanse of level ground; unbroken, save by one thin line of trees, which scarcely amounted to a scratch upon the great blank; until it met the flowing sky, wherein it seemed to dip; mingling with its rich colors, and mellowing in its distant blue.

There it lay, a tranquil sea or lake without water (if such a simile be admissible) with the day going down upon it: a few birds wheeling here and there: and silence reigning paramount around. But the grass was not yet high; there were bare black patches on the ground; and the few wild flowers that the eye could see were poor and scanty. Great as the picture was, its very flatness and extent, which left nothing to the imagination, tamed it down and cramped its interest. . . .

It was lonely and wild, but oppressive in its barren monotony. . . . In travelling the prairies, I would often glance toward the distant and frequently receding line of the horizon, and wish it gained and passed. It is not a scene to be forgotten, but it is scarcely one, I think, (at all events, as I saw it), to remember with much pleasure, or to covet the looking-on again, in after life.

In 1842, James Kirke Paulding, retired Secretary of the Navy and close friend of ex-President Van Buren, made a leisurely tour of the South and West, accompanied by Van Buren. Paulding's vivid three-paragraph description of the Illinois prairies, as he viewed them in 1842, was published in 1867 by his son, W. I. Paulding:

The prairie has a character, a physiognomy, and an atmosphere of its own. Just around you it is all reality; at a distance it is all doubt, delusion, mystification. Distances are magnified, or diminished; what seems close by, is often a great way off; and what shows dimly afar, is almost within reach of the hand.

What, in passing over, seems a perfect plain, exhibits in perspective a succession of light waving hills rising one above another pencilled in the skies. It is always level under your feet and yet you see a perpetual succession of little eminences, behind, before, and all around. At one time you behold a solitary house looming upon a rise, which, when you approach it is a flat expanse, apparently without beginning or end; at another a distant wood, whose straight line of deep foliage darkens the sky in which it seems to stand self-supported: — at all events, beneath is vacancy.

Occasionally, you see something sailing across this ocean of land, distinguishable almost as far off as a ship at sea. This is a wagon, freighted with the goods and chattels of a pilgrim journeying to the land of promise, and manned by a troop of lusty children. At first you can see nothing but the peaked ends of the wagon-top, covered with linen or canvas, shaped like gaff-topsails, and one cannot resist the impression always conjured up by the strange resemblance which an open prairie-scene bears to an ocean on which now and then a vessel heaves in sight. Hence these wagons are aptly called Prairie Schooners.

That mystical, phantasmal appearance of those immense prairies of Illinois populated by their giant grasses, when first encountered by white men, was noted and confirmed by the staid scholars of the Illinois State Department of Conservation in this paragraph, introducing their handbook, *Prairie Plants of Illinois*:

> Prairie is a vegetational community dominated by native grasses. Subordinate to the grasses are many colorful herbs that delight the eye of the traveler and observer. Interesting patterns are also created by the

rippling motion of the grasses under the wind, and shadows by the sun and clouds. The vastness of the land, its rolling topography, motion of the grasses, and changing light and shadows give the illusion of the ground heaving and swelling, and appealed to the same emotions as did the endless oceans.

More recently, a good description of the Illinois prairie as it appeared a century and a half ago was prepared in the 1950s by the distinguished scholar of the University of Chicago, Dr. Robert Havighurst:[5]

> Beyond the Wabash the Grand Prairie began its long sweep westward. Here the gloom of the forest ended in space, light, distance. Every traveler halted at sight of the prairie, as though he stood on an ocean shore.
>
> On the edge of the great Illinois grasslands, fertility shouted from the wind-rippled bluestem and rank bull grass, the tangle of pea vines in the hollows. On the swells profuse cornflowers mingled with waving stems of blazing star and bluebells. The prairie lay many-colored under its bending sky.
>
> For two hundred miles the grassland, broken by thickets of bottom timber along the Kaskaskia, the Illinois, the Spoon River, and the Sangamon, rolled on to the Mississippi. In this country timber was rare, infrequent groves rising like islands from the sea of grass. Some of Illinois' early place names designated the exceptional woods — Downers Grove, Troy Grove, Little Grove — as in Ohio the exceptional "plains" were distinguished.
>
> Northward, toward the long loop of Lake Michigan, the forest began again. The "oak openings" of Wisconsin and Michigan were meadows framed with

---

[5] An essay in *The Romance of North America*, Houghton Mifflin, Boston, 1958.

timber. And half-way up Lake Michigan came the deep, unbroken woods.

John Madson, previously quoted, has been for many years an affectionate devotee of the Middle Western prairie grasses, and he knows a great deal about them. Madson, like Havighurst, described the shocking suddenness experienced by the pioneers as they first encountered the great prairies:

> In many tallgrass prairies, the break between forest and grassland was shockingly abrupt. There was no gradual thinning of trees, no transition in which prairie grasses mingled with open groves. A man would walk through forest among many of the same flowers and trees that he had known in Pennsylvania, and then suddenly enter a border of wild plum, red-haw, and crabapple several yards wide, with an outer edge of hazel, dogwood, and coralberry that was canopied with wild grape. He would break through a narrow belt of sunflowers, and then out into an open world of limitless sky and distance. At his back were the familiar trees and flowers of the Old States; out front were prairie coneflowers and compass-plants, and a vast sea of grasses in an entirely new plant association. In ten strides he had passed from one world to another, across what was probably the sharpest, clearest boundary between any of the major floristic provinces of the New World.

In the 1830s nearly two-thirds of Illinois consisted of these remarkable natural grasslands. Gerhard listed and described 125 separate and distinct prairies existing in Illinois about 1850. All of these 125 individual prairies were encompassed within, and were intrinsic fragments of, what geographers of the 19th Century frequently called "The Grand Prairie of Illinois." Until well into the 20th Century, Illinois was often termed "The Prairie State."

The nickname designated the region lying between the Wabash and Mississippi Rivers.

Starting at the Illinois-Indiana boundary north of where the Embarrass River empties into the Wabash, and extending all the way north to Lake Michigan, the map of 1850 would have shown an immense prairie, almost devoid of trees.

This prairie was plentifully dappled with hundreds of islets of trees, in Illinois always called "groves." That grassland canopied all of Illinois to the Mississippi River in approximately a northwesterly sweep, almost to the Wisconsin border. Its only interruption was a broad heavily timbered strip paralleling the Illinois River and a narrower strip along the Rock River. The aggregate area of this vast grassland exceeded 20,000 square miles, not including the many smaller but still impressive prairies south of "les Grandes Prairies d'Illinois."

Nowhere On Earth Was There Another Great Meadow Like Illinois'

Illinois' Grand Prairie was unique; nowhere else in the Americas — indeed, nowhere else in the world! — have natural meadows ever existed exactly like those once luxuriating in Illinois. It required a unique concatenation to bring them into being and to sustain them.

First, they needed soil of extraordinary fertility. Second, they required a climatic cycle agreeable to the peculiar Illinois grasses, with ample rainfall. Third, they maintained immediate proximity to the hardy primeval forest, which was forever groping eager fingers westward, trying to capture new land. Finally, a controlling factor was the practice among Illinois Indians of burning off prairie grasses every fall. This they did in order to drive game into the woods, where it could be more easily hunted in winter.

Gerhard believed that Central Illinois' fabulously rich soil nourished such massive root systems beneath the native grasses that the prairies were able to survive these annual burnings. This is confirmed by Madson, who states that "in tallgrass prairie every cubic inch of soil surface is a mass of rootlets. Half a square meter of big bluestem sod may contain nearly thirteen miles of fine hairs and rootlets." Studied in recent years by botanists, the deepest of the big bluestem roots have been found to penetrate six feet or more beneath the surface. When air-dried, these root systems weigh more than four tons per acre.

When Central Illinois pioneers in later years first attempted to plow the prairie sod, they often were forced to hitch from five to eight yoke of oxen to a single plow (a specially built sod-breaking plow, able to withstand the tremendous strain), before the colter would cut through the massive, foot-thick 10,000-year-old turf. Madson went on to explain that:

> The symbolic grass of tall prairie, an official stamp of prairie authenticity, is the big bluestem or *Andropogon Gerardi*.
> This is one of the great dominants of true prairie, the most universal of the prairie's tallgrasses and a marvel to the early settlers who plunged into it and left accounts of big bluestems so tall that it could be tied in knots across the pommel of a saddle. That, and the stories of bluestem pastures so dense and deep that cattle vanished in them and could be found only if a herdsman went to high ground or stood in his saddle to watch for telltale movement in the sea of towering grasses. Such anecdotes are so common that they are trite; yet there's no reason to doubt them.

Madson, like Gerhard a century earlier and other 19th Century explorers of the Illinois prairies, found himself impressed by the profusion of indigenous prairie flowers populating the Illinois country. Says he:

> In terms of families, genera, and species, the tall prairie carries an incredible roster of native flowers. All the great families are there: *Iridaceae, Orchidaceae, Leguminosae, Euphorbiaceae, Labitatae, Scrophulariaceae, Rosaceae, Umbelliferae,* and many others. But all of these pale in terms of frequency and number of individuals when compared to the great family *Compositae* — the daisy family. Someone has said that tall prairie should not be called "grassland" but "daisyland," for the summer prairie is a flaming riot of goldenrods, ironweeds, bonesets, fleabanes, daisies, coneflowers, sunflowers, asters, blazing-stars, rosinweeds, compass-plants. The daisy, in some form or other, is as characteristic of tall prairie as are grass and grasshoppers.

Approached from the east, as mentioned by Havighurst, the prairies appeared first in slender strips of grassy meadows along the south shore of Lake Erie. Farther west, the country bordering the upper Wabash was interlaced with meadows, and most of the land around the lower curve of Lake Michigan was prairie. As for Northern and Central Illinois itself, "This whole region was nothing but a vast prairie, intersected by strips of woods, mainly on the banks and valleys of rivers," stated Havighurst.

Documentary evidence of the almost-unbelievable tallness of Illinois' primeval prairie grasses was published in 1826 in a book written during the 18th Century by Victory Collot, a French adventurer who explored the Illinois Hinterland in the late 1700s. Said he (translated): "The vegetation of the soil was so luxuriant, that a man on horseback is covered by the height of the grass. We measured some stalks which were twenty-one feet high!"

These grasses which made Illinois prairies unique, were — botanically speaking — themselves unique. The first white man to inspect the prairies found the grasses growing sometimes to spectacular heights, particularly in the sloughs or "swags," as Illinois' early farmers called swampy depressions on the prairie.

They found large tracts in middle Illinois boggy, miry and pocked with muddy sloughs and small ponds. After tilling made the soil dry enough to work, the earth often was astonishingly fertile, but an almost incredible amount of drainage would be necessary in years to come before the land could be satisfactorily farmed. It is estimated that the total mileage of drainage tiles now undergirding Illinois farms, if laid end to end, would circle the world five times — about 125,000 miles!

According to Dr. Arthur Watterson, former Head of the Geography Department at Illinois State University, Normal, these ancient prairie grasses had been growing for more than 10,000 years before the French explorers of the late 17th Century looked upon them.

Those tremendous Illinois tallgrasses that Professor Watterson said had been living — perhaps continuously! — for 10,000 years, possessed powerful life force. Their seeds, given hospitable environment, sprouted eagerly, sinking deep roots into the soil while rearing into the sunshine strong young stalks. The ease by which Illinois tallgrasses could be reseeded guaranteed their survival.

Beginning in the 1960s, Illinoisans interested in ecology and natural history embraced enthusiastically the whole herbaceous family of their state's famous prairies. The great Illinois prairie tallgrasses are coming back.

Before the white men intruded, Illinois' unique primeval grasses occupied more than 20,000 square miles of land. The white men's touch has been catastrophic. Forgotten remnants of the pre-historic tallgrass prairies surviving today in Illinois, still growing undisturbed from their ancient roots, can be found sometimes in thin strips paralleling a few of the state's very oldest, remote and little used roads or occasionally in the ancient sod left undisturbed alongside old railway rights-of-way and also sometimes in very old, often abandoned, rural cemeteries.

What A Young Methodist Circuit Rider May Have Thought about Illinois' Tallgrass Prairies in the 1830s

What were young Crissey's private thoughts when he first rode across hundreds of miles of Central Illinois' astounding grasslands? He left no written description; but, being the sensitive man his career records show him to have been, it is not too difficult for one possessed of imagination and some knowledge of Illinois natural history and geography to reconstruct the young clergyman's feelings as he and his horse penetrated the mysteries and the beauties of Illinois' virgin prairies.

Autumnal tawniness tinctured the landscape from horizon to horizon, for the year 1831 was far advanced when the young circuit rider entered upon airy grassy plains embracing tendrils of woods — small far out sentinels detached from that vast sea of primeval forest to the east. Of a mellow autumn morning, with the Indian Summer haze standing over the virgin Illinois prairie, he found its beauty intense and piquant.

It is easy to visualize why young Crissey, and other circuit riders who preceded and followed him exulted in those golden autumn mornings on the prairie trail: relaxed in his well-worn, comfortable saddle, his faithful horse beneath his crotch, he jogged along, his thoughts upon God and nature. He felt grateful to the kindly people behind him and to the expectant people awaiting him on ahead.

Topping a rise, all around he gazed upon the vast prairies bathed in early November-gold sunshine. At the end of summer, yet before the annual winter burnings, the high grasses he saw no longer stood tall, but by then lay bent over by the autumn winds, their myriad stalks matted together, looking like an immense yellow-green mattress. Although far from as spectacular as the grasses would appear to him in mid-summer 1832, nevertheless, the immensity of the vistas impressed the young clergyman deeply.

Yonder in the distance, he observed, nestled a grove of trees, enveloped now in amethyst. Here and there — always near the woods — light blue smoke curling from the chimney of a low gray cabin betokened a pioneer home. Shocks of corn standing off there looked like Indian teepees; and, on the far horizon, the dim purple of a forest strip appeared from a distance for all the world like a rocky seacoast seen far away.

These things focused vivid, colorful images upon the sensitive mind of young William Stoddart Crissey. As an old Methodist preacher living with his grown children in a little white frame cottage at Decatur, Illinois, he continued to cherish these mental pictures. Those virgin "grandes prairies d'Illinois," which had astonished Sieur de La Salle two hundred years before, had incised his memory indelibly.

And understandably! For 10,000 years they had canopied these Illinois level lands with their prodigious grasses. Probably young Crissey in the 1830s did not yet realize the full magnificence of Illinois' great prairies; but, by the time he was an old man, very likely he had come to know that what he had traversed on his preaching circuit half a century before had been one of the natural wonders of all the world!

II

THE CIRCUIT RIDERS REACH TOWARD ILLINOIS TERRITORY

When the first Methodist preacher entered that territory in the Mississippi River Valley now embraced within the state of Illinois,[1] George Washington was President, and when the first Methodist circuit riders came, Thomas Jefferson was in the White House.[2]

In 1793, Joseph Lillard of Kentucky, formerly a traveling Methodist preacher, crossed the Ohio River into Southern Illinois, gathered a few scattered Methodists into a little class, appointed a local leader for them, and then returned to Kentucky. In 1803, the Western Methodist Conference, meeting that year at Mount Gerizim, Kentucky, appointed Benjamin Young of Virginia to carry the Gospel to the Indians and white inhabitants of the Illinois wilderness. At the end of his first year, he reported 67 members of the Methodist Church residing in Illinois Territory.

These two "horse preachers" were the far outriders of a skillfully organized brigade of invincible Soldiers of the Cross, soon to push northward into the Illinois country. Far off on the Atlantic shore, this unique Methodist missionary campaign was being launched. It made inevitable the ultimate arrival of Methodist circuit preachers at Bloomington, Pekin, and at all the larger

---

[1]More properly that portion of the Northwest Territory later allocated to the state of Illinois. Hereafter, when events prior to 1818 are mentioned, this qualification will be understood.

[2]To be precisely accurate, it was not until after restoration of the Capitol during Madison's administration, following its burning by the British in 1814, that the term "White House" came into use; after the President's residence was painted white to disguise soot and smoke stains inflicted by the fire.

grove settlements which were beginning, in the second decade of the 19th Century, to populate the Illinois Heartland.

But this invasion, later so irresistible, very nearly died aborning. The Methodist Episcopal Church derived from and was closely identified with the Church of England; consequently, in the final quarter of the 18th Century, the angers ignited by the revolt of the colonies against their mother country threatened to snuff out Methodism in America. Not until after the famous Christmas Conference at Baltimore in 1784, which cut colonial Methodism loose from its English allegiance, did suspicions cease among many Americans that the Methodist Church was "Tory."

In that year of 1784, Methodism was almost unknown in New England, and it had scarcely penetrated beyond the Appalachian Mountains. The Episcopal and Congregational denominations were immensely stronger, while the Presbyterians and Quakers were flourishing, especially in Pennsylvania, New Jersey and Delaware.

The Remote Illinois Hinterland

Away to the west, across a vast primeval forest, lay the future state of Illinois — a wilderness of huge trees and great grasses. Soon it would be proclaimed a part of the new Northwest Territory, declared by the federal government in 1787 to be public domain. This vast Northwest Territory encompassed all lands westward from the mountains to the Mississippi River, and southward from Canada's border to the Ohio River.

Mad Anthony Wayne, George Rogers Clark, Vincennes, Kaskaskia and Cahokia are names vibrant with the dramatic happenings which secured Illinois for the American Union. Those episodes of the closing 18th Century decisively shaped the eventual peopling of Tazewell, McLean, DeWitt, Logan and Woodford Counties. Those historic struggles opened the broad stage across which the Methodist circuit preachers were soon to ride. Lacking those military and political events, they would not have come. Nevertheless, the military and political history of the Illinois frontier cannot be retold here. However, we must note a significant pattern; namely, while those events were unfolding, dedicated standard bearers of the Methodist Episcopal Church were tenaciously following frontiersmen into Illinois. There, they organized means to preach Christ's Gospel to Illinois pioneer families, wherever such could be found.

All of the Illinois Country, in the beginning, was administered by the old Western Conference of Methodism, organized in 1796. Everything west of the Appalachian Mountains was included within it. During those years, little churches (almost exclusively Protestant, and most of them Methodist) were beginning to appear in Northern Ohio, skirting the shore of Lake Erie, as well as at many interior settlements and along the Ohio River. Simultaneously, Methodist churches were organizing in western Virginia, in the Cumberland Valley of Tennessee, at scattered settlements in Mississippi, and quite plentifully in Kentucky.

Far off Illinois in 1796 was still virgin wilderness. The area which we have designated the Illinois Heartland was then inhabited by Kickapoo and Pottawatomi Indians and a few Delawares. An important Kickapoo town and fort stood in the southeast corner of what is now McLean County. West of the Mississippi River lay Spanish-French territory, hospitable only to Catholics until after President Jefferson purchased Louisiana in 1803.

In 1812, Illinois, insofar as it concerned the Methodists, became part of the newly defined Tennessee Conference. Four years later it was assigned to the Missouri Conference, which then encompassed all of Missouri and Illinois, plus Western Indiana. Methodist circuits were flourishing here and there throughout this spacious region, constantly expanding, following ever close upon the heels of pioneers. In 1815, five Methodist circuit riders were preaching in Illinois. They ministered to settlements along the Mississippi and Ohio Rivers, except for occasional missionary excursions northward to visit the Indians.

Francis Asbury

Francis Asbury

The Tennessee Conference — at one time, as we have noted, the mother Conference to all Illinois Methodism — in 1815 convened at Bethlehem Meeting House, Wilson County, Tennessee. That Conference was historic, because the venerated Bishop Francis Asbury, patriarch of American Methodism, then 70 years old, was present. Almost incredibly, he was completing his 60th journey across the formidable mountains to counsel with his western parish. Bishop Asbury first penetrated into the great forest west of the Appalachians in 1788.

He was, at the time, 43 years of age. Asbury had been born in Staffordshire, England, and received there a good elementary schooling, but he never approached the intellectual brilliance of the Wesleys. After studying Methodist literature, young Asbury at the age of 18 was licensed as a local preacher. At 21, he was received into the Wesleyan Conference, and four years later, in 1770, John Wesley dispatched Asbury as a missionary to the British Colonies in North America. Methodists in America then numbered fewer than 400 and were scattered chiefly around New York and Philadelphia.

When the American Colonies revolted against their mother country, Asbury sided with the Americans. Although John Wesley remained staunchly loyal to the Crown, his affection for Methodists across the sea moved him in 1784 to appoint Asbury General Superintendent of the new Methodist Episcopal Church in America. The appointment was confirmed by a conference of Methodist preachers. Four years later Asbury construed their official approval as conferring upon him the office of Bishop, although John Wesley never so ordained him, and objected vehemently to Asbury's self-ordination.

Nonetheless, Asbury's instinct had been correct, for the sheep of his flock were few and scattered along the forested and mountainous frontier. They needed a strong authoritative spiritual father. Asbury was that kind of a leader — conservative, autocratic, of iron will; but withal, intelligent and able to compromise as occasion required. All his biographers agree on his dominant source of strength: his amazing devotion to prayer. At one time in his career, Asbury forced himself to pray three hours out of every day; at another time, he set aside daily seven stated periods for prayers; and at another, he spent 10 minutes out of every waking hour in prayer.

Francis Asbury outrode John Wesley! In all, it is estimated that he covered 275,000 miles — most of those miles wilderness trails. He crossed and recrossed the Allegheny Mountains 60 times. The circuit which this Prophet of the Long Road covered every year has been described thus by one of his biographers:

> From Maine to Virginia, through the Carolinas, wading through swamps, swimming the rivers that flow from the eastern slopes of the Alleghenies to the Atlantic, on down to Georgia, back to North Carolina, through the mountains to Tennessee, three hundred miles and back through the unbroken wilderness of Kentucky, back again to New York, to New England, then from the Atlantic to the Hudson, over a rough road, mountainous and difficult, on to Ohio. . . .

The Homeless, Road-Weary, Old Wanderer Finds A Home, At Last

His visit in 1815 to Wilson County, Tennessee, was destined to be the beloved Bishop's last far journey. He died in Virginia five months later. Halford E. Luccock and Paul Hutchinson, in *The Story of Methodism* (The Methodist Book Concern, New York and Cincinnati, 1926), relate his end with touching pathos:

Slowly the old man made his way into Tennessee, where once more he essayed to preside over a conference. It proved his last Conference session. He placed his hands for the last time on the heads of men to set them apart for the ministry; he read for the last time the marching orders of a brigade of his devoted army. Then he wrote, with faltering pen: "My eyes fail. I will resign the stations to Bishop McKendree. I will take away my feet. It is the fifty-fifth year of ministry, and forty-fifth of labor in America. My mind enjoys great peace and divine consolation."

From the 1815 Tennessee Conference, he went back to the familiar road. He seemed to have no definite objective. He had no home to which to go. So he just kept going. As night came on he stopped with friends who eagerly vied with one another for the honor of keeping him. Once and again he stayed over a few days with those who would not permit him to proceed immediately. Back to the southern end of his familiar circuit, in South Carolina, he made his way, then northward. On the seventh of December, 1815, he made his final entry in his *Journal:* "We met a storm and stopped at William Baker's, Granby." But though his record stopped, the journey did not.

The idea seems to have taken hold of him that he should reach Baltimore in order to resign his office in person at the session of the General Conference soon to meet there. Although he was now so sick a man that a few miles of travel utterly exhausted him, he kept pushing on. Finally, late in March, he reached Richmond, in Virginia, where he was placed in a chair on a table beside the pulpit of the Methodist Church, and preached his last sermon.

The next Sunday, after he had reached the home of an old friend about 20 miles from Fredericksburg, still on his way to Baltimore, he died. The end came as he sat in a chair, resting his head against the hand of the young preacher who had been his traveling companion.

"The brave pilgrim's journey," says Doctor Ezra Squier Tipple, author of *The Prophet of the Long Road*, "is over. The greatest itinerant of the ages has come at last to the end of the Long Road, and behold there is a House at the end of the Road, and a light in the window and a welcome. At last the man without a home has found his Home."

Bishop Asbury, in bronze, travels the long, long road at the national capital.

Jesse Walker

In the early annals of Central Illinois Methodism, the name of Jesse Walker occurs and recurs, echoes and re-echoes. In all probability, it was he who first rode into the Illinois Heartland bearing a Bible and proclaiming his Lord.

To this heroic Christian frontiersman, Jesse Walker, the Methodist Episcopal Church in Illinois is more deeply indebted than to any other man. In Illinois, Jesse Walker was the earliest pioneer who carried John Wesley's church into the wilderness.

Jesse Walker started early. Kentucky and Tennessee Territories were the first lands west of the great Appalachian barrier to be settled by Americans previously confined to the Atlantic Coast. Jesse Walker was a product of those frontier families who settled on the Cumberland River around Nashville.

Walker was 20 years old before he experienced conversion in July 1786, and joined the Methodist Episcopal Church. His obvious sincerity and enthusiasm made him at once the class leader. His circuit preacher persuaded Walker to accompany him around the circuit, and later urged Walker to qualify himself for ordination and go forth as a horse preacher. At that time, Walker felt himself totally unfit because he was only an impoverished farmer, barely able to read and write, supporting a wife and several children.

As he related of himself, the voice of God's Spirit constantly spoke to his soul, "Go ye into all the world and preach the Gospel." Finally, in 1802, he yielded and joined the Western Conference of the Methodist Episcopal Church during its session at Strothers, Sumner County, Tennessee. Walker's preaching skill was never better than mediocre, but he had been set on fire by the mysterious flame of God's Holy Spirit. He was never able to interpret theology nor debate the doctrines of the Bible, but his love for Jesus burned with such heat that those who heard him never forgot him.

One of those who as a boy had heard Jesse Walker, many years later said of him, "Old Jesse Walker could tell the story of Jesus on His cross with such pathos and eloquence as to melt the hardest heart. He brought sinners to their knees, weeping."

Illinois Governor John Reynolds (1830-1834) knew Jesse Walker and described him thus: "Mr. Walker was a man of great energy and courage. He was very warm and excitable, and generated great excitement in his congregations. He was a short, well-set man. He walked erect and possessed great firmness, energy and perseverance. His complexion was sallow, his eyes blue, small and piercing. He was not a profound scholar, yet he constantly studied the Scriptures, and he understood human nature."

Another and even more vivid description of Jesse Walker, penned by acute and educated observer Bishop Thomas Asbury Morris of the Ohio Conference, a fellow churchman who worked with Walker in Kentucky and Illinois, depicted Jesse Walker during his prime years on the Illinois frontier in these words:

Jesse Walker

That readers may form some faint idea of the personal appearance of our hero, let them suppose a man about five foot six or seven inches high, of rather slender form with a sallow complexion, light hair, small bue eyes, prominent cheekbones, and pleasant countenance, dressed in drab colored cloths, made in the plains style peculiar to the early Methodist preachers, his neck secured with a white cravat, and his head covered with a light-colored beaver, nearly as large as a lady's parasol, and they will see Jesse Walker as if spread out on canvas before them.

As to his mental endowments, he was without education, except the elementary branches of English imperfectly acquired, but favored with a good share of common snese, cultivated some by reading, but much more by practical intercourse with society, and enriched with a vast fund of incidents, peculiar to a frontier life, which he communicated with much ease and force.

His conversational talent, his tact in narrative, his spicy manner, and almost endless variety of religious anecdotes, rendered him an object of attraction in social life. Unaccustomed to expressing his thoughts on paper, he kept his journal in his mind, by which means his memory, naturally retentive, was much strengthened, and his resources for the entertainment of friends increased. He introduced himself among strangers with much facility, and as soon as they became acquainted with him, his social habits, good temper, unaffected simplicity, and great suavity of manner for a backwoodsman, made them his fast friends.

As a pulpit orator he was certainly not above mediocrity, if up to it, but his zeal was ardent, his moral courage firm, his piety exemplary, and his perseverance in whatever he undertook was indefatigable. Consequently, by the blessing of God upon his labors, he was enabled, in the third of a century, to accomplish incalculable good as a traveling preacher. But few men, even of his day, performed more hard labor or endured more privation than Jesse Walker, and certainly no one performed his part with more cheerfulness or perseverance.

From the session of the Western Conference at Ebenezer, Nollichuckle, Tennessee in 1806, Jesse Walker was sent northwestward to help minister to the new Illinois Circuit. His Presiding Elder, William McKendree, accompanied Walker to Illinois Territory. Walker was profoundly impressed with the prodigiously tall grasslands he encountered in Illinois, with its salubrious climate and fertile soil. He told his Presiding Elder that in Illinois a great work for the Lord could be performed. Soon thereafter, Walker found himself appointed to pastor the Illinois Circuit. Dr. James Leaton thus described Jesse Walker's leave-taking from Tennessee and his entry into Illinois:

Reaching home about noon, by ten o'clock the next day he was ready to start with his family, a wife and two daughters, for his new field of labor, a distance of at least two hundred miles. Their only mode of travel was on horseback. After a tiresome jouney through the wilderness, in which they were greatly detained by storms and high waters, and suffered much from cold and hunger, they at length reached the Turkey Hill settlement, in St. Clair County, a few miles from which he located his family, and where he continued to reside for a number of years.

His parsonage was an old log cabin belonging to a Brother Scott. It had a plank floor and a stick chimney, with the hearth so low that the edge of the floor made seats for all the family around the fire. As soon as possible he entered on his labors, and it was not long before souls were converted. On New Year's eve [1807] he held a watch-night meeting, probably the first held in Illinois, and in connection with the meeting he held also the first Love Feast.

In 1824, the Methodist General Conference created for the first time an independent Illinois Conference, by splitting off from the Missouri Conference the states of Illinois and Indiana, plus adjoining fringes of Wisconsin and Iowa. When the first Illinois Conference came into being, that tract of Central Illinois here frequently designated its Heartland contained perhaps as many as fifty or more tiny frontier villages. Each settlement hugged an island of towering trees, while surrounding each of the groves lay the immense Illinois prairie — a rolling sea of grasslands.

North of these lonely little outpost settlements, all of Illinois between the Mississippi River and Lake Michigan lay a silent wilderness, uninhabited by white men, void of roads, unknown. The new Illinois Conference gathered all this region into its immense Sangamon Circuit.

Peter Cartwright

This spacious charge was assigned to a rugged and picturesque traveling preacher and Methodist Presiding Elder, who bore a name destined forever to be remembered by Illinois Methodists — Peter Cartwright. In the summer of 1824, the Reverend Cartwright, then 39 years old, moved his family by wagon from the state of Kentucky, to Fort Clark , now Peoria, Illinois, thence up the Sangamon River Valley to a little settlement west of Springfield.

Charles L. Wallis, who supplied a spirited introduction to the Centennial Edition of Cartwright's autobiography, published in 1956, wrote this colorful one-paragraph vignette of the famous Illinois circuit rider:

Contemporaries describe him as a man in maturity of medium height with a square, two-hundred-pound frame, and considerable physical strength. They quoted him as saying that he had a constitution that could wear out a dozen threshing machines and that he considered himself to be one of the Lord's breaking plows. He was distinguished by a dark complexion, unruly hair, high cheekbones, a resolute jaw, and deeply set, small, piercing black eyes — "a very bold and formidable look." He habitually wore a white hat with a broad brim which, an Illinois acquaintance speculated, had never been replaced.

Wallis opened his Introduction with this encomium to the Methodist circuit riding preachers by the renowned American historian, Edward Eggleston: "More than anyone else, the early circuit preacher brought order out of chaos. In no other class was the real heroic character so finely displayed." In the history of early Illinois Methodism, one rough-hewn bully of a horse preacher towered over all others. Much of the data about Peter Cartwright which follows will be drawn from his famous autobiography.[3]

He was born in Virginia two years after the Revolutionary War ended. His boyhood was lived in the wild mountainous country of western Virginia, not many miles from the Kentucky border. Cartwright inherited a physique and mentality ideally suited to his life-long career as the belligerent yet tender-hearted horse preacher who conquered the wilderness by sheer loudness of his bull-bellow voice, his tenacity, his astounding vitality, his animal strength, but more than all else, his faith in God. He left on the Kentucky, Indiana and Illinois frontiers of the early 19th Century a picturesque image, never to be erased.

---

[3] In 1984 the Abingdon Press of Nashville published a handsome paperback edition of the autobiography originally copyrighted in 1956 by Pierce and Washabaugh.

Peter Cartright

On top of a superb body sat a big rugged head, topped by a shaggy thatch of iron gray hair. His long black eyebrows shaded two deep-set eyes, black and shining with emotion. When angry, old Peter's eyes seemed to snap with fire as his voice rose to thunder. The Lord could not have chosen a preacher better suited to subdue the dangerous bullies and Godless ruffians who often intimidated settlers in Kentucky, Indiana and Illinois. His method of restoring peace when a ruffian tried to disrupt one of his preaching services was to seize the intruder, march him outside and thrash him with his big fists.

At a boisterous campmeeting, Peter Cartwright at 16 experienced a profound conversion to Jesus Christ as his personal Saviour; he dedicated his life work to spreading the Gospel. Two years later he was ordained a junior preacher and appointed to ride a circuit on Bishop McKendree's Kentucky District.

Cartwright was politically a fervent Jackson Democrat. By the year 1840, he had acquired so many friends, most of whom were Democrats, that he got himself elected twice to the Illinois General Assembly. By 1846, he believed himself able to get

43

elected to the United States Congress. The Democrats nominated him. What then happened is delightfully recounted by Luccock and Hutchinson, as follows:

His opponent was another Kentuckian who had also moved from that State to Indiana, and finally had settled in Illinois. He was as unusual a character in his way as Cartwright was in his. He had successfully resisted the efforts of Cartwright and all the other preachers of the period to induce him to join a Church, and, in fact, the common report of the neighborhood was that he was a skeptic. His following seemed to Cartwright to consist principally of the unregenerate. So Cartwright felt it well to combine a good deal of preaching with his campaigning.

One night Cartwright's opponent wandered into the meeting he was holding, and took a back seat. The preacher was hot after souls that night, and, after he had put all the fervor he could summon into his appeal, he called sinners to the mourner's bench. He even dared to do a thing which he had done time and again in camp meetings. He singled his opponent out and called on him by name. "If you are not going to repent and go to Heaven," he asked, "where are you going?"

The gangling politician thus addressed took his time in getting to his feet, but once there he answered, with apparent confidence, "I am going to Congress, Brother Cartwright." The event proved him to be right. For Cartwright's opponent was Abraham Lincoln.

In his 72nd year, old Peter Cartwright wrote out his own life story, which has since become something of a Methodist classic. There is no better way to verify the old man's prodigious labors than to quote now briefly from his closing chapter:

I have traveled eleven circuits, and twelve districts; have received into the Methodist Episcopal Church, on probation and by letter, 10,000; have baptized, of children 8,000; of adults, 4,000. I have preached funerals of 500. . . .

I can come very near stating the number of times that I have tried to preach. For twenty years of my early ministry, I often preached twice a day, and sometimes three times. We seldom ever had, in those days, more than one rest day in a week; so that I feel very safe in saying that I preached four hundred times a year. This would make, in twenty years, eight thousand sermons. For the last thirty-three years, I think I am safe in saying I have averaged four sermons a week, or at least two hundred sermons a year, making, in thirty-three years, 6,600. Total, 14,600. . . .

Thank God that during my long and exposed life as a Methodist preacher, I have never been overtaken with any scandalous sin, though my shortcomings and imperfections have been without number.

Pray for me, that my sun may set without a cloud, and that I may be counted worthy to obtain a part in the first resurrection, and may, O may I meet you all in Heaven! Farewell, till we meet at the judgment!

III

HOW IT WAS ON THE CENTRAL ILLINOIS FRONTIER IN THE 1830s

Every night during his year's ministry on the Tazewell Circuit—with only rare exceptions—the Reverend Crissey slept in the family cabins of his parishioners. His meals were eaten with these people. Most of his winter evenings were spent around their firesides. In warmer weather, too, he fellowshipped with them, sharing their hospitality, often talking cheerfully with the families during the long summer twilights, as they sat together out-of-doors.

Except for his lonely hours on the trails and his busy hours of pastoral work, the life of young Crissey that year was in many ways the life of the people he served. Therefore, to fill in and around this reconstruction of his experiences and the environment he lived in, we need to visualize in detail how the people lived who inhabited the Central Illinois frontier of the early 1830s.

Among pioneer families newly settled along any frontier two elements of nature — both wholly beyond their control — constantly engaged their alert interest, namely, weather and climate. Young Crissey arrived on his Illinois appointment near the end of the very year that had visited upon his parishioners a weather phenomenon that they all remembered as long as they lived. During their conversations with the young parson, references to it were very frequent.

The Big Snow

The winter which ended prior to young Crissey's arrival on the Tazewell Circuit was remembered for generations as "the most terrible winter ever felt in the Northwest." One of its effects was virtually to wipe out Central Illinois wildlife. Consequently, Crissey at no time during his repeated trips around the Illinois Heartland saw many wild animals. They had starved to death in the long-to-be remembered "Big Snow."

Proof of this was plainly visible to the young clergyman that autumn of 1831. At half a dozen places, secluded in the deep woods, Crissey observed from his saddle, patches of white, not unlike old snowdrifts. Curious, the circuit rider investigated them, and was shocked to discover them to be deer skeletons; thousands of bones heaped together whitening the ground — the pitiful remains of herds which had huddled together the preceding winter while the terrible blizzard closed in, only to starve when the deep snowfall made it impossible for them to graze or travel. Sometimes the boneyards covered a full quarter acre. Scattered frequently along the wooded sections of his trails, Crissey observed many other animal skeletons — all dramatic aftereffects of the havoc wrought by the storm, which old timers half a century later would still be talking about.[1]

The Big Snow began falling upon a vast region spanning the Mississippi Valley, the night of December 29, 1830. It continued falling steadily into New Year's Day. When it finally ceased, snow had accumulated to a depth on level places of four feet or more; drifts were sometimes 20 feet deep. Allensworth reported that, within the six weeks following the Big Snow, new snowfalls occurred 19 times in Tazewell County, and that snow covered the Central Illinois countryside until April 1831. For weeks, skies over the region were continually dark and cloudy,

---

[1] Among the Illinois Indians, old men and squaws of the 1820s described to the first settlers another winter equally severe, which it is estimated probably occurred about 1765. Prior to that date Illinois had been inhabited by herds of buffalo and elk. The terrible blizzard of the 1760s killed them off. This fact was confirmed by the numerous buffalo and elk bones still to be seen when white settlers arrived. After the fearful snow and cold of the 1760s, most animals native to Illinois came back; but the buffalo and elk were never seen in Illinois again.

day after day. High winds blew much of the time and temperatures remained bitterly cold — "so cold," some contemporary descriptions say, "that no snow melted for weeks, even on the south sides of cabins."

As mentioned, such terrible weather killed most of the wild animals. Fortunately, no persons died because of it, although human suffering was intense and universal. Many Illinois farmers of the early 1830s still depended for their winter food on corn and game. The storm cut off supplies of both. It was customary for Illinois farmers of that time, when their corn was ripe, to cut the stalks and shock them, leaving the ears in their husks. The ears were then shucked out in the fields, as needed. This was practical because almost no farmers of the time possessed barns or bins for storage.

But the Big Snow played havoc with this comfortable method. To gather a little corn for the table, the farmer found himself compelled to lead his horse into his field, with sacks thrown across its back. Where he sighted a tassel, he burrowed into the snow until he could pull off the ear. It was a slow, bitterly cold chore, repeated every day.

Firewood — especially because of the numbing cold — confronted him with a second emergency. During the icy freeze-up he solved it by venturing forth with his ax, heading for the nearest trees. He chopped off the exposed top, dragged it home, and cut it up for his fireplace. This feat was made possible by the icy crust which encased the deep snow — safe enough to support a man. The following April, after the snow had melted, the farmer, in astonishment, no doubt, looked upon tree boles all around him towering up high enough to be cut down and split into fence rails.

Even with the coming of thaw, the fearful winter was not finished. Charles Chapman adds another weather datum about 1831 so unusual as to be almost unbelievable. He states that "Frost came every month of the year of 1831." Farming began very late that spring, and the corn crop in Central Illinois was a failure,

48

which explains its extremely high price during the winter of 1831-1832. It is small wonder, indeed, that Central Illinois pioneers who lived through the Big Snow for the rest of their lives dated events as occurring such and such a time "before the Big Snow" or "after the Big Snow." It was something worth remembering.

Young Crissey's first time around his new circuit in October 1831, was a three-week-long struggle against mire, thickets and driftwood at the fords. The myriads of flies, continuous in warm weather, had remained after the first frost. The previous winter's tremendous accumulation of snow had left — even as late as the following fall — some of Crissey's trails loblollies of black mud. Creeks and rivers all around his circuit had been in flood that year, often out of their banks, and heavy debris and driftwood were scattered everywhere. All during that wet, frosty summer of 1831 brooks and rills had overflowed continually.

It was not a comfortable beginning for Crissey's Illinois ministry. But he was a young man of will and dedication. The motives which drove the youthful preacher on from station to station week after week were infinitely stronger than the mere discomforts which he personally suffered. Eventually, he would look back on the beginning of this ministry with deep satisfaction.

The Houses They Lived In

Even in the two largest towns on his circuit — Pekin and Bloomington/Blooming Grove — almost all habitations were of logs. Pekin, however, by contrast, contained more than a score of frame cottages made of crude, rough-sawed planks. And Pekin in 1831 boasted one brick house. Log cabins, of necessity, usually were small, although James Allin's double house in Bloomington, and John Patton's on Money Creek, were more spacious.

Isaac Funk's second cabin, built in 1832, in which the Reverend Crissey sometimes preached, was a somewhat better cabin than most. It measured 18 feet square. It was constructed of hewn logs, notched and dove-tailed closely on the corners, the chinks sealed with dried mud that had to be renewed every fall. Its roof was overlapped by heavy 2-foot by 2-foot square clapboards. It had a puncheon[2] floor, which fact set it apart from most cabins of the time, which had only dirt floors. Opposite the heavy plank door was one window, glazed with greased paper, which also needed frequent repairs. The entire ground level within the Funk cabin was one big room. Above this was a low ceiled loft, reached by a ladder.

A huge fireplace and chimney occupied almost all of one inside wall. The Funk chimney was built of small logs, protected from heat by a lining of stone and mud. (This "protection" obviously was faulty, inasmuch as Funk's first three cabins on the site burned down.) The Funk hearth was so wide it devoured logs three feet thick, which burned sometimes as long as a week. Nevertheless, huge as the fireplace was, on cold winter evenings

---

[2] "Puncheon," a very common word in frontier times, nowadays is unfamiliar. A puncheon was a heavy log, roughly trimmed, and smoothed by axe on one face. Laid snugly side by side, over the earth, smooth faces uppermost, a puncheon floor was sound, warm and dry.

the family — to quote an expression common on the frontier — "roasted on one side and froze on the other." The Funk fireplace had a sunken hearth, depressed 18 inches below the floor level. This handy arrangement eliminated the need for extra chairs.

Crissey's route covered a tenuous three-week circuit of 250 miles across parts of five counties. Wherever feasible, the circuit rider followed segments of the ancient Indian trails, because they afforded him the easiest and most comfortable riding. American Indians, like the canny buffalo before them, were expert trail breakers. Their routes were never straight, but always followed more or less level contours, which, although longer, avoided exhausting grades.[3]

Wildlife

The year just before young William Stoddart Crissey appeared upon the Tazewell Circuit, the prairies and groves covering the Illinois Heartland had been abundantly populated with birds, animals and game.

There were flocks of wild turkeys, partridges, prairie chickens and quails. The woods concealed herds of deer, and innumerable foxes, raccoons, "ground hogs" (woodchucks), oppossums and squirrels. Myriads of rabbits made their homes on the prairie. Skunks and weasels, too, were numerous everywhere, while every creek supported its colonies of beavers, otters, minks, and muskrats. All creeks and rivers were teeming with edible fish.

Almost always at night, the staccato barks of prairie wolves could be heard out in the grass. When a full moon excited them, howling wolves often awakened sleeping families and started the settlers' dogs barking for miles around. One old Illinois Tazewell County pioneer depicted the uproar by this

---

[3] During the second half of the 19th Century, railroad civil engineers surveying rights-of-way often followed closely these same ancient trails, laid out in prehistoric times by the buffalos and the Indians.

picturesque simile: "Suppose six boys, having six dogs tied, whipped them all at the same time, and you would hear such music as two wolves would make."

In the 1830s, the Illinois prairies were thickly populated with wolves. Margaret Young of Elm Grove Township, Tazewell County, was a girl in her teens at that time, and remembered once counting seven prairie wolves, all visible at once, as she watched from her father's cabin door. Deep within the big groves lurked a few of the larger black timber wolves. Not infrequently, particularly up in the primitive backwoods of Woodford County, wildcats were heard caterwauling, and, occasionally, panthers and bears were seen.

Overhead, the sky was sometimes blackened by prodigious flights of passenger pigeons. The roar of their wings, like thunder, could be heard several miles away. Incessantly, all through the summer and autumn, crows, blackbirds and blue jays kept up their noisy talk from the trees. Near all water courses, numerous flocks of wild geese fed and gabbled.

Underfoot, the beauty of the summer prairies to the early settlers was less appealing — especially to their womenfolk. The ground beneath the grass sheltered many snakes. Most Illinois snakes were harmless, but they grew to remarkable sizes. W.S. Radford, a pioneer settler of Pekin, remembered "seeing one timber blacksnake ten feet long." Of genuine danger were the prairie and timber rattlesnakes. With few doctors, usually far away, a rattler's bite could be extremely serious. On the trail during the warm weather of 1832, the Reverend Crissey's horse, every once in a while, shied or reared at the warning buzz of a rattler. It was always an unsettling experience.

Frontier Furniture

Outside the two towns on Crissey's Tazewell Circuit, all families lived in log cabins. Furniture inside these rude dwellings was, of necessity, in character with the buildings. The most conspicuous article was a big high bed for the father and mother fluffed up in winter by a goose feather ticking, weighted down by home-made quilts — some of them highly artistic. Under the big bed was a trundle bed for the small children (almost no pioneer couple was childless). A growing family living in a small cabin soon confronted an almost desperate problem of congestion, usually resolved by adding rooms or building a bigger house.

A board table, used constantly for every kind of duty, occupied the center of the cabin. Along the walls might be two or three split-bottomed chairs. Back in one corner almost always stood a spinning wheel, sometimes two spinning wheels, the big one for woolen yarn, the little wheel for flax. Over the fireplace or above the door hung a musket and powder horn or perhaps a "long-rifle" brought from Kentucky or Tennessee, always a cherished possession, because target practice was a favorite sport on the frontier, and a long rifle could outshoot a musket any day.

The cabin's simple furniture was completed, usually, by a small chest or trunk, transported lovingly overland by the woman of the family from her girlhood home back East. Its mysterious contents on the perilous journey included dishes, pewter or silverware, and a few goblets, and, almost invariably, a mirror.

Kitchen utensils in the Funk cabin were typical of the time. All were of heavy iron, styled and adapted for open hearth cooking: a "spider" — a long-handled deep frying pan with a lid and eight-inch legs, which raised the vessel above the coals, two or three kettles of assorted sizes, and a Dutch oven for baking.

Each cabin's hearth was the very navel of the family it sheltered, for without fire, frontier survival was impossible. The hearth fire, therefore, was pampered and beloved, almost as if it were a living presence. Every cabin strived to keep its fire alive. Even in hottest summer, its embers slumbered beneath a blanket of ashes. If, by great misfortune, the fire died, it had to be rekindled from sparks struck off by hitting a piece of flint sharply against a small bar of steel. The hot sparks, tenderly nurtured against dry shredded wood, could be blown into flame. Often, fire borrowed from a neighbor was transported in a covered metal bucket or kettle. It was not until well into the 1840s that phosphorous matches arrived on the Illinois frontier.[4]

This They Called "Belly Timber"

Food in the 1820s and early 1830s on the Illinois frontier comprised cracked corn, cooked in a variety of ways, fresh and dried fish, freshly killed venison, wild turkey, passenger pigeons, rabbits, squirrels and, once in a long while, bear steaks. In summer there were wild blackberries and strawberries. In early spring, the hard maple trees provided sweet sap from which the settlers boiled down sugar and syrup. Often, in summer wild honey could be taken from the bee trees.

Nearly always, there was a scarcity of what the pioneers called "bread stuffs." Grist mills in the Tazewell Circuit region of the 1830s, were few and often far away.[5] Consequently, frontier housewives doled out their white flour sparingly. Hot biscuits were a very special family treat, reserved only for Sunday or "company." Probably, our young clergyman, since he always qualified as a special guest wherever he stopped, ate a great many hot biscuits! "Light bread" was sometimes attempted by pouring boiling water over white wood ashes to leach out the lye, after which the rinsed ashes were used as a substitute for baking powder.

The one staple food item the Illinois pioneers craved most, but seldom enjoyed, was "store-boughten" coffee. Genuine

---

[4] The first U.S. patent for matches was issued in 1836 to Alonzo Dwight Phillips of Springfield, Massachussetts. Its combustible head was a mixture of phosphorus, chalk and glue.

[5] Most of these mills on the prairie were powered, not by water or wind, but by a horse walking a treadmill. The miller's customary toll for grinding grain was "one bit (12 $\frac{1}{2}$ cents) per bushel."

coffee could be purchased at Springfield, Pekin, Bloomington/ Blooming Grove, Old Mackinaw Town and Wesley City. But it was discouragingly expensive, while most pioneer families possessed very little ready money. Coffee, too, therefore, was something the family hoarded. Coffee was brewed only on Sundays or when entertaining guests. Some frontier housewives, in desperation, tried making their own home-grown coffee substitute by roasting and grinding okra beans. Lacking aroma, flavor and stimulant, it was never popular. In Bloomington/Blooming Grove and Pekin, provisions were more varied and ample. But even in those places it was a decade before genuine coffee became an always accessible staple.

Another item in Illinois frontier cookery was as hard to come by as coffee, but, unlike coffee, salt was indispensable. Among settlers at Bloomington/Blooming Grove, salt came from the well-known salt springs near Danville. Salt was packed horseback into the settlement over the trails, and sold at high prices. Frequently, too, men and boys visited the Danville salt spring and bought the evaporated salt following a trip to a grist mill.

By the early 1830s, the more enterprising settlers in the Tazewell Circuit region were beginning to raise cows and chickens — which greatly improved the scope of their wives' menus. Many pioneers had come to Illinois from the East and the South, driving a few cows with them, along with their horses and oxen. Milk, cream and butter, therefore, were not uncommon foods on the frontier tables. Refrigeration, of a sort, was occasionally possible by constructing a spring house. But artesian springs occur usually in hilly or mountainous terrain, and Central Illinois, by and large, was prairie country with few springs.

Almost every frontier home possessed at least one dog, often several, and not infrequently a house cat. Often, in a rail-fenced pen nearby were to be seen a few sheep which produced the family's wool. Raising them necessitated a ceaseless battle against wolves, and many sheep were lost in the war. If a farmer

55

was keeping sheep, a dog on the place was all but indispensable. A wolf could kill a dog, but the dog's usefulness lay not in fighting, but as sentry.

Wearing Apparel

Clothing was simple and strictly practical, roughly tailored out of wool, flax, cotton or tow-linen. In summer, most men wore a crude hat plaited from rye, oats or wheat straw. Summer shirts and pants were of cotton, flax or tow-linen cloth. In winter, men and boys wore woolen clothes, almost always homespun. In the 1830s, a few buckskins were still to be seen. Overcoats, caps and mittens often were of fur, although hats of beaver felt could be purchased where there were stores. Boots and shoes were hand-made by local or traveling cobblers. All summer long, boys (and sometimes their fathers, also) went everywhere barefooted. At Christmas time, frontier boys usually expected to receive a pair of "red-topped" boots.

Illinois pioneer women wore dresses home-made of "linsey-woolsey." It was a durable cloth woven as the women of that day described it, "the chain of linen, the filling of wool." Weaving it required a loom, but in every neighborhood there was always at least one loom used frequently by every family. The typical maid on the early frontier yearned for a calico dress, which most of them managed to acquire before they were married. Their mothers were overjoyed to receive occasionally from town a bolt of muslin.

Hard work on the frontier was almost continuous and often back-breaking. In Bloomington/Blooming Grove and Pekin, at Springfield and Old Mackinaw Town, were shops and stores and a growing variety of trades which kept the townsfolk busy. But more than nine out of 10 frontiersmen in Central Illinois in the 1830s were farmers.

Clearing land, improving buildings, planting, tending and harvesting crops, raising cattle, hogs, and sheep: these duties filled the farmer's day from dawn to dusk. In the Tazewell Circuit region, a new settler coming to Illinois could expect to invest in his land, on the average, about 10 years of toil and self-denial, before he could finally achieve a dependable financial security. In the language of the 1830s, "It takes ten years hard work to reach easier times."

These early Illinois farmers, like their progeny 120 years later, wrestled with the problem of overproduction. Their soil was so fertile, their seasons so salubrious, that quite early they found their harvests too big. They had no room in which to store surplus grain, no place to pasture their ever-enlarging herds. Market prices for grain hardly paid for hauling it. On the Pekin market in the late 1830s, wheat sold for 25 cents per bushel, dressed hogs for $1.10 per hundredweight. It was an era, not so much of "tight money" as of "no money." On the Illinois frontier, very little currency circulated. Consequently, much trade was barter-swapping commodities without the exchange of money.

Because these Central Illinois farmers found themselves growing too much, they began limiting their plantings to the amount of grain which their families and livestock could eat. At times it seemed a discouraging and unrewarding life. Yet, all was not toil. There were amusements and many happy hours of recreation. The men of a Sunday afternoon usually would get together and race horses, argue politics, pitch horseshoes or compete in target practice. Trips to the mill were a welcome break in the monotony, and every now and then a cabin full of neighbors would gather to sing and play favorite games.

The Loneliness Was Almost Unbearable

Many as were the hardships on the frontier, none was harder to endure than the loneliness of it. To ward off the depressing solitude, frontier families attached prime importance to public gatherings of all kinds. They came eagerly, across many miles, sometimes through vile weather, just for the pleasure of "seeing folks."

Favorite occasions were cabin-raisings and log-rollings. These would pull together men folk for miles around, with their wives and children. The men pitched into the hard work while the women cooked a big meal. At sundown the meal was eaten with much jollity. Rustic games and square dancing followed. Corn huskings brought both sexes into the work at the same time. Banter, gossip and laughter kept the circle entertained. Finders of red ears collected kisses all around the barn. Quilting bees and apple parings,strictly feminine parties, were thoroughly enjoyed.

Of quite a different relish, but, in its way, enjoyed fully as much as the rustic jollifications, was the visit, once every three weeks during 1831 and 1832, of the Methodist circuit rider. Invariably, his visit was considered an important occasion, and was looked forward to with pleasure. The circuit rider brought spiritual refreshment, and also a welcome breath of news from the world outside.

What manner of folk were these men and women who emigrated into the Illinois wilderness, and eventually civilized it? A description of their behavior has been left by James Haines, one of the earliest settlers in Pekin:

All were common in speech, some rude in manner, few boisterous, mostly quiet in speech and slow in movement. Very little refined as now gauged. In learning from books — outside the Bible — hymns, song music and school books. Intercourse between intimates and close relations, frank, laconic, abrupt, good natured; with acquaintances only, and strangers, inquisitive, genial, tolerant. These characteristics I recall in men mostly. The women conformed in milder degree to each phase of speech, manner and action.

Obviously, among such people, the Reverend Crissey was conspicuous, not only because he was accorded unusual respect as an ordained minister of the Church, but equally because he was, by comparison, a scholar. Most Central Illinois settlers were literate, but — excepting the lawyers at the county seats, and the few scattered doctors — almost none had attended college.

Life on the Illinois frontier in the 1830s was strenuous and hazardous. Heavy lifting, back-straining work, use of crude tools, day in and day out, brought mishaps and injuries. And when accidents came, skilled medical care was slow to arrive, or almost impossible to find. Consequently, grave illnesses were ever to be dreaded. Frontier life was especially hard on children. The old cemeteries, populated with infants' graves, attest to how many sickly babies and children suffered and died. Usually, only the robust survived. Married women, too, on the American frontier endured much and usually died in middle years or sooner. They bore many babies, and their day-to-day work was hard. Many were heroic souls, cherished by their families, martyrs to the frontier, but they did not think themselves ill-used.

Diseases of the Frontier

Considering the ever-present dangers, the exposure, the lack of protection and sanitation, it is remarkable that there was not much more illness. Malaria among Illinois pioneers during the

1830s was perennial and was especially bad each fall in settlements near the rivers and sloughs. In places like Pekin, almost everybody grew pale and jaundiced every autumn. Malarial chills attacked every other day at regular, predictable intervals. After a severe siege of chills and fever, the victim felt languid, stupid, sore and depressed, and recuperated slowly.

Winter exposure and overwork brought on colds — sometimes pneumonia, considered very deadly. Poultices, homemade salves, herbal brews, and Indian medicines often were the only remedies. Whiskey, among frontier families, was a respected and almost universal medicine. Virtually every cabin cherished "a little brown jug" of strong liquor, somewhere on the premises. Notably, however, addiction to strong drink among the Central Illinois frontiersmen was extremely rare.

Felling timber was peculiarly dangerous work on the Illinois frontier, perhaps because of the tremendous massiveness of Central Illinois trees. It is rather startling to read in early Illinois accounts how frequently woodsmen were killed or crippled by falling trees. On the frontier, all accidents, indeed, were doubly dangerous.

The ways of bacteria were not yet understood, the cause of infection mysterious. Always present was the menace of "lockjaw"(tetanus) and blood poisoning. No dependable cure for them was known. Typhoid fever was another mysterious disease — mysterious because nobody then suspected that contaminated drinking water was its source. Sometimes it swept away entire families.

A supply of pure water was always a problem on the Central Illinois frontier. Wherever possible, pioneers tried to situate their cabins near springs or flowing streams. As soon as barrels could be bought in town, every pioneer woman tried to have one or more standing under the cabin eaves to catch and store rain water. In summer, stagnant rain water became alive with "wiggletails," mosquito larvae. They were considered harmless.

Before drinking the water, the settlers sieved out the wiggletails using a cloth mesh. It was a generation before most farm homes achieved dug cisterns, and years later still before drilled wells and pumps became common.

Naturally, frontier kitchens had no reliable refrigeration. Neither did the cabins have screens. There was no systematic garbage disposal, no plumbing, no sanitation facilities. Every family had its privy, set back some distance from the house, in a secluded niche. House flies bred in excrement, offal, manure, rotting garbage. All summer long, flies swarmed over kitchen utensils, tableware, dishes and foods. The frequency with which old-timers wryly described the plague of flies indicates their appalling numbers. One man who traveled through Woodford County one summer in the 1840s tells of seeing cabin ceilings at night literally black with roosting flies. The prevalence of summer diarrhea and dysentery is not surprising.

At the time young Crissey rode into McLean County the countryside had not yet thrown off its lingering debility from the summer's unusually severe epidemic of "fever and ague," as all frontiers people then called it. Crissey's arrival after October frosts saved him from the dreaded disease. Prior to the young preacher's appearance, almost everybody in Blooming Grove and Bloomington had suffered long bouts with the fever and ague. Esek Greenman of Bloomington said that in the summer of 1831 "out of twenty-four persons, members of three families in the village, twenty-three were sick with the fever and ague."

All of Central Illinois during frontier years and long afterwards was pocked with innumerable swamps, bogs and shallow pools of stagnant water — all prolific breeding places for mosquitoes. The perennial summer sickness across Central Illinois continued to be the dreaded fever and ague until the stagnant waters were finally dried up by extensive tiling, late in the 19th Century.

Old records prove that Illinois frontier folk, for about a quarter of a century after the first primeval prairie sod was broken open, suffered another scourge almost unendurably painful to man and beast. Unquestionably, the young circuit rider suffered this strange scourge during his summers' circuit riding pastorates in 1832, 1833 and 1834, although no written records from him or his Presiding Elder mention the green-headed, blood-sucking flies. Every summer in the 1830s, myriads of these ferocious insects attacked every live animal they could smell out. They were as big as honey bees, and when squashed, their bodies were often gorged with blood.

So excruciatingly painful were their bites, that most frontier families, during the late summer months, stayed indoors as much as possible. These terrible flies drove horses wild, causing runaways. Some horses even died from the insects' torment. Where the green-headed, blood-sucking flies came from has never been satisfactorily explained. Some believed that they evolved somehow mysteriously from the virgin prairie sod, then being plowed for the first time. In any case, the horrendous pests largely disappeared a decade or two after the ground had been farmed for a while.

Henry Clay Tate, long-time editor of Bloomington's daily newspaper, *The Pantagraph*, in his history of McLean County, quoted from early McLean County settlers this vivid first-hand description of those ferocious blood-sucking flies and the prevalence of rattlesnakes at that time:

> Weeks in the year large green-head flies attacked horses and oxen so vigorously that they prevented travel by day. At this season the early settlers traveled at night, and even then the flies were bad on moonlight nights. They were so thick and so bad that they would kill a young horse if it were turned loose. The flies would cause the animal to run wildly as they bit and sucked its blood. The insects bred in the long prairie grass and they vanished as the prairie grass gave way to bluegrass.

Rattlesnakes were another unpleasant part of the early settler's environment. In 1827, Robert McClure killed 330 of them in that one year in the Stout's Grove area. James Turner Gildersleeve once found a rattler curled up on his hearth. Judge John Edward McClun wrote in his description of early life in the county that "rattlesnakes crawled through the town, and now and then a bull snake, that monster of the prairie, would crawl into the very heart of the city."

He Witnessed the Astounding Flights of the Passenger Pigeons

Young Crissey's never-ceasing peregrination around his 250-mile-long circuit all through the summer months of 1832 inflicted on him, agonizingly, discomfort from the blood-sucking flies, from malarial mosquitoes — especially along the swampy regions of Logan County — and from poisonous snakes. But those journeys at the same time rewarded him with forest and prairie beauties and exciting glimpses of animal life.

The most spectacular phenomenon witnessed by the boy preacher that summer was the astounding visitations of the passenger pigeons. One main flight pattern for the passenger pigeons in the 1830s originated along the eastern lake shore of Wisconsin, then passed over Illinois. One eye-witness observer wrote:

As the birds alighted in the forest the noise they made was like a great windstorm. Tree limbs became so crowded with birds that great branches crashed to the ground under the sheer weight of their numbers. Every tree became loaded with crudely built nests, with from 5 to 50 in a single tree. As a result of the great crowding at the nesting site, the constant flopping of pigeon wings created a roar like a waterfall. And within a few days the dung, like snow, lay several inches deep on the forest floor.

Contemporary ornithologist Arlie W. Schorger, in his recent study, *Passenger Pigeon, Its Natural History and Extinction*, estimated that when North America was discovered, the continent supported up to 5 billion of the birds, comprising maybe 40 per cent of North America's total bird population. Another recent historian described them thus:

For more than 200 years they covered the sky with their great migrations. John James Audubon, the naturalist-artist, in 1813 reported a flight of pigeons in which "the air was filled with them; and the light of noonday was obscured as by an eclipse." Riding from his home at Henderson, Ky., on the Ohio River, to Louisville, a distance of 55 miles, he observed pigeons passing overhead all day, and noted that the migration continued for 3 days in succession. He estimated that the pigeons in a flock a mile wide, passing overhead for 3 hours, numbered 1,115,130,000. A flock this size would consume 8,712,000 bushels of mast — beechnuts, chestnuts, and acorns — in a single day, he said. Yet the flock Mr. Audubon described was only a small part of the 3-day migration he observed.

Tragically, the last passenger pigeon died September 1, 1914, at Cincinnati's Zoological Garden. The fate of the passenger pigeon retold that same, weary, outrageous story of mankind's ruthless annihilation of nature's creatures, indigenous everywhere. It was at Petroskey, Michigan, in 1878, that the last great slaughter of passenger pigeons occurred. That spring, as soon as the nestlings, or squabs, were almost mature enough to leave their nests, an army of killers moved in with wagons, nets, guns, axes, beds and camping equipment. Some men camped for days at the pigeons' breeding place. For a week the thundering of firearms sounded like a battle. Fledglings were knocked from their nests with long poles, and smaller trees cut down. The ground came to be strewn with dead and struggling birds, mixed with the wreckage of hundreds of thousands of eggs.

Rail depots in Chicago, Cleveland and New York were glutted with barrels of iced squabs and pigeons. It was estimated that the Petroskey massacre destroyed 1,500,000 pigeons. The next year the pigeons did not return, nor the next nor the next. Never again was a vast flight of passenger pigeons observed, only here and there a few scattered flocks.

Like the American bison whose immense herds once blackened the western plains, the pigeons were not inexhaustible. But, unlike the buffalo, the very last passenger pigeon succumbed. A boy near Sargents, Ohio, shot and killed the last wild passenger pigeon, March 24, 1900. The specimen which died at the Cincinnati Zoo in 1914 had been hatched in captivity.

Those 19th Century Americans who looked upon the prodigious flights of the passenger pigeons witnessed one of this continent's most spectacular phenomena. Nothing like it had ever been seen before, and its like will never be seen again. The young Methodist clergyman, riding his circuits across Central Illinois in the 1830s, was one of those fortunate enough to have participated in this spectacle. Being the reverent, thoughtful young man that he was, surely he marveled at the Eternal's handiwork as the birds darkened the sky over his head.

Hard and dangerous as life was on the Central Illinois frontier in the 1830s, there was immense zest to it. The settlers reveled in freedom as untrammeled as could be found anywhere on earth. Moreover, these families from Pennsylvania, Virginia, Ohio, Kentucky, Tennessee, Indiana and other states, who located in McLean, Tazewell and adjacent counties, soon discovered that they had homesteaded some of the most fertile land in America. Hundreds lived to become wealthy.

IV

THE CIRCUIT RIDER'S LIFE ON THE ILLINOIS FRONTIER IN THE 1830s

The most potent force motivating these pioneer horse preachers was an unshakable faith in the importance of their work. Such sacrifice and loyalty as the circuit riders experienced would not have been possible were it not for an inner compulsion in them far stronger than opposing considerations: family, personal comforts, material security, often their own health. Even so, as a matter of fact, the turnover among early Methodist circuit riders was very high simply because only a few years of such unending hardship literally wore them out.

Moreover, the financial support given the traveling preacher was so meager that an itinerant could scarcely keep himself and his horse in decent condition, to say nothing of a family. Among the Illinois frontier Methodists of the 1830s, the very thought of having to support also a circuit rider's wife and children was abhorrent. Early Methodist records tell of gruff objections by parishioners against a preacher's taking a wife. Traveling ministers were discouraged in plain language from considering marriage. Like Saint Paul, they were expected to remain celibate in order to be freer to minister to their arduous work.

Not surprisingly, loneliness and hardship, aggravated sometimes by lack of appreciation on the part of parishioners, cut short many an itinerant's enlistment. Crissey's tenure is a fair example. He remained in circuit work from 1830 to 1834, and in 1848 was forced to retire permanently from the ministry because his health had been ruined by the hardships he had endured while riding the circuits. However, from his little cottage in Decatur, he continued active thereafter in his church and in civic affairs for many years.

Nearly always, the itinerant preacher in frontier Illinois did his traveling from point to point during the mornings, after breakfasting with his host. Upon arrival at his new charge in the forenoon, his day's work usually followed somewhat this schedule: Preaching began about noon. The sermon was expected to last not less than one hour, preferably longer. Pioneer families considered it scarcely worth while to travel long distances to hear a short sermon. After preaching, the pastor visited with his congregation. He then met the local class, made up of earnest men, women and children studying the Scriptures, the Methodist Discipline and the catechism. These classes continued, even while the circuit-riding minister was absent. On the Tazewell Circuit, during the three weeks while Crissey was elsewhere, a local lay preacher conducted the class instruction.

Perhaps half an hour of chaffer and fellowship followed the ministerial duties, after which the pastor went to the home of one of the local class members for dinner — an arrangement agreed on in advance among the members. Often this entailed another horseback journey over rough or muddy trails from one to five miles long, lasting sometimes more than an hour.

So, it was usually between 3 and 5 in the afternoon before "company dinner" for the preacher was served. By this time the traveling parson — having eaten nothing since early breakfast — could be expected to have a ravenous appetite. Not infrequently, therefore, he ate too much. This caused among Methodist circuit preachers a very common complaint: "dyspepsia" or indigestion. Modern medicine might call it "the circuit rider's occupational disease."

The evening was spent in the host's log cabin, in cool or winter weather around the fireplace, the pastor entertaining his host's family with talk about interesting events along the circuit and political happenings he had heard discussed elsewhere. Since he traveled constantly, he knew much to talk about. The circuit rider was always welcome because his visit brought both news and entertainment into the lonely frontiersman's home.

The following morning, after a hearty breakfast, the circuit rider was on his way again towards his next appointment. The daily travel between points was seldom less than six miles, often much farther. Walking his horse at a leisurely pace of five miles an hour in good weather, the circuit minister could expect to spend at least an hour and a half in his saddle every morning, and he usually spent longer. He enjoyed these summer mornings on horseback. They were exhilarating intervals for meditation and planning, periods of prayer and inner refreshment.

But not all mornings were fair. Regardless of weather, however, his circuit duties urged him on. There was no tarrying even when rain squalls drenched the rider to his skin, and shallow creeks became transformed within a span of minutes into angry torrents often genuinely dangerous for a lone rider to cross. In springtime, thaws softened the ground until in places it turned into quagmires that threatened to swallow horse and rider.

Hardest, of course, were the winters. At times, after November, the circuit rider in Central Illinois could expect deep drifting snows and almost continuously raw, bone-chilling winds. Through heavy drifts the lonely rider's horse plunged and struggled. The rate of travel then was much slower, and to make the task more painful still, gales of freezing wind shriveled man and beast.

"As a Good Soldier of Jesus Christ"

Yet, through it all, the Methodist circuit rider pushed on and on, urged by his sacred resolve to "endure hardness as a good soldier of Jesus Christ." Sustained by hope as seeing Him Who is invisible, faithfully and fearlessly, he carried his spiritual lantern along the frontier. So young William Stoddart Crissey rode his circuit across the Illinois prairie that first year of Bloomington's new life.

The circuit rider on the trail was constantly in personal danger.

The Tazewell Circuit in 1831-1832 embraced all of McLean and Tazewell Counties, and portions of what are now DeWitt, Logan and Woodford Counties. It was contained within the Sangamon District of the Methodist Episcopal Church, serving the new state of Illinois. Peter Cartwright was its Presiding Elder. Cartwright's name would be remembered long afterward by

Illinois historians by reason of the Illinois Congressional election of 1846, in which Cartwright contested Abraham Lincoln — and lost.

More than two dozen "preaching points," scattered along a great meandering loop of approximately 250 miles, constituted the Tazewell Circuit. Its itinerant pastor endeavored to preach at each point at least once every three weeks. At each point, he encouraged his local leaders, reviewed his classes and officiated at weddings, baptisms and other functions which required an ordained minister.

The pastor of the Tazewell Circuit traveled entirely by horseback, because usually a saddle horse was the only conveyance available, and because certainly a saddle horse was the only carrier able to surmount obstacles along the way. His books, papers, clothing and personal necessities were snugly balanced in leather saddle bags cinched across his horse's flanks. Many points on the circuit in 1831-1832 were connected by ungraded trails traversing the virgin prairies and skirting groves of timber strung along the circuit, like beads on a rosary. Usually, even the trails were only rough bridle paths.

Often, between certain preaching points on his circuit, the young pastor found it shorter to cut straight across the open unmarked prairies. During summer and autumn months in Central Illinois, when the weather was fair, this was not hard to do, because the countryside was level. Outside the timbered groves, it was overgrown with wild prairie grasses, saddle high or higher. These spacious virgin prairies had been rippling under summer winds for eons of time. It was not without reason that Illinois very early acquired the name, "The Prairie State."

At short intervals along banks of streams at that time there were dense groves of primeval timber — hundreds of thousands of huge oaks, tulip trees, beeches, chestnuts, walnuts, elms and sugar maples. The Central Illinois black loam was so fertile and deep that all vegetation flourished luxuriantly, disciplined only by the cold winters. Forest giants 150 feet tall and 25 feet in circumference were not unusual.

The spectacular prairie interwoven between dense timber of Central Illinois in the 1830s inspired the place names adopted everywhere by the early settlers. Among the preaching points on the Tazewell Circuit, at least 17 bore names to which "Grove" was appended: Blooming Grove, Funk's Grove, Big Grove, Randolph Grove and numerous others. These old place names — many still in use — reflect clearly the nature of the Central Illinois country-side in the 1830s. A traveler would have discovered here and there little clusters of log cabins standing in clearings hacked out of the thick groves, which always hugged a creek or river. Every now and again he would have seen ebony black soil, plowed or sown with crops. All in between the islets of trees, as far as the eye could see, the traveler in the 1830s looked upon spacious seas of grass — prodigious in height and amplitude.

In spring and summer, Crissey admired their endless green waves, rippling under the prairie breezes; in winter, when not covered by snow, he saw them blackened by burned over ashes. However, during the autumn before the fires had been set, young Crissey observed the prairies looking like immense mat-tresses woven of yellowish green stalks of tall grasses, blown down and matted together by the ceaseless wind. All through the many fair days of spring and summer — but especially through the golden weeks of October's Indian Summer! — the magnificent Illinois prairies uplifted the young preacher's spirit and compelled him silently to praise the Great Maker for His handiwork. During winter, by contrast, the lonely prairie was not a happy place to abide.

Indians

American Indians in Illinois history never played roles of strength, as did some aborigines in certain other states and

71

colonies. George Rogers Clark's two expeditions against the Shawnees, in 1780 and 1782, helped secure the Southern Illinois frontier for the Americans during the Revolutionary War. But Clark's expeditions were not major campaigns, and the Indians' participation in them was never a decisive factor.

The Black Hawk War of 1832 frightened many pioneer families who had settled in Central and Northern Illinois. And some lives were lost (see Chapter VII). But, in a military sense, that campaign, too, was a small affair. Thereafter, the Indians rapidly disappeared from the Illinois scene. By the time young Crissey arrived at Bloomington to take over his duties on the Tazewell Circuit, nearly all the local Indians had moved elsewhere.

At one time, however, they had been populous in the Illinois Heartland. The Pottawatomies, allied to the Shawnees under the great Tecumseh during the first decade of the 19th Century, had been the most numerous and the most powerful among the tribes in the Northwest Territory. After Tecumseh was killed at the battle of the Thames, in Canada in 1813, most Pottawatomies moved beyond the Mississippi River. Scattered enclaves of Pottawatomies continued for a time to live in Northern Michigan, Northern Ohio, and in Illinois north of the Kankakee and Des Plaines Rivers.

It seems possible that Crissey met no Pottawatomies on the Tazewell Circuit. Black Hawk's Sacs and Foxes had not long before been formidably strong in the Rock River Valley of Northern Illinois, but disappeared after 1832. Since they never ventured as far south as the Tazewell Circuit region, it is doubtful if Crissey ever saw a Sac or Fox. He did, however, encounter the Kickapoos.

During 1831-1832 there were remnants of the Kickapoos still living near the Vermilion and Sangamon Rivers, and in the Mackinaw Valley along Panther Creek. Once, the Kickapoos had been generally feared by the whites because of their chronic hostility toward all settlers. They had the reputation of being fierce, warlike and treacherous. Crissey passed fairly near to one small Kickapoo village as he traveled the backwoods country along Panther Creek in what is now Woodford County. The Indians never molested him.

The Kickapoos were fairly numerous in 1831 and 1832 at Ollendorf's Mill over in Logan County. Crissey met them there more often than at Panther Creek in Woodford County. How they may have appeared, if he ever got a good look at them, was vividly described in 1830 by Christopher C. Ewing of Ollendorf's Mill. When Ewing wrote his word picture, the Kickapoos were present in sufficient numbers to be a nuisance. Kickapoo braves were forever begging whiskey and tobacco from the white men, and when refused grew threatening. Given the opportunity, they had no scruples at stealing whatever they wanted. Ewing wrote this about the Kickapoos as he remembered them around Ollendorf's Mill in the early 1830s:

These savages were a fearful sight to us boys. They were the first Indians we'd ever seen. Some were painted different colors. Others had heavy rings in their ears, or notches cut in them. . . . They were bad tempered and quarrelsome.

When a deer would come in sight, the entire squad of braves would rush for their ponies, and pell-mell after it, shooting from the backs of their ponies. As soon as the deer fell, it would be slung across the back of their ponies and brought to camp. . . .

When their dinner was prepared of venison and soup, the warriors . . . around the pot in a circle, spoon or ladle in hand . . . rushed for the pot, and rapidly began to devour its contents. Their habits were disgustingly filthy.

The Summer of '32 Was A Bad Time

At every preaching place all summer long in 1832, Crissey encountered frontiersmen and their womenfolk crowding around him; and always they asked the same questions: "What do you hear about Chief Black Hawk?" and "What is seed corn selling for?" and "Do you think there'll be enough seed corn to plant our crop next spring?"

On the Illinois frontier during the fall, winter and spring of 1831-1832, seed corn was alarmingly scarce and commanded an exhorbitant price. Not infrequently farmers paid $2.00 per bushel (in buying power, equivalent to maybe 10 times that sum today). The scarcity was a delayed aftereffect of the fabulous Big Snow of the year before, which had left farmlands wet, soggy and cold. The Illinois corn crop of 1832 had been a disastrous failure.

All during the year of 1831 and the year following, the shadow of Chief Black Hawk and his fierce Fox Warriors cast a chill over Central Illinois towns and farms. All the way from Peoria to the Wisconsin state line settlers were more or less constantly afraid.

Ever since the British defeat in the War of 1812, Indians of the Northwest Territories had retreated sullenly, yielding their lands grudgingly before the white man's encroachment. Finally, they crossed the Mississippi. Near where today stands Davenport, Iowa, the Sacs and Foxes inhabited an important Indian town.

Returning from their spring hunt in 1830, Black Hawk and his people were dismayed to find their town site preempted by white settlers who had even plowed over the Sacs' ancestral burying grounds — an intolerable insult. Infuriated, Black Hawk and his people went away for a year, brooding over this indignity. The following spring they returned, demanding that the whites go. Panic among some of the whites led to acts of violence against the Indians, and these led in turn to bloody battles and massacres in Northern Illinois.

All that summer of 1832 Indian alarms raced frequently along the Mackinaw Valley. At Pekin, Walnut Grove, and on the Mackinaw River near the present site of Lexington, temporary block houses were manned.

Old block house that stood west of Lexington, Illinois.
Built in 1832 for protection against Indians.

75

That the youthful horse preacher, ministering during the spring and summer of 1832 to his little flocks of Methodists scattered across Central Illinois, was keenly aware of hostile Indians, was verified many years later by his daughter, Margaret Crissey, a spinster living at Decatur. Miss Margaret was interviewed by the Decatur daily newspaper in November 1924. Although at the time in her eighties, she remembered clearly hearing her father tell of seeing Indians several times that summer of the Black Hawk War.

Always, old Reverend Crissey told his daughter, the Indians were on horseback and riding their ponies swiftly away from where he paused in his saddle and watched them. He was not afraid of them, and none ever approached him. If an Indian had accosted him, the Indian would have been greeted with courtesy, kindness and good will.

Old Miss Margaret Crissey told the reporter of other incidents she remembered hearing her father talk about. One night on the Tazewell Circuit Crissey found it impossible to cross a flooded creek. With darkness coming on, he searched for a deserted log cabin. There he slept through the night alone, his horse tethered outside, as prairie wolves howled in the distance.

On another occasion, when the Mackinaw River was on a rampage, Crissey decided the only way to cross the river was to dismount, leave his horse behind, and wade across the dangerous ford on foot. He did so, carrying his heavy saddle bags high on his shoulders to protect books and records from getting wet. Once across, the young preacher tramped the last four miles through the high prairie grass on foot, carrying his heavy bags. But he arrived on time for his appointment.

Last Year of the Tazewell Circuit

In spite of personal hardships on the Illinois frontier, and Indian alarms, Crissey's year on the Tazewell Circuit was described by Leaton as "a successful one." He held two camp meeting revivals during the summer of 1832, the first near the present site of Tremont; the second in Randolph Grove close to the Kickapoo Creek. The latter was an important meeting, with Presiding Elder Cartwright present, as well as most official members of the circuit. Local preachers assisted during both meetings.

On one of the Sunday afternoons, the old history relates, young Crissey preached from the text "An enemy hath done this," developing his sermon around the character and works of Satan. That particular sermon left an indelible impression. It was the sort of Scriptural theme which especially appealed to Crissey, whose tastes — Leaton noted — "tended somewhat towards the mystical."

The Illinois Annual Conference of 1832 which convened September 24th at Jacksonville, redefined the Conference to include only territory within the state boundaries of Illinois. Bishop Soule presided. Previously, the western portion of Indiana had been a part of the Illinois Conference, which then contained four districts. The 1832 Conference added two new districts, one focused at Quincy, the other at Chicago. The Illinois Conference in 1832 was served by 35 traveling preachers, who ministered to about 10,000 Methodists. The Reverend William Stoddart Crissey was the last pastor traveling the old Tazewell Circuit because at the 1832 Conference the Tazewell Circuit was divided into the new Bloomington and Pekin Circuits. At the September 1832 Conference, Crissey was transferred to the Jacksonville Circuit, which then embraced Morgan, Cass and Scott counties. There he encountered dangers a good deal more menacing than wild Indians.

Plague!

Newspapers reaching the Illinois frontier that spring of 1833 frequently reported that cases of the dreadful Asiatic cholera had broken out in eastern coastal cities. Ominously, these reports confirmed that the awful scourge had somehow crossed the Atlantic Ocean. But Illinoisans felt themselves to be very remote from the plague, so did not worry about it.

Subtly, silently and unsuspected, the killer germs soon found their way into Illinois. In Morgan County, one day early in that summer of 1833, a family of travelers from the East, en route to the Far West in a big canvas-covered wagon, stopped at a farm homestead, asking help for the mother lying inside the wagon, deathly ill. Naturally, the strangers were given shelter and comfort. Two days after arrival, the woman died. A few days later, several of her children sickened and died. When the father also took sick and quickly died, the host family became thoroughly frightened. From their homestead, neighboring families contracted the disease. Its easily recognizable symptom was violent diarrhea. Feces and all bodily excretions from the cholera patients were ferociously infectious. There was no cure, no escape except flight.

When people inhabiting the country which the Reverend Crissey was traveling all during the summer of 1833 suddenly became aware that the dreadful Asiatic cholera had invaded the Illinois prairies, they were appalled. As news about it filtered into Illinois families, gradually they became aware that their Morgan County plague was a faraway backwash of the terrible pandemic which originated in India in 1817, then spread by way of Persia and Russia into Europe.

With frightful speed the mysterious contagion leaped from farm to farm, from village to village. The whole countryside became paralyzed with dread. In tiny Jacksonville alone, more than 60 persons died; throughout Morgan County, nearly 100 deaths from Asiatic cholera occurred. In these days, more than a century and a half later, the canopy of fear, through which young Crissey rode day after day in 1833, is an experience so dreadful that no one today can really sense what it meant.

Truly, Crissey's danger that summer of 1833 is quite inconceivable nowadays. But perhaps we can help the reader recreate the temper of Morgan County, Illinois, during the 1833 summer by transposing the mortality statistics of 1833 to the population statistics of McLean County in the 1980s. We must imagine more than 3,000 deaths within Bloomington and Normal occurring across the brief span of a single summer. To magnify the hysteria, one should imagine that the cause of this horrendous sweep of death was traced to the invasion of certain appallingly dangerous germs imported from some mysterious and faraway continent, perhaps Central Africa. Finally, worse still, doctors were helpless. There was no cure.

Under such conditions the panic and horror that would paralyze McLean County, Illinois, boggle one's imagination! Obviously, there cannot be a very close parallel here, since frontier living in Morgan County in the 1830s was immensely different from sophisticated living in Bloomington-Normal in the late 20th Century. Nonetheless, the temper of the people would bear similarities.

Although Menaced by Cholera Every Day, Crissey Never Missed an Appointment

This, then, was the countryside environment across which the young circuit rider rode on day after day, from appointment to appointment, all summer long in 1833. To his credit, the panic everywhere around him did not dismay him. Clothed in unshakable faith that his Lord provided "a shield unto them that put their trust in Him," Crissey fulfilled his duties without interruption. Even though he realized that traveling from post to post, meeting each day new possibilities of contagion, immensely heightened his personal risk, he rode on every day that summer, never missing an appointment.

Interestingly, an aspect of the young circuit rider's pastoral work during that summer of Asiatic cholera was that the Methodists of the Jacksonville Circuit increased in number. Leaton wrote that "they enjoyed a general advance in most appointments."

Our young minister's sensations, thoughts and reveries as he traveled across the Illinois Heartland in the 1830s, can be imagined from a description left by a contemporary and colleague of his, the Reverend J. H. Dickens of Jacksonville, Illinois. The Reverend Dickens rode the Jacksonville Circuit a few years after Crissey served it.

J. H. Dickens was born in Tennessee early in the 19th Century, and moved to Illinois in 1830. He lived most of his life in Morgan County. "Father Dickens" — as he was affectionately addressed in his old age by a host of Morgan County friends — once described his personal feelings while riding his Methodist circuits in the 1830s. Father Dickens' picturesque comments about the Jacksonville Circuit, no doubt, could just as accurately have been spoken by William Stoddart Crissey about the Tazewell Circuit:

> Those days were such as tried men's souls, their mettle, their nature. I would like to take some of the young preachers around some of those circuits. One of them was three hundred miles around. Flies were terrible, mud bottomless. There were no bridges, no ferries, no canoes. Sometimes I would swim, sometimes swim my horse; and in winter I crossed on the ice. Those were times of trial. But some of them were the happiest days I ever spent.

If heroism be a compound of courage, selfless sacrifice and loyalty to an ideal, then in a modest sense, most of the early Methodist circuit riders were heroes. Young Reverend Crissey's unflinching faithfulness to duty in 1832 and 1833 bespoke that same spirit which has always sustained Christ's great Church Militant.

If English hymnologist Percy Dearmer had known about the dedicated Methodist circuit riders faithfully pastoring their little flocks all across the American Middle West during the early

19th Century, these gracious and moving verses that he penned more than 100 years later might appropriately have been their eulogy:

Unknown and unrewarded,
    Their very names have died:
Thy true Church, Lord, through the ages,
    The remnant by Thy side.
These pure in heart did see Thee,
    From dross of self refined.
They spent their lives for others, Lord —
    Courageous, peaceful, kind.

Wise they were, and simple,
    And meek yet strong and sane.
Beloved and loving were they, Lord;
    Joyous laughter in their train.
Fame they spurned, and riches,
    A nobler path to choose.
They glorified Thy Kingdom, Lord;
    They proclaiméd Thy Good News.

How McLean County Appeared to Its First White Settlers

The new Illinois county of McLean (created by the State Legislature only on December 25, the year before), when the young Methodist horse preacher, William Stoddart Crissey, rode into it for the first time in October, 1831, appeared to his eyes as a vast prairieland clothed with prodigiously tall grasses.

Here and there he noted thickly timbered groves of trees each grove straddling a stream of flowing water. The groves were not numerous enough to change young Crissey's concept that McLean County, Illinois, was one almost unbroken immensely vast prairie, its luxuriant grasses growing astonishingly tall — some towering 12 feet into the air. The young Methodist preacher's first impression of the county was accurate. McLean, Illinois' biggest county, covered 1174 square miles, of which about 12 % was wooded, leaving more than one thousand square miles of contiguous prairies.

Soon, young Crissey would realize that McLean County, Illinois, was a gently rolling land, devoid of hills or valleys. Only 310 feet separated the county's highest altitude of 960 feet above sea level (in the eastern sector a few miles north and east of present-day Arrowsmith), from the county's lowest altitude of 650 feet near the county's southwestern corner.

Thus, from its eastern summit, the big county's terrain drained away across easy slopes: northwestward down the valley of the Mackinaw River; in the opposite direction drainage seeped away comfortably along the valley of Kickapoo Creek. The beginnings of the Sangamon River originated near the center of the county, and flowed slowly off to the southeast. McLean County along its western townships drained by easy runoffs into three creeks, all named "Sugar" (because of proliferations along each creek bed of big hard maple trees).

Waterways and timbered groves notwithstanding, the physiognomy of Illinois' largest county in the early 1830s was that of one homogeneous prairieland, immensely vast, growing towering grasses, as far as eye could see.

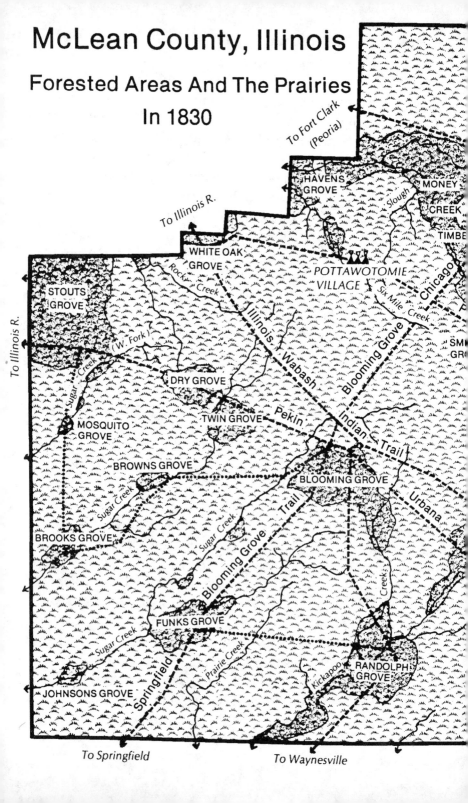

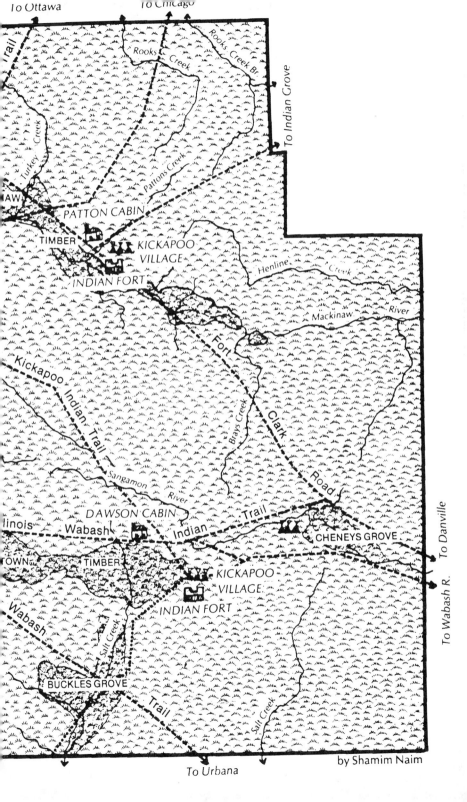

To Ottawa

To Chicago

Trail

Rooks Creek

Rooks Creek Br.

To Indian Grove

Turkey Creek

Pattons Creek

AW

PATTON CABIN

TIMBER

KICKAPOO VILLAGE

INDIAN FORT

Henline Creek

Mackinaw River

Fort

Kickapoo Indian Trail

Braus Creek

Clark

Sangamon River

Road

linois

DAWSON CABIN

Wabash

Indian Trail

To Danville

TOWN

TIMBER

KICKAPOO VILLAGE

CHENEYS GROVE

Wabash

Salt Creek

INDIAN FORT

To Wabash R.

BUCKLES GROVE

Salt Creek

Trail

To Urbana

by Shamim Naim

V

DAY BY DAY
AROUND THE TAZEWELL CIRCUIT

Beginning Week: The Long Trail Beckons Again

First Sunday: Dr. Leaton considered *BLOOMINGTON*[1] the starting and ending point of the Tazewell Circuit. However, the rider stopped there no longer than elsewhere, one day only. Indeed, apparently he never stopped. The preacher who rode the Tazewell Circuit that year was responsible for serving 25 "preaching points." His schedule allowed him 21 days in which to traverse his more than 250 miles around the route. Wherever he was, and regardless of delay, weather or obstacles, he was always aware that tomorrow a different congregation ahead would be expecting him.

When young Crissey arrived at the James Allin log house about sunset one October evening in 1831, his ears were assailed by a clamor of noise coming from a scene of busy activity a few hundred yards north of where he dismounted. Crissey was witnessing the beginning of a new county seat village destined a century later to be one of Illinois' major cities — Bloomington. But at that moment the new village was still in gestation. Only at Christmastime the year before had the state's General Assembly officially authorized the new county, and stipulated that a seat of government should be created for it. Its name and site were not then determined.

Soon after Crissey came to Bloomington, David Trimmer settled there and opened a blacksmith shop near the square. In a few weeks he was joined by Henry Miller, who was a wheel-

---

[1] Place names that appear in bold small capitals indicate modern towns corresponding to "preaching places" where the circuit rider slept overnight.

wright. Miller in 1835 installed a turning lathe, powered by his own foot. Among the objects he turned out that the Bloomington housewives especially appreciated were spinning wheels. James Allin's general store occupied the southeast corner of East and Grove Streets. Asahel Gridley's store stood on the opposite corner. It testifies to the friendship between them that, although competitors, they lived under the same roof and never quarreled. In 1831, Bloomington had two doctors, joined the next year by a third, and in 1834 by a fourth.

In May 1831 the Post Office established at Blooming Grove in 1829 was transferred to Bloomington. Allin was appointed Postmaster and operated the mail facility from his store. The United States Mail in 1831 arrived at Bloomington once a week, by stage from St. Louis, where Mississippi River steamboats delivered the mail from New Orleans, an ocean port.

Who was Bloomington's First Ordained Clergyman?

The first sermon by an ordained clergyman heard by Bloomington people was preached Sunday, October 9, 1831, but it was not delivered within the new village's legal boundaries. The preacher was 20-year-old William Stoddart Crissey, who had arrived at Bloomington only two days earlier. That same Sunday when Crissey preached near Bloomington, the Reverend Stephen R. Beggs, then traveling pastor of the Tazewell Circuit, returned to Bloomington. At once the Reverend Beggs was introduced by James Allin to the youthful new circuit rider who was to supersede him.

Since the Tazewell Circuit was so immense, it was indispensable that the older and experienced pastor escort the new man completely around the entire circuit, pointing out trails and hazards, and at every preaching place introducing Crissey to local Methodist leaders. That pathfinding trip by the two preachers consumed three weeks, and it was not until Sunday, November 6 that the young clergyman got around to preaching to a congregation assembled within Bloomington itself.

Crissey's October 9th sermon was delivered at the farmhouse belonging to John Canaday, about one and one-half miles southeast of the Courthouse Square. Crissey preached the first sermon by an ordained Christian clergyman delivered within the precincts of Bloomington Sunday morning, November 6, 1831. The place was James Allin's big double house, standing on the corner of South East and Grove Streets.

James Allin's double house, in which Crissey
preached Bloomington's first sermon.

Early the next morning, after eating a hearty breakfast with the Allins, the youthful clergyman saddled his horse, buckled and cinched his double saddle bags across the animal's rumps, mounted, and with a friendly wave, cantered away toward Smith's Grove. This was Crissey's second appointment and his first Monday out on the big Tazewell Circuit, which stretched some 250 miles before him.

First Monday: About seven miles northeast of Bloomington (and one mile north of the present site of *TOWANDA*), at Smith's Grove on Money Creek was a small Methodist society —

88

the Reverend Crissey's first preaching place out on the Tazewell Circuit after leaving Bloomington. Religious worship at this appointment near Money Creek, according to Leaton, was "at a private house." To get there, the young circuit rider rode the well-marked Springfield-Fort Dearborn Road across the prairie.

The John Trimmer family moved to Smith's Grove in 1826. His widow and children were still there in the fall of 1831 when the Reverend Crissey arrived. Henry Moats, a young man from Ohio, arrived in 1829 with his family. In 1830 came David Smith from North Carolina, of German extraction, for whom the grove was eventually named. Soon thereafter came another young settler, Jesse Walden from Kentucky, who located near the Trimmer place. Richard Fling, a carpenter, settled at Smith's Grove in 1831. It was in one of these cabins that the Reverend Crissey preached in 1831 and 1832.

First Tuesday: Leaving Smith's Grove, the young circuit rider guided his horse northeast upon the Springfield-Fort Dearborn Road. At a shallow place in the Mackinaw River, long known as the Ford Crossing, Crissey's horse splashed across the river, then turned sharply left, toward the northwest. Paralleling the dense timber that bowered the river, Crissey rode almost 10 miles, following the Fort Clark Road through the tall grass. Presently, he arrived at a small settlement of scattered cabins (the site was about six miles down stream from where *LEXINGTON* now stands).

Most of these families were Methodists. As usual, these cabins were not close to each other, but well separated, paralleling the fringe of timber. Jacob Harness from Ohio had settled here in 1825. The next spring came Jacob Spawr of Pennsylvania, and his aged father, Valentine Spawr, a veteran of the Revolutionary War. During the next four years several others moved into the Money Creek Settlement: John Steers, the Van Buskirk family, General Joseph Bartholomew of Indiana, another old soldier who had distinguished himself in the Revolutionary War and later Indian wars. Others who came were M. N. Barnard, Jess Stretch, and Benjamin Ogden from Ohio.

To these settlers, once every three weeks, came the youthful evangelist, bringing Christ's comfort and ministry. Leaving this appointment Wednesday morning, Crissey retraced his previous day's travel over the Fort Clark Road, until he came to the important settlement surrounding John Patton's cabin.

An Important Colony of Methodists

First Wednesday: "The chief society on the Mackinaw" according to Leaton, throve among the neighbors of John Patton, who in 1829 had erected a log house near Patton's Creek at the edge of Mackinaw Timber , which was the largest coherent mass of forest in McLean County.

John Patton, an Irish American, was a skilled mechanic and artisan, whose feisty Gaelic humor quickly won him friendship among the Indians. He was an ardent Methodist whose house was for years the accepted preaching place of the neighborhood.

The year before, several families had settled in this vicinity: John Haner and three sons; Conrad Flesher, wife and several children; and the Brumhead brothers, Isaac and Joseph. Duis reported eight families living in the Patton neighborhood in 1830.

Near John Patton's house (two and one-half miles southeast of the site of Lexington) lived the family of young Joseph H. Hopkins, "whose [subsequent] labors for Missouri Methodism are so well known," according to Leaton's notes. "Brother Joe," then only a boy, "delighted in waiting on the preachers who visited his father's house," said Leaton. The young Reverend Crissey, himself scarcely out of boyhood, was the focus that year of Joe Hopkins' adolescent admiration. It is easy to imagine that the young pastor and the admiring boy enjoyed many happy visits together.

Leaton mentioned a society of United Brethren in the vicinity, "and between them and the Methodists was a good deal of strife for the ascendancy." Leaton mentioned also another "appointment on the Mackinaw above Pattons at which there was preaching occasionally." It seems probable that this was at the site of the new Henline Fort, erected in 1832 on Henline Creek for protection against Chief Black Hawk's warriors, who threatened from the north.

First Thursday: Leaving the Pattons, the Reverend Crissey rode through the thick Mackinaw Timber, then again splashed across the river at the Ford Crossing. From there he rode his mount southeastward down the Fort Clark Road. Presently, leaving the timber behind, the road emerged into a broad grassy prairie. When the weather was clear, Crissey could see Cheney's Grove, his destination, far ahead.

Upon arrival at his First Thursday appointment about noon, Crissey had traversed almost 20 miles since he had eaten breakfast with the Pattons that morning. It was one of the three longest links on the circuit, and brought him to its easternmost point.

On the banks of the upper Sangamon River, in the grove named for him, lived Jonathan Cheney's big family of eight children, plus half a dozen other kinfolk. Cheney, a Virginia man, settled at the grove in 1825. His was an exuberant and happy family. Most of his children in later life accumulated substantial wealth and left an honored family name. At this grove were also Robert Cunningham, his wife and numerous children. He was a veteran of the War of 1812, from Indiana, and settled near the Cheneys in 1829. The Cheney and Cunningham flock comprised Crissey's first Thursday congregation. The tiny settlement in time grew into the present town of *SAYBROOK*.

First Friday: Fording the upper reach of the Sangamon River, Crissey turned his horse westward until he came to the well-traveled Illinois-Wabash Indian trail, which ran from the Wabash River in Indiana to the Illinois River near Fort Clark (*PEORIA*). After perhaps an hour's ride, he passed about two miles north of the Kickapoo Indian fort and village on the eastern tip of

Old Town Timber. By 1831 it was largely abandoned. But even if the Kickapoos had been there in numbers, he would not have minded. Crissey respected the Indians. He felt no fear of them, and they never molested him.

Prior to 1829, Illinois' native Indians, the Kickapoos and a few Delawares, had been numerous throughout most of McLean County. Sometimes mischievous and annoying, on the whole they were friendly or at least passive. The hostile and dangerous Pottawatomies had departed, many of them to as far away as Mexico. In 1831 and 1832 only two passages on the Tazewell Circuit were still frequented by Indians — the Ollendorf's Mill neighborhood in the thick woodlands about Sugar Creek, in what is now Logan County, and the primitive hilly backwoods around Panther Creek, north of Stout's Grove, in the area now in southeastern Woodford County. During the skirmishes in 1832 against Chief Black Hawk and his Sacs and Foxes of the North, tensions toward all the Indians mounted among the white settlers, until most of the Indians in McLean and Tazewell Counties were removed to Kansas Territory by federal government order.

McLean County's First Settlers

Heading westward, Crissey passed the Dawson place on Salt Creek in the margin of Old Town Timber. This was an eight-mile-long strip of woods, averaging about three miles wide, running due east and west. John Wells Dawson was a Kentuckian of English extraction, who had been a wagon master with American troops during the war of 1812.

In November 1821, Dawson, with wife Ann (Cheney) and two young sons, joined a fellow veteran of that war, John Hendrix, with wife Jane (Brittin) and their two you sons, for the long tek through Ohio, Indiana and into Illinois. They traveled in two covered wagons pulled by oxen. Hendrix was a farmer and cattleman. He brought along considerable livestock (five milk cows, 19 young cattle, three horses and 25 sheep). They followed the Ohio Trail into Illinois and turned south to Sangamon County where both families had relattives. They arrived at Christmastime.

In April 1822, the two men rode north and selected sites one mile apart on the edge of a handsome stand of hardwoods, later named Blooming Grove. The Dawson and Hendrix families were the earliest Caucasian settlers in McLean County. They visited each other every Sunday for mutual encouragement and fellowship.

The Dawsons moved to Old Town Timber in 1826. Beside the trail, Dawson built an inn for westbound travelers that he operated for many years. It was this Dawson location that the 20-year-old circuit rider greeted as he passed by going west.

The Hendrix family stayed in Blooming Grove the rest of their lives. Six more children were born to them. their livestock prospered and they became leaders in the development of the area.

Following the shallow headwaters of Salt Creek, young Crissey continued jogging on his horse two miles westward along the Indian trail before he attained his day's destination. This was the little colony of Methodists at "Old Town," a name attached to the settlement in remembrance of an ancient Indian village that had once occupied the site (not far from the present village of PADUA). Here was a scattering of half a dozen log cabins hugging the big trees. By now, the Reverend Crissey had put 10 miles behind him during the morning since leaving Cheney's Grove, where he had eaten breakfast. But for the most part he had ridden a well-beaten trail along high dry ground, so the journey was easy. Much of the way the trail skirted the northern edge of the forest. To his right, hour after hour, stretched a vast prairie, gently rolling northward beyond the horizon.

The first settler to locate in the Old Town Timber moved there in 1826 from Blooming Grove — William Evans by name. He located on Kickapoo Creek near the western tip of the woods. Then came William Maxwell from North Carolina, with his three sons, in 1829, John Bishop one year later, and Jeremiah Greenman from Ohio in 1831.

Old Town Timber's most celebrated pioneer, Jesse Frankeberger from Ohio, arrived in 1829, settling near the present site of Padua in McLean County. He was a born evangelist and devoutly religious. Excepting for his lack of schooling and ordination, Frankeberger would have made an exemplary Methodist circuit rider. All Methodists who came to Old Town learned to love and depend on him. For years the Frankeberger cabin was the recognized "preaching place" for the settlement. His barn often housed the Methodist Quarterly Conferences. Frankeberger was the local preacher, but his labors for the Lord were by no means circumscribed by his neighborhood. Charles Merriman stated that Frankeberger was

> ... a man of good sense and a good manager. He owned and managed a large farm, and preached wherever he was wanted all over this part of the country, from the Mackinaw to Monticello, in the houses or barns or groves, wherever he could collect a few together, riding miles to attend an appointment, and returning home without a dinner.

First Saturday: Leaving Frankeberger and other stalwart Methodists at the Old Town Timber Settlement, the young circuit rider, each first Saturday morning, entered the thick timber, following a brushy, lightly traveled trail for almost a mile, emerging into the grassy valley of the Kickapoo Creek. Skirting the western edge of Buckles' Grove, he is brought after an hour's canter to a lonely little cluster of cabins, lurking under the shade of Conaway's Grove. Despite its smallness, the settlement comprised a vigorous Methodist society.

James Harvey Conaway, of distant Irish ancestry, was born in Kentucky but moved with his parents to Illinois when he

94

was eight years old. Pausing in 1819, in Vermillion County, Illinois, the Conaways arrived in McLean County in February 1828. Subsequent settlers at the grove, to whom young Crissey preached in 1831 and 1832, named their settlement, as customary, after the first family to arrive: Aquilla Conaway and his wife, Rachel Barnett Conaway, and their son, little Jim.

Lawson Downs of Tennessee arrived in 1829. Henry Jacoby moved from nearby Randolph Grove in 1830. That year also brought Thomas Toverca from Tennessee, who had been persuaded to come to Illinois by his old friend Gardner Randolph of Alabama and Tennessee.

Toverca was an important acquisition to the Methodists, because much of the spiritual fire among the Methodists at Conaway's Grove derived, undoubtedly, from Thomas Toverca. He was a veteran of the War of 1812, a born fighter, and brimming with animal vigor. Although unlettered, his fame "as an exhorter of power," as one historian described him, spread far. It was enthusiasm such as Toverca's that enabled the Methodists to conquer the Illinois frontier.

Leaton added this very human touch to his description of church life at Conaway's Grove: "a local preacher named Reuben Clearwater, moved from Indiana this year and settled in this society. He was a fair preacher, but not always on the best terms with the itinerants."

Christmas Eve, 1831, at Conaway's Grove, Illinois

Christmas Eve in 1831 overtook the young Methodist circuit rider at Conaway's Grove in southern McLean County. Crissey already had met the Conaways and their Methodist neighbors three times, the first being in October when his predecessor, the Reverend Stephen R. Beggs, had introduced him. At that time, the older man had done the preaching. But on Saturday, November 12, and again three weeks later, on Saturday, Decem-

95

ber 3, Crissey had arrived alone, and by himself had preached, conducted the Methodist Class and took care of all other church business needing his attention.

His visit at Conaway's Grove, Saturday, December 24, was his fourth. But this visit was a very special occasion, and everybody attended the Christmas Eve service: The Downs family, Henry Jacoby, Tom Toverca and other neighboring families and children. That evening, in the Conaway's log cabin the youthful minister conducted a special service of worship honoring the eve of Christ's birthday. The little cabin was crowded to suffocation with fathers and mothers and their children. The mothers had decorated the cabin with evergreen boughs plucked from the timber. The fireplace was roaring with fresh logs. Remembering the early December darkness, several women brought extra candles. When these were lighted and placed around the cabin walls, up high enough not to tempt children, the interior, already pink from the flaming fireplace, took on a twinkling glory, such as no cabin in the grove had ever experienced before.

After carols and Christmas hymns sung by everybody, the young minister talked briefly about the wonder of the first Christmas Eve: the virgin birth, the Heavenly chorus, the humble shepherds, the three Wise Men who had followed the miraculous star from faraway Persia. It was a sacred moment every person there would remember long afterward.

Womenfolk had baked cakes for the occasion and had made coffee, a rare treat! Most of Crissey's parishioners at Conaway's Grove that evening had brought their pastor small gifts, all modest, for nobody was wealthy. Their Christmas presents were homemade mittens, a woolen throat muffler, hand-woven socks and homemade candy from maple sugar rendered from local "sugar trees."

Half a century later, recollection of his first Christmas Eve as he rode his first Illinois preaching circuit remained ever clear in old Father Crissey's memory, still — after fifty years! — bathed in the strangely luminous aura that miraculously always sanctifies every eve of the Savior's birth.

VI
DAY BY DAY
AROUND THE TAZEWELL CIRCUIT

Middle Week: The Loop Farthest Out

Second Sunday: By now, the Reverend Crissey had covered the first week of his three-week circuit, but he was still in McLean County, with two more preaching points to serve before leaving it. His second Sunday out of Bloomington found him among the Methodists at Randolph Grove, on the west bank of the upper Kickapoo Creek, midway between the present sites of *DOWNS* and *HEYWORTH*.

In 1823, Gardner Randolph of Alabama, together with his young brothers-in-law, Alfred and Severe Stringfield of Tennessee, and their families, located at the grove later to be identified with them. The Stringfields' widowed mother joined them there a year or two later. Mrs. Stringfield was a Baptist. Her husband had been Episcopalian. However, the enthusiasm of the frontier Methodists captivated the Stringfield boys, so they joined that church and became devout Methodists. Another young settler here was Thomas Officer Rutledge of Georgia, who came in 1825.

This was one of the most vigorous Methodist colonies along the entire Tazewell Circuit. It possessed considerable religious leadership of its own. Dr. Leaton said this about it:

> One of the first settlers in the county, Bro. William Hodge, was a leading member of this class. He died a few years ago in Bloomington. Here, too, was a Bro. Stringfield, a local preacher, who was one among the first settlers in the county. He was originally from Tennessee. He was a reliable man, mild in disposition generally

acceptable as a preacher and somewhat useful, but not as energetic as some of the rest of the local preachers.

Christmas Day, 1831, on the Tazewell Circuit

The young circuit rider's first Christmas Day as an Illinois Methodist circuit rider befell him at one of his strongest stations, and the day also was a Sunday — which always hallowed the people's sense of worship. It could not have come at a better time or place.

Sunday morning, December 25th, Crissey, after enjoying a hearty breakfast with the Conoways, saddled his horse, re-packed his saddle bags (a little fuller than usual because of last evening's gifts), bade his host and hostess good-bye, and pointed his mount westward toward Randolph Grove, only a 90-minute ride away.

In the Randolph's log cabin that Christmas Sunday noon-time, there was enacted something of a repetition of last evening's celebration with the Conoways and their neighbors, except this time attendance was substantially larger. More families attended the preaching, which was focused upon the old familiar Gospel texts. The music was wholly Christmas pieces, carols and hymns, all sung with joyous gusto, and, of course, without instrumental accompaniment, for on the Central Illinois frontier in 1831 no musical instruments existed.

The Randolph cabin had been beautified by generous sprays of cedar and spruce, stripped out of the grove and tacked to the walls and over the big fireplace. After the preaching, class was conducted, and pending church business attended to. Then in the early afternoon came the moment all had waited for: every housewife had brought with her a basket, bulging with good things to eat. Happily, all shared and exchanged dainties — the young circuit rider seated in their midst, the lion of the occasion. After the robust meal came presents to the young preacher from

99

the Randolphs, the Stringfields, the Hodges, the Rutledges and half a dozen others. Although their gifts duplicated those received the evening before, his never-lagging enthusiastic thanks concealed the fact.

As the early December twilight settled over the forest, the families departed, one by one. Behind them that evening they left a young man wreathed in smiles, warmed in heart. This first Christmas Day of his Illinois ministry was ever after cherished by William Stoddart Crissey, until the year of his death in distant 1888, even though the many intervening years by then had led him around two other preaching circuits and into the pulpits of important Illinois churches, and on into a soldier's uniform as Army Chaplain in Tennessee and Georgia, not forgetting those two days in May 1856, at Bloomington, when he had fraternized with Abraham Lincoln. All those experiences, he often said in his old age, were important; but none quite equalled the sweetness of his first Christmas on the Illinois circuit.

Second Monday: Riding almost due west, soon leaving the timber behind, Crissey at this juncture entered a broad prairie. He followed a fairly well-marked trail, washed on both sides by seas of recently rugged primitive grass, but by Christmastime reduced to blackened char where the fires had burned it. *FUNK'S GROVE*, his destination, lay almost due west, some five miles away.

About two-thirds of the way across this prairie he had to ford Prairie Creek, but it was a shallow stream. However, a constant worry during most of the year to Crissey while crossing the prairies was the frequency of treacherous sloughs. In the 1830s, and for many years after, Central Illinois prairies were interlaced with watery sloughs concealed in summer beneath prodigious stands of grass. These bogs afforded no safe footing for horse or man. Although they were seldom soft or deep enough to wholly engulf animal or rider, they were nevertheless dangerous, particularly for a man alone. A solitary rider needed to be

100

wary, but so long as he kept to the trail, the ground beneath his horse was solid. In winter the travel across the prairies was safer, since the frozen ground contained no pitfalls. Heavy snow, on the other hand, presented a formidable obstacle of a different kind.

On most days Crissey could sight Funk's Grove across the wide prairie as soon as he left the Randolph trees. At Funk's Grove the Methodist society was small. "The preaching," Leaton said, was "at the house of one of the Funk's." Because there were several Funks living around this small grove, this meant constant rotation by the young minister, in order that each family in turn could share the pleasure of entertaining him — for the itinerant pastor's call always brought not only spiritual refreshment but also interesting news from other McLean County neighborhoods. Entertaining a visitor was considered a rare privilege at that time in frontier communities.

Here, at this little settlement near the southwest corner of McLean County, the young Reverend Crissey was the guest and pastor that year of two families, both progenitors of distinguished Illinois dynasties: the Funks and the Stubblefields. Both families had come out from Ohio seven years before the young circuit rider met them. They chose to settle on the margin of a handsome stand of hardwoods watered by Sugar Creek.[1]

Two brothers, Absalom Funk and Isaac, 10 years his junior, came out first, in May 1824, accompanied by a neighbor they had known back in Ohio, William Brock. In December that same year, the father, Adam Funk, recently bereaved of his wife, joined Absalom and Isaac, with two other of his sons, John and Robert Peoples, and also a daughter, Dorothy. With his daughter came her husband, Robert Stubblefield, a muscular 200-pound six-footer—pioneer of what in a generation or two would become a renowned family. Later a fifth Funk brother, Jacob, settled at

---

[1] The numerous Sugar Creeks in early Illinois always denoted minor water courses flanked by innumerable hard maples, or "sugar trees," from which maple sugar could be extracted.

Fort Clark, now Peoria, while another brother, Jesse, left his father's grove, and moved on east to Randolph Grove.

All these early Funk pioneers who entered Illinois in the 1820s were people of character, vigor and independence. All of them prospered, but it was Isaac who was destined to be the patriarch of one of the most influential families in Central Illinois. In 1825 he married a Fort Clark girl, Cassandra ("Cassander," they called her) Sharp, like Isaac a recent immigrant from Ohio. When young Reverend Crissey first preached at Isaac and Cassandra Funk's cabin in the fall of 1831, he found a year-old baby and two little boys playing there. Eventually there were 10 children. Isaac became in time one of Illinois' largest landholders, a millionaire cattleman, and a state senator. In 1831 and 1832, said Leaton, the Reverend Crissey preached regularly once every three weeks "in one or another of the Funks' homes."

Besides the Funks, the little congregation at the grove that year also included Mr. and Mrs. Robert Stubblefield and their large brood of stair-step children, perhaps as many as 10 by the fall of 1831, when the Reverend Crissey first appeared at the settlement. Robert Stubblefield, a Virginian, had fought in the War of 1812. In Ohio, he first married the sister of Adam Funk, Sarah, by whom he had four children. Then, after Sarah's death, he married Adam's daughter Dorothy, who mothered nine more. The eldest of the Stubblefield offspring, Absalom, was 16 when he first heard Crissey preach in Isaac Funk's cabin late in 1831.

Robert Stubblefield was a deeply religious man, and always attended worship services wherever they were accessible. Undoubtedly, it was he who arranged the first preaching service at Funk's Grove. The Reverend Peyton Mitchell, a Scotch Cumberland Presbyterian minister living over at Stout's Grove some 12 miles north, was the preacher. The place was Robert Stubblefield's cabin. The date is not recorded, but it antedated Crissey's arrival by several years.

The young circuit rider's work during his year on the Tazewell Circuit helped build up the momentum that in 1833 culminated in the organization of the first Methodist Church at Funk's Grove, under the Reverend William Royal, who succeeded Crissey. The founders of this church, which was to become perhaps the most historic Christian congregation in McLean County, comprised, among others, Adam Funk and his brother Robert Peoples, Robert Stubblefield and his son John, and Mrs. William Brock. Ultimately, the congregation found its home in a substantial white frame church building overlooking the shaded Funk's Grove burying ground. That building, trim and white, and lovingly cared for, still stands on the bank of Sugar Creek, about a mile west of Funk's Grove village.

Second Tuesday: From the Funk-Stubblefield neighborhood, the young minister turned his horse southwestward toward DeWitt County.[2] He traveled at first for some nine or 10 miles on the well-marked Springfield-Bloomington-Fort Dearborn Trail. But because that trail continued southwestward toward St. Louis, presently he was forced to leave it in order to intersect the Big Grove settlement at Kickapoo Creek, across the line in DeWitt County, close to the present site of *WAYNESVILLE*.

Near where the Springfield-Fort Dearborn Road entered Logan County, the young circuit rider made a sharp turn to his left, leaving the trail and continuing three miles through the prairie, with the spacious wood of Big Grove visible ahead. Again, the Reverend Crissey found himself traveling across breezy grassy lands, encountering only sparse woods along Prairie Creek, which he presently crossed a second time. Ahead lay another of those large islands of dense timber characteristic of Central Illinois until several decades after the 1830s.

---

[2] Here, and wherever else county names are mentioned, the present county lines are definitive, not the county lines as they existed in 1831-1832.

Shugart Mill and the Eccentric Sylvania Shutleff

There, the young itinerant preacher was welcomed on this Tuesday by a society of 30 or more members, considered then a substantial congregation. Religious worship here began in 1825, when five or six people gathered occasionally on the dirt floor at Prettyman Marvel's log house and listened to a passing preacher. By 1831, when young Crissey arrived, the settlement had developed, for by then it possessed a tiny one-room log store, operated by Greenman & Dunham, selling "notions and groceries." On nearby Kickapoo Creek, in 1829, a water-powered grist mill had been built. It was operated by two brothers, Zion and Edom Shugart. The Shugart Mill had been started on Kickapoo Creek by the eccentric Sylvania Shurtleff, who soon abandoned it to the Shugarts. Shurtleff was the first white man to settle near Big Grove.

Unquestionably, Shurtleff's odd doings were described to young Crissey, and laughed at during many evenings as the young pastor visited around the firesides of his parishioners at the Big Grove settlement. It is even possible that Shurtleff may have attended some of Crissey's church services, but, considering his half-wild nature, that seems improbable. Born in remote Vermont, he appeared in the early 1820s in the Central Illinois wilderness. Shurtleff was an incurable wanderer, forever restless, one of that rather numerous tribe of rootless American frontiersmen, solitary men who felt cramped and crowded if a neighbor lived within gunshot-hearing. Almost never did one of them marry, settle down permanently and rear a family . They were truly the frontier breakers, but their impact was shallow. Somehow, Shurtleff won the confidence of the dangerous Pottawatomi and in 1823 was initiated into their tribe. Four years later he drifted to Big Grove, and two years later built the mill on Kickapoo Creek, which he abandoned later to follow the frontier farther west.

In 1825 Prettyman Marvel, his wife Rebecca and their two babies came to Big Grove from Georgia. They were joined in a few days by John Barr, Mrs. Marvel's brother, who settled several miles west. Others in the Reverend Crissey's society at Big Grove in 1831-1832 were James Scott, his wife and two sons, who had come out from Indiana in 1827. Another early settler there was Abraham Onstatt of Kentucky who arrived in 1829. John J. McGraw of Kentucky, came in 1830, with his father-in-law, Tillman Lane, who brought with him his wife and seven children. (In later years Tillman Lane became a DeWitt County Judge.) John B. Jones, with his wife and five children, arrived in 1830 from Indiana. One year later came William W. Dunham, formerly a New Englander, from Ohio, with his wife and five children. That same year, George Isham of New Hampshire arrived with his wife and two children. The preaching here at Big Grove, Dr. Leaton stated, "was at a private house" — unquestionably the cabin home of one of the above-mentioned settlers.

Second Wednesday: Prettyman Marvel's settlement on Big Grove in DeWitt County virtually straddled the boundaries separating DeWitt from McLean and Logan Counties. From Prettyman Marvel's people, the young clergyman rode directly westward along the northern edge of Big Grove, then angled his horse toward the Springfield-Chicago Trail, which he presently rejoined. Naturally, wherever feasible around his circuit, Crissey chose to travel the trails and roads, rather than to breast the virgin prairie alone and without guide. Several miles beyond where the trail forded Kickapoo Creek, the circuit rider again turned his mount sharply left, in order to traverse the open prairie, separating the Randolph Neighborhood from the Springfield - Fort Dearborn Road.

Riding south by west across some miles of open prairie, presently Crissey glimpsed ahead a spacious grove of giant maple trees. Through the middle of the grove flowed Salt Creek — already, he came to know, a formidable stream flowing westward and eventually emptying into the Sangamon River on the border of Menard and Mason Counties.

There, in the southeastern quarter of Logan County, hugging the big maples of Sugar Grove that shaded Salt Creek, the young circuit rider came onto the Randolph Neighborhood, several miles northeast of the present site of *MOUNT PULASKI*. It was pure coincidence that Crissey encountered a second Randolph settlement only three days after he had preached at Randolph Grove in McLean County. Apparently the two families were not related, for they migrated to Illinois from areas in the South far distant from each other.

About the time of the Big Snow, Brooks Randolph, James Randolph and Willoughby Randolph, all Virginians, arrived on Salt Creek with their families. A little son of James Randolph and his wife, William Patton Randolph, born in Virginia in 1829, was destined to become one of the best educated pioneers of Central Illinois. Eventually, William Patton Randolph attended three colleges, and for years practiced law at Lincoln, Illinois. All the Randolphs were Methodists, and the young preacher was often a guest in their cabins. That these Virginia Randolphs were well-bred, and commanded the respect of their neighbors, seems evident by the fact that the community, but a year or two after their arrival, came to be known as the Randolph Neighborhood, even though other families had settled there seven or eight years earlier.

One of the very first families settling at Sugar Grove was John and Ruth Downing and their half-grown sons, James and Robert, who came in 1822 from Ohio. They, too, were Methodists. Then in 1823, Samuel McClure, William McGraw, William Long and their families came and built cabins near the Downings. During the next few years came David Lowert, James Morrow, Alfred and Edmund Sams, from Tennessee, and Montgomery Warrick. Another Virginia family — the Vandeventers, John and Abram, and their wives — arrived in 1828, just ahead of the Randolphs. That same year, Preston Pendleton and his wife, from

Kentucky, settled here on Salt Creek. The year 1828 also brought Eli Fletcher of Kentucky, and his wife, Marian, a Virginia woman. Mr. Fletcher returned to Kentucky for one year to settle his affairs. Then in 1829 he came back to Illinois and settled permanently on Salt Creek. The Fletchers also were Methodists.

These were some of the people to whom young William Stoddart Crissey ministered during late 1831 and until September 1832, as he patiently worked his way westward across the farthest-out loop of his 250-mile circuit.

Much of this long loop into what was then Sangamon County traversed low, boggy country. The terrain away form the streams was hummocky and rough. Mosquitoes and flies in these areas were an all-summer-long abomination to both horse and rider. Here especially, but also everywhere else on the circuit, from mid-summer to first frost, the green blood-sucking flies tormented man and beast, almost unendurably. It must be assumed that the young circuit rider that summer and early fall of 1832 did not escape the green flies. There is no record that he ever complained.

The Methodist society at Randolph Neighborhood was small; therefore, it was practical to serve two appointments that same day. His second preaching place after the Randolph Neighborhood was a tiny congregation of not more than half a dozen members, the Latham Settlement at far away Elkhart Grove. After preaching to the Randolphs and their neighbors, reviewing their class work and attending other duties, Crissey remounted and rode directly across the broad prairies of central Logan County, between the Deer Creek Timber on his right and Sugar Grove on his left. He first came to Salt Creek, which he forded, or swam across if the water was in flood. Miles further on, he did the same at the Lake Fork of Salt Creek. By then, on the horizon ahead, the timbered heights of Elkhart Grove loomed against the skyline.

Serving Two Appointments the Same Day,
20 Miles Apart

Double appointments on the Tazewell Circuit imposed extraordinary strain on the itinerant pastor that year, especially, since three of them were clustered within a space of four days. This first double appointment on Salt Creek in Logan County greeted the minister after he had just ridden over miles of prairie and timber country, third of the four extra-long links in the Tazewell Circuit. However, neither young Crissey nor any other circuit riders who carried the Gospel along these difficult trails ever complained at the time of the hardships.[3]

A few miles west of Lake Fork of Salt Creek stood in the 1820s — and for countless centuries before that — perhaps the most picturesque grove of hardwood trees in all Illinois, its impressiveness greatly enhanced by the unique knoll 120 feet high, one and a half miles long, and half a mile wide, on which the big trees grew. The Indians called it "Itaska," meaning "a patch like an elk's heart." There were springs there, too, and glades of fine grass. Since pioneers entered Illinois always from the south or east, it was inevitable that "Elkhart" (as the early settlers spelled it and as its place name on Illinois maps continues to be spelled) should attract some of the region's first settlers.

Richard Latham of Kentucky, spied out the beautiful *ELKHART* knoll during a trip into Illinois, probably in the summer of 1823. In September of that year he arrived there with his family and household goods loaded into several big wagons. Here afterwards, he built a little horse-powered treadmill — the first mill of any kind in that area of Logan County. Prior to Latham's mill, people had laboriously hauled their wheat and corn all the way to Edwardsville, 75 miles to the southwest.

---

[3] In their later years, as superannuated clergymen discoursing with young preachers while they toasted their shins in front of comfortable fireplaces during winter evenings, they loved to expatiate on their frontier sufferings.

Latham became in time fairly prominent in the little community, which came to be linked with his name. President John Quincy Adams, in the late 1820s, appointed Latham United States Indian Agent, which compelled him for a time to move his family to Fort Clark. Latham, however, was not the first settler at the Elkhart Grove. Charles Turley of Kentucky, with his wife, Elizabeth, and a large brood of children, were pushing into Illinois in the summer of 1823, when they discovered the picturesque Itaska knoll. They promptly started building a cabin there.

The third pioneer family to make its home in Latham's Settlement during that important discovery year of 1823, was Daniel Lantis, with his wife and children, from Ohio. Several years later, Lantis built a dam and a water-powered saw mill on Salt Creek not far from Elkhart. This was the mill that sawed the lumber from which Robert Musick, another early settler, constructed his board house, another first of its kind in that region.

By the time the youthful Reverend Crissey arrived in the late fall of 1831, several other families had built cabins at Latham's Settlement, including Jacob Moore, a weaver and blacksmith, who came in the 1820s. Crissey's congregation here was tiny. To the serious young preacher, however, every soul earnestly yearning for Christ was worth whatever personal sacrifice it cost to bring the Word to him. The spectacular beauty of the noble trees densely timbering Elkhart knoll doubtless helped compensate the young circuit rider for the sparsity of his flock.

Second Thursday: After spending his second Wednesday night with friends at Latham's Settlement, Crissey the next morning turned his horse northeast, following the well-traveled Springfield-Fort Dearborn Road. These two Wednesday appointments on Salt Creek in Logan County marked the southernmost extremity of the Tazewell Circuit.

Since the Springfield-Fort Dearborn Road skirted Elkhart Grove and Latham's Settlement, Crissey, upon leaving this southernmost preaching place on the circuit, chose, of course, to urge his mount along the well-marked road. Inasmuch as more than 30 miles separated Latham's Settlement from Ollendorf's Mill, his next appointment, the 26 miles of trail which he was able to use that Thursday morning, provided him with a very timely convenience.

Ollendorf's Mill on Sugar Creek, not far from the Tazewell-Logan County Boundary, was Crissey's destination. The site was about four miles north by west of the subsequent village of *LAWNDALE*. To reach the mill, the Reverend Crissey was compelled to turn his horse off the Springfield-Chicago Road, and proceed through the prairie grass for about five miles. Nestling against the small timber called Ollendorf's Woods, and adjacent to Sugar Creek, he found the important little community designated Ollendorf's Mill, named after the North Carolinian who in 1826 had built there a grist mill.

From North Carolina in 1826, Christopher Ollendorf, his wife Elizabeth and their two grown sons, Benjamin and Joseph, removed to Illinois and settled on Sugar Creek, almost on the old boundary line between Sangamon and Tazewell Counties. There, the father and sons built the first grist mill in that region. It was destined to become a well-known landmark to three generations. Its burrs were hewn from Sugar Creek boulders. After the father's death in 1829, the two sons continued for years to operate the mill, and around it grew up an important settlement of Illinois frontier folk. The preaching at Ollendorf's Mill settlement, according to Leaton, "was at the house of Brother Kenny."

Within this region along Sugar Creek lying between Logan and Tazewell counties, pioneers settled first in 1823 — the same year the Latham family discovered Elkhart knoll. In the summer of 1827, the John Reed family arrived from Kentucky. Sometime during the late 1820s, three more new families came to the Ollendorf Mill region in Illinois and established homes: Ezekiel Bowman and his people, from Ohio; Ezekiel Hopkins, wife and children, from Indiana; and Robert Musick, also from Indiana.

Musick built for his family the first sawn-board house erected in the Ollendorf Mill neighborhood, obtaining his lumber from the new Lantis sawmill on nearby Sugar Creek. Musick enjoyed the unusual. He himself verged on the comical, and was regarded by all who knew him as a "character." Years before, Musick had lost a toe by some accident, and since he and many other white men of the time wore no shoes during the warm season, Musick's missing toe was common knowledge. Especially, children and the Indians were fascinated by it. Indians always addressed Musick as "Man-Without-Toe." Musick liked the Indians and they liked him. He was the deadliest marksman in the Ollendorf Mill Settlement and enjoyed demonstrating his skill. Whenever he could, Musick challenged the Indians to test their shooting against his. At these practice duels, it was seldom that Musick failed to beat them.

In 1830, the year before the Reverend Crissey made his first appearance at Ollendorf's Mill, the Ewing family arrived from Tennessee. There is evidence that the middle-aged couple, John and Elizabeth Ewing, and their half-grown son, Christopher, were people of alert, imaginative minds. The father had fought in the War of 1812. Christopher, the son, in later years wrote the best extant description of the Kickapoo Indians, as he observed them around Ollendorf's Mill.[4]

Second Friday: Leaving the Ollendorfs and their neighbors, Crissey continued riding on almost due north. This was the second longest leg of his circuit, almost 15 miles. Fortunately, the Reverend Crissey in 1831 and 1832 was a youth in strong health, for this middle span of his second week on the circuit would have

---

[4] Ewing probably wrote his description just prior to Crissey's arrival in 1831, since, at the approach of the Black Hawk War in 1832, most of the Indians inhabiting the region served by the Tazewell Circuit decamped for safer regions. About 1830, however, the Kickapoos were fairly numerous and often meddlesome.

proved unbearably exhausting to an older man. Even he must have considered it an ordeal. During his second Wednesday Crissey had filled double preaching appointments, first at the Randolph Neighborhood, then 12 miles away, at Elkhart Grove. Leaving Elkhart Grove the morning of his second Thursday, he had ridden on the well-trodden Springfield-Chicago road for 15 miles, its convenience interrupted only where the road crossed Salt Creek.[5]

A Vast Land of Giant Grasses

Between Ollendorf's Mill and Old Mackinaw Town, Crissey traversed the widest prairie anywhere on the Tazewell Circuit. The 20 miles of it which he crossed once every three weeks comprised but a small part of its whole area. Beginning at Dry Grove and Twin Grove, over in McLean County, this great prairie stretched westward all the way across Tazewell County and into Mason County — up to 50 miles of grassland, treeless except for a few insignificant clumps of timber and slender strips of trees paralleling the creeks. Between Ollendorf's Woods on the south and Stout's Grove on the north, this tremendous prairie measured almost 30 miles. It encompassed, therefore, at least 1,000 square miles of Illinois' finest and most spectacular tall grasses, its vast expanse unbroken by any sizeable islands of trees.

His route from Ollendorf's Mill to Old Mackinaw Town, even though it traversed mile after mile of towering grass stalks — often in summer so tall that the rider could barely peer across their tops — was easy for him to follow, because the year before he came onto the circuit, his predecessor, the Reverend Stephen

---

[5] Salt Creek was misnamed; it carried more water than Mackinaw River and drained five counties. Where the Springfield-Chicago Road forded, Salt Creek was one hundred yards wide and often deep and swift. I have found it impossible to verify how people following the Road got across Salt Creek. Because of its depth, conceivably, a raft-paddle ferry operated, although the sparse traffic would scarcely have justified a ferry.

R. Beggs, had pioneered the way many times. The prints of Mr. Beggs' horse's hooves could still be seen in November 1831, when young William Stoddart Crissey first rode into the great prairie alone.

Many years later, during his retirement at Decatur, Illinois, the old circuit rider, whenever he reminisced about his year on the Tazewell Circuit, always remembered vividly his sensations as he and his horse crossed that immense grassland. In midsummer, 1832, he had seen it as a seemingly limitless ocean of green towering stalks of grass, sprinkled with fragrant flowers, billowing in the incessant breeze with bird calls filling the air.

When he saw it first in October and November 1831, already the autumn winds had blown down the tall stalks, tangling them into an airy greenish-yellow mattress, blanketing the landscape as far as his eyes could see. By Christmas, the appearance of the prairies he found to be drastically and depressingly transformed into blackened wastes; for even into the 1850s, Illinois frontiersmen customarily burned off the old grass, usually early in December. After Christmas, falls of fresh snow obliterated the ugliness.

But the onset of winter not only beautified the landscape, it brought frigid winds and sometimes bitter cold. Unfortunately for the young Reverend Crissey, he always crossed this vast prairie, traveling from south to north, usually into the teeth of the wind. In his old age, doubtless he still remembered certain plodding journeys in the saddle across that immense, lonely and arctic prairie — huddled within his heaviest overcoat, a homemade wool muffler wound about his throat, a fur cap pulled far down over ears and brow — when both man and beast, chilled to their bones, suffered. Unquestionably, however, during such ordeals, young William Stoddart Crissey invariably whispered to himself as he plodded on, those strong words of the Great Apostle to the Gentiles, "I reckon that the sufferings of this present time are not worthy to be compared with the glory which shall be revealed to us."[6]

After four to six hours' in the saddle, the young circuit minister discerned big Mackinaw Grove to his left, and at its northern end, Old Mackinaw Town, his destination. But Old Mackinaw Town was not for him a place to pause for rest. Immediately, after finishing his duties there, he was compelled to repack his saddle bag, remount, and ride another four miles across the prairie to the little settlement of *TREMONT*. In all, between the Randolph Neighborhood in Logan County, and Tremont in Tazewell County, during three days and nights, young Crissey found this southernmost loop of his circuit the most exhausting segment of its 250 miles.[7]

After his trail entered Tazewell County, ever northward he rode, for probably two hours, before he forded Little Mackinaw Creek. Still on north he rode until he arrived at the Mackinaw River.

An Old, Old Town, Once Famous, Now Almost Forgotten

There stood Old Mackinaw Town, the first county seat of Tazewell County, and for a few years the busiest place in the county. In 1827, white men first settled in the picturesque grove

---

[6] *Romans*: 8:18.

[7] The three Bloomington physicians asked to conjecture the nature of Crissey's prolonged and ever-worsening illness that eventually compelled him to leave the ministry all agreed that he probably contracted tuberculosis of the lungs, and that the hardships of this circuit work caused his breakdown. The disease, they surmised, may have infected him as early as 1832. If so, the killing pace of his second week on the Tazewell Circuit must be assumed to have started the undermining of his health.

overlooking the river. Indians told them of their old tribal tradition that the site centuries before had been occupied by a village of the ancient Mackinaws — an Indian nation long since extinct. So, for years, the white men gave their settlement the nostalgic name, "Old Mackinaw Town."

At first, the settlement flourished. Its log courthouse, built in 1828, hoisted on pilings with hogs wallowing underneath, was still its civic center in 1831-1832, when young William Stoddart Crissey preached there. His congregation included some, and perhaps most, of the following community leaders: the Hittle family from Pennsylvania and Ohio, who settled at Old Mackinaw Town in 1830; Mordecai Moberly, semi-official "village father," Postmaster, County and Circuit Recorder and Clerk and also County Judge; the families of Rufus North, John Bogardus, and J.C. Morgan. In the early 1830s there may have been 25 families or more situated in or near Old Mackinaw Town. The village by 1831 contained several stores and shops. It was a trading center for families living as far east as Bloomington and Blooming Grove.

The Methodist society at Old Mackinaw Town, however, was small, so the pastor, after conducting his work, remounted and turned westward for a second appointment of the day. Near Old Mackinaw Town, Crissey forded the river, then pushed on westward to a little settlement on Dillon Creek, located near Elm and Pleasant Groves, not far from the present site of Tremont. The Tremont colonies from Rhode Island and New York, which enriched Tazewell County by half a hundred prosperous and well educated settlers, did not appear in Illinois until three years after the Reverend Crissey had finished his pastoral work in Tazewell County. (See Chapter IX.) Hezekiah Davis from Virginia and his family doubtless listened to Crissey's sermons in 1831-1832. Davis had arrived in 1826, and the year following purchased a nearby tannery and moved it to Pleasant Grove. Others living nearby in 1831-1832 were James Chapman and his family, the first settlers, Michael Trout, David Lackland, William Sterling and the Broyhill brothers, William and James.

This second Friday was the most exhausting lap on the circuit. "Here was an important society. During part of the year the preaching was at the house of a Bro. Eads, a prominent citizen, who afterward moved to Peoria," said Leaton in his narrative.

Second Saturday: Some eight miles southwest down the Dillon Creek and Mackinaw River Valleys, following a rough trail all the way, the young traveling preacher reached the Sand Prairie neighborhood, four or five miles south of the present site of *PEKIN*. Here just north of the river, avoiding the barren sandy prairie on the opposite side, were two small religious societies that he visited that same day, preaching, counseling, reviewing the classes and encouraging his people in both settlements.

Several families had settled as early as 1824 close to the timber along the north bank of the Mackinaw River. Perhaps the best remembered among them was Major Isaac Perkins, who lost his life in 1832 fighting Chief Black Hawk's Indians. In 1828-1829, Daniel Ramkin and James Reese, both from Pennsylvania, had arrived. Crissey's worship services were held in the log house built about 1826 by Gideon Hawley, also an Easterner.

At Sand Prairie, the Reverend Crissey reached the outermost southwestern point on his circuit. By the route he had traveled, he was then about 150 miles out of Bloomington. From there on he would be winding his way back toward Bloomington and Blooming Grove. At Sand Prairie he must have realized that he was far from home — if, indeed, he thought of Bloomington as "home," for the circuit rider knew no home, really, other than his saddle.

VII
DAY BY DAY
AROUND THE TAZEWELL CIRCUIT

Final Week: The Way Back to Bloomington

Third Sunday: William Stoddart Crissey's final Sabbath appointment on the circuit that year was at Pekin, an important settlement, laid out in 1829 on the east shore of the Illinois River. In 1830, Pekin became the new county seat of Tazewell County, replacing Old Mackinaw Town. Pekin was easily the most important preaching place on the Tazewell Circuit. The youthful Reverend Crissey first saw Pekin in the fall of 1831, from horseback. He was favorably impressed with the thriving river port as he rode northward into the town over the rough trail that connected Pekin to Springfield.

He found Pekin by far the most populous town on the Tazewell Circuit. By the time he first saw it, more than 1,000 people were living there. Its business section in November 1831 boasted more than a score of stores and shops. Most of them were constructed of rough-sawed planks. Some were even painted! All seemed well stocked with goods brought up the river from St. Louis. The young Methodist minister's ears noted the incessant noises of hammer, maul and ax echoing throughout the town.

Pekin occupied an excellent site for a town, on the East bank of the Illinois River, just where the stream rounded a big bend clockwise, flowing first southeast then swinging all the way around to the northwest. Cooper's Island, a short distance off shore, provided a dependable breakwater that protected the town during the floods that occurred every spring.

The young Methodist minister was met at Pekin by Jacob Tharp and his sons, Jonathan and Northcott, all enthusiastic

117

Methodists originally from Pennsylvania. Jonathan Tharp had built the first cabin on the site of Pekin in 1824. Two years later his father and brother joined him and built a second cabin nearby. It was in one of the Tharp cabins in 1826 that Pekin's first worship service had been conducted.

As in all river towns, Pekin's business life focused toward the water. Front Street ran roughly north and south along the brink of the 30-foot embankment that paralleled the river. At low water in October, this embankment lay back 100 yards or more from the water, but during spring floods, the river lapped its base.

Running eastward back into the woods, which closed in a quarter mile away, streets were laid out, approximately 100 yards apart. By 1830, most of the best land in Pekin had gravitated into the possession of five men — all sensible leaders and men of means and good character: William Haines, Thomas Snell, Nathan Cromwell, William Brown and David Bailey. Crissey came to know them all, because it was customary wherever he preached for all the leading families of the community to attend his worship services. The Methodists, for some years after Pekin was settled, were the only denomination providing Pekin with regularly scheduled church services. At Pekin, during William Stoddart Crissey's itinerary, these occurred on Sunday every three weeks.

Indulging a bit of whimsy, probably with the connivance of their womenfolk, Pekin's leading citizens, when the town was platted in 1829, bestowed feminine names upon all east and west streets in town, naming them after their wives and daughters: "Elizabeth Street," after Mrs. Thomas Snell, "Anna Eliza Street," after Mrs. Nathan Cromwell,[1] and "Jane Street," after Mrs. John

---

[1] It was Mrs. Cromwell, obviously an imaginative and extroverted woman , who chose the town's singular name: "The New Celestial Pekin." The story — admittedly apocryphal — tells that Mrs. Cromwell calculated that her new town in Illinois occupied the position on the earth's surface precisely opposite to that of China's capital, a miscalculation later found to be some five thousand miles in error. (Actually, that site on the earth's surface diametrically opposite Pekin, Illinois, is near the center of the Indian Ocean.)

G. Adams. There was also a "Lucina Street," one named "Amanda," another "Sabella," and half a dozen more.

By the fall of 1831, when Crissey first rode into Pekin, probably as many as 200 cabins and cottages lined these little, dusty, but gracefully named, streets. Everywhere except in the very middle of the streets, stumps still protruded. Few shade trees survived the pioneers' axes. Settlers coming out of the vast forests of eastern America ruthlessly chopped down trees around them, in order to open up space to live in. Two generations and more were to pass before Middle Westerners finally came to appreciate the comfort and value bestowed by shade trees.

The Methodist circuit rider was guest in Pekin's first, and at that time only, brick residence, built just the year before by Jacob Tharp. Several blocks east of Front Street, at "Tharps' Place," the brick house stood conspicuously among its neighboring log cabins and plank-board cottages. It was in Jacob Tharp's new brick house that Crissey first conducted his worship services, meetings and classes in 1831. Soon after the new Snell Schoolhouse at Elizabeth and Second Streets was finished, the Methodists borrowed it for their Sunday meetings. The Snell Schoolhouse was a frame building erected the same year, largely by the energy — and money — of Thomas Snell. John S. Snell, his son, became Pekin's first school master.

When Reverend Crissey first met them, the people of Pekin believed that their "Celestial City," as they were beginning occasionally to call it, was some day going to be "the biggest city in all of Illinois." In 1831, that goal did not appear too far-fetched, for Pekin was the most important town on the Illinois River and the fastest growing. Peoria, upstream some 10 miles, had not then been incorporated and contained but half a dozen frame buildings and fewer than 20 cabins. Almost everybody called the settlement there "Fort Clark," named way back in 1813 after the great George Rogers Clark. In 1831, Pekin's civic future did, indeed, appear assured and impressive. Unfortunately, it was a premature vision, soon to be shattered.

The blow fell one afternoon the following May at an inconsequential creek in Ogle County — later to be renamed by Illinois historians "Stillman's Run." In the brief course of a few hours, nine of Pekin's best known men were shot down and scalped by Chief Black Hawk's warriors. Among those killed was John G. Adams, one of the most prominent men in town. Major Isaac Perkins was another well-known Pekin leader who was shot and killed by the Indians that day. Both Adams and Perkins were officers, commanding a motley company of some 300 volunteers from Tazewell and Fulton Counties who had marched north, resolved to drive Black Hawk and his Sacs and Foxes back across the Mississippi.[2]

Brashly overconfident, disorganized and impetuous, the whites rushed into battle against the Indians. Black Hawk's warriors overwhelmed them and sent them flying terrified toward their homes. The bodies of the Illinoisans who fell that afternoon were left behind to be scalped. The next day their mutilated corpses were buried in unmarked graves, where they had fallen.

---

[2] For generations before Illinois was settled by the whites, the Sacs and Foxes had occupied the picturesque Rock River Valley. In the later 1820s their chieftain was Black Hawk, an Indian leader of distinguished wisdom and integrity. Pressured by the encroaching whites, Black Hawk had signed a treaty with white traders, agreeing to give up his people's ancient homelands and retire west of the Mississippi River. In the spring of 1831 Black Hawk brought his people back across the river and into the Rock River Valley. His reasons for this move are obscure, but that his intentions were peaceful was plainly evident by the fact that he was accompanied by womenfolk, children and old people, something which no Indian war party ever permitted. The Sacs and Foxes conducted themselves quietly on this visit. Their very presence, however, alarmed the whites. Hotheads insisted that the Indians be pushed back across the Mississippi, and a campaign was organized to accomplish this. Not until he was first attacked by whites did Black Hawk strike back. The consequences, as usually has been true in conflicts between red men and white men, were for the Indians tragic, for the whites perfidious.

When the appalling news reached Pekin, the shock was traumatic. Captain Adams had commanded the Tazewell County volunteers as they had gaily marched off the week before. His wife, Jane Adams, was known to everybody in Pekin as a community and church leader. Upon learning that her husband had been killed in battle and that his body had been abandoned to mutilation by the Sacs and Foxes, Mrs. Adams' mind collapsed. During the remainder of her life she never fully recovered her reason.

The shocks suffered by others differed only in degree. All that summer day the entire town remained stunned by the awful catastrophe. Pekin never recovered its old, ebullient spirit. Pekin's shock was enormously intensified by fear. All summer long, Pekin men largely forgot their regular work, while they labored frantically to fortify the Snell Schoolhouse. Every week they anticipated an invasion by Black Hawk's vengeful warriors, not knowing that the Indians had fled into Wisconsin.

Such was the tragically fractured and frightened frontier river town of Pekin that the young circuit rider ministered to that summer of 1832. We can be sure that the somberness of Pekin's grief and fear after May 1832 colored the tone of the Methodist pastor's preaching and Bible studies as he tried to comfort his stricken flock. Most of the nine men killed he had known personally and several he remembered affectionately as members of his class at Pekin.

This sudden and horrible snatching by death compelled the little town's families to meditate upon eternal things. For consolation, the more thoughtful ones turned to God's Word. Most Pekin families owned a Bible, and often it was the only book they owned. But it was mainly to their pastor, youthful as he was, that they looked for comfort. He ministered it to them. That was his work. He was grateful that God deemed him worthy to be used.

Third Monday: Leaving Pekin, Crissey turned his mount northward, following a path skirting the timber that paralleled the Illinois River. On the river's eastern bank, opposite Fort Clark, he found his little congregation. Several times that summer of 1832, Crissey ferried across to the western bank of the Illinois River, near the foot of Lake Peoria, its broadened channel. The place where he landed was not then called Peoria. That name in 1832 was almost never mentioned. In fact, the town of Peoria was not incorporated until 1835, although the legislature had authorized it in 1831. The little settlement 10 miles up-river from Pekin and on the opposite shore was spoken of as Fort Clark. It had been so called ever since the erection there of an old frontier defense many years before. The old name regained acceptance in 1832 during the Black Hawk War, when the fort was rebuilt, even though it was never garrisoned. Occasionally during the summer of 1832, Crissey took the liberty of ferrying over the Illinois River to Fort Clark, and "preaching there in the house of his former member, Brother Eads," stated Leaton.

At other times, the young minister met with a small but fervent Methodist society on the Tazewell County side of the river. Vigorous Methodist seeds must have been planted there, because a generation later the settlement chose to identify its Post Office as "Wesley City." But when the Reverend Crissey stopped there, it was known as "Fond du Lac." Earliest settlers there who, with their families, made up the Reverend Crissey's little congregation included Jacob L. Wilson from Indiana, who came in 1824; Cyrus J. Gibson, Elza Bethard, Thomas Camlin and Joseph Schertz. The community was proud of its new water-powered sawmill, opened in 1828 on Farmer's Creek.

Each third Monday, when the young preacher arrived, work at the mill stopped long enough for Crissey to deliver his sermon to the people assembled to hear him. The mill shed was his auditorium. As usual, after preaching, he reviewed the classes, catechized new candidates, counseled with local leaders, performed any weddings or baptisms required, and then dined and spent the night with one of the local families. Early the following morning he was in the saddle and away.

Third Tuesday: Following a well-traveled dirt road northward through the timber paralleling the eastern bank of the Illinois River, then turning inland at the ferry landing over the well-traveled Fort Clark-Danville Road, the Reverend Crissey continued on northeast across the prairie.

As soon as he emerged from the trees shading the Illinois River bluffs, he found himself ascending a gradual slope rising to a grassy plateau, which opened upon a spacious prairie. From that vantage point he viewed an immense ocean of towering grass, without a tree in sight. For more than an hour's travel the horseback rider saw nothing but a sea of giant grass. Here was the meadowland that explorers in Illinois ever since Joliet, Marquette and LaSalle had observed as a peculiarity of this region.

Only one shallow stream, Farmer's Creek, intersected this plateau. A few sparse trees marked the course of Farmer's Creek. Two small groves guarded its source. After two hours' travel, he came to a lonely little settlement nestling on the fringes of Wrenn's Grove and Holland's Grove, which eventually consolidated under the current place name, *WASHINGTON*.

Wrenn's and Holland's Groves was a joint settlement, begun in 1825, when William Holland, formerly of North Carolina, built a cabin there. Holland worked as a blacksmith to the Indians. He married three times, sired 21 children and died in his 91st year. When Crissey came in 1831, 17 families resided near the two groves. The first religious meeting at the settlement was held in 1828 when the indefatigable Methodist missionary, Jesse Walker, preached in the Holland cabin. Crissey, in the fall of 1831, preached in one of the larger cabins among those belonging to the society.

The Preacher Takes a Bride

Leaton interjected a modest touch of romance at this point, mentioning that the Heath family was prominent in Holland's and

Wrenn's Grove Methodist society. William Heath, his wife and family of daughters had moved to Wrenn's Grove from Ohio in 1830. One of these daughters was destined to play a role in the history of the Tazewell Circuit. The year prior to Crissey's arrival, his predecessor, the Reverend Stephen R. Beggs, had interrupted his ministerial duties to court one of the Heath daughters once every three weeks. Probably he was able to see the young lady only one day out of every 21, but that proved sufficient, for the Reverend Beggs proposed, was accepted and took her to wife.

Since weddings were the most important social affairs the frontier afforded, one's imagination is titillated at the picture there at lonely Wrenn's Grove, Illinois, during the summer and early fall of 1831, while this young circuit riding minister persistently but discreetly courted his Miss Heath. One can imagine the growing gossip about it, the exciting announcement of their engagement, and, at last, the sensational wedding itself. The minister who read the service is unrecorded, but in all probability it was none other than Peter Cartwright, Mr. Beggs' Presiding Elder. It is a pleasant and revealing little vignette.

At the Holland's and Wrenn's Groves, Leaton mentioned, "A young relative of the [William Heath] family, Zadok Hall, a local preacher, came out from Ohio during the year, and at its close was recommended to the annual conference."

Third Wednesday: From Holland's and Wrenn's Groves, Crissey rode his horse eastward more than 10 miles across more treeless prairie, but following, all the way, along the Fort Clark-Danville Road. A couple of miles west of lower Walnut Creek, the circuit rider left the road and turned sharply northward toward little Walnut Grove. In winter, this high ground was swept by icy gales. Then, it was truly a lonely road. At Walnut Grove, near Walnut Creek, in what is now southern Woodford County, nestled another small society beneath and on the edge of a forest of thousands of towering black walnut trees. The tiny backwoods settlement there was destined eventually to become *EUREKA,* the county seat.

The young circuit rider no doubt enjoyed this third week on his circuit, because of its dramatic contrasts, which followed one another in quick succession: Sunday on the bustling river front at Pekin he found more people at one center than anywhere else on his circuit; Monday he traveled along the broad Illinois River; Tuesday he found himself crossing another wide prairie, high, windy and lonely; then Wednesday, he plunged into the edge of the wildest region anywhere on the Tazewell Circuit.

Crissey's two-day incursion into the southern tip of Woodford County brought him face to face with the most primitive country of Central Illinois in the 1830s. Eastward from Walnut Grove, only six or seven miles away, glowered the fearsome Big Painter Woods,[3] avoided by all white persons, because its dense timber reputedly concealed several lairs of the dangerous big cats. Also, in the 1830s Big Painter Woods sheltered bears and a few of the big black timber wolves, which were heavier and fiercer than the smaller prairie wolves numerous elsewhere. The grove covered some 30 square miles of extremely rugged, rocky hills, all canopied with giant hardwood trees that had been growing there for thousands of years. Panther Creek and its East Branch trisected Big Painter Woods.

Much of this ground was rough and rolling, and steeply eroded by rocky streams flowing into the Mackinaw River, while over it spread a dense canopy of gigantic hardwood trees. Here was a magnificent outpost of the ancient North American forest primeval, not indigenous to most areas of Illinois, but just here flourishing tremendously.

Isolated from traffic lanes, and crowded before a sinister forest, it was inevitable that the region should remain a wilderness much longer than communities to the south and east of it. Walnut Grove, for instance, where the Reverend Crissey entered this primitive region, was still minus a Post Office as late as 1850. It

---

[3] Universally along the Illinois frontier in the 1830s, the colloquial noun, "Painter," was used to designate the wild panther.

was still without a store, blacksmith or wagon shop more than 25 years after these conveniences had appeared at Pekin, Old Mackinaw Town and Blooming Grove.

Pioneer families discovered Walnut Grove only three or four years before Crissey's arrival. The three Moore brothers, Charles, John A., and Campbell, from Kentucky, were living there in 1828, when passers-through reported "a few families at Walnut Grove." John Moore did not stay, but penetrated some miles further southeast to Panther Creek.[4]

To Walnut Grove, John Dowdy and his wife, Eliza, came about 1829. Mrs. Dowdy soon after gave birth to the first baby born in the community. Tragically, as too often happened to frontier women, the mother died a few months later. Others at Walnut Grove to whom the Reverend Crissey preached in 1831 and 1832 included Isaac Black and the Richardsons, James and Aaron, from Indiana, all of whom arrived in 1830.

Walnut Grove's most distinctive settler had preceded them — the Reverend Oatman, a minister ordained by the Disciples of Christ, a new denomination formed during the early 19th century in Kentucky, Ohio and Indiana. The Reverend Oatman preached the first sermon at Walnut Grove, and in 1832 organized a Disciples Society, attended originally by seven members. "Elder Oatman," as he became known, contributed such durable faith and labor to his community that, out of the spiritual seeds he planted, in 1847 grew the Walnut Grove Academy, which in 1855 became Eureka College.

In 1831 other settlers arrived: Caleb Davidson and his father, William Davidson from Kentucky; William P. Atteberry, also from Kentucky; and Matthew Bracken from Ohio. Doubtless,

---

[4] The name projected quite dramatically the savage character of the surrounding country then, and even today. About a mile from the mouth of Panther Creek, until almost into the 20th century, a deep dark, sinister cave on the left bank of the creek housed successive generations of panthers. The cave was the object of many fearsome folk tales among early settlers.

the young Reverend Crissey preached to most of them, and during his year on the circuit, won their friendship and support, even though many of them were primarily loyal to their own Disciples Society.

Third Thursday: Bidding good-bye to his friends at Walnut Grove each third Thursday morning, young Crissey guided his horse down a narrow trail traversing a small prairie. For two hours he rode his lonely way through the tall grass, emerging finally onto the most primitive and remote of all his appointments. Here, hugging Panther Creek and shrouded to the east by savage wilderness, the youthful clergyman encountered the tiny but noisy Willis Mill. Whenever it was operating, young Crissey no doubt smiled to himself, recognizing afar off the mill's groans and grumbles. Willis Mill was the focus in 1831-1832 of whatever civilization existed in the remote and dangerous Panther Creek region. Because of the loneliness Crissey's arrival always came as a welcome break in the solitude.

The creek had been named after a family of panthers whose den was not far away. Bears and timber wolves, too, were known to inhabit those rugged woods. At that time Indians felt at home there, and frequently hung around the little mill. However, Crissey never saw them there, and, if he had, would have greeted them in friendship. Wolves had been numerous in the Panther Creek valley two years before Crissey came, but the Big Snow the preceding winter had starved out most of them as well as most of the deer and small game.

On Panther Creek, John Moore built a tiny mill of logs, powered by one horse walking a treadmill. Farmers from as far as 40 miles away hauled their grain to "Moore's corn cracker." About 1831, Moore sold his mill to Francis M. Willis, a new settler just arrived from Kentucky. Willis enlarged and improved the mill, and operated it profitably. His severest worry was from mischievous Kickapoos who, up here near the big woods, remained numerous and bold until frightened away during the Black Hawk War.

Living near the mill that fall, when the young circuit rider first came down the trail to get acquainted, were the following families: John Moore, first settler and builder of the horse mill; Francis M. Willis, who bought the mill in 1831; James M. Richardson, and his brother, Aaron, who had moved down from Walnut Grove. (In 1836, Willis laid out in southwestern Woodford County, the site of Bowling Green, a village that existed for one generation, then disappeared.)

Settlers along Panther and Walnut Creeks enjoyed getting together in summer under the big walnut trees. During the summer of 1832, on at least one occasion, Crissey held a two-day outdoor religious meeting, and Leaton mentioned a visitor: "Here, a two-day meeting was held at which Brother Beggs preached an excellent sermon from the text 'All Scripture is given by the inspiration of God.'" It may be assumed that the visitor was prompted to come, in part by the new Mrs. Beggs' desire to visit her family at nearby Wrenn's Grove.

Third Friday: Panther Grove lay in a kind of broad peninsula between two fords, one crossing Panther Creek, the other crossing Mackinaw River. Although quite passable by a man on horseback throughout most of the year, heavy rainfalls rendered the fords difficult and dangerous. This hazard existed at many fords on the Tazewell Circuit, but was particularly dangerous near the mouth of the streams when they carried heavy flows of water. It is on record, however, that the Reverend Crissey never missed an appointment during the year 1831-1832; but there must have been occasions when he needed all his resources to arrive on time.

Soon after leaving the Panther Grove settlement, Crissey re-entered McLean County. Skirting heavily forested country all the way for several miles, his horse headed southward. At that time a big stand of timber covered northwest McLean County and lapped amply across into Tazewell and Woodford Counties. It was called, in McLean County, Stout's Grove. Here, awaiting him, was a thriving settlement and Methodist society, the 22nd he had visited since leaving Bloomington 19 days before.

Ephram Stout, a farmer from Tennessee, with his grown son, Ephram, Jr., selected this handsome grove in 1825 as the place where they wished to settle. Another son, David, joined them a year later, and soon thereafter the mother and wife with several additional children came on to complete the family. Because this settlement stood near the much-traveled "Old State Road," the Pekin-Urbana Trail, it was soon a well-known location and grew rapidly. It included the present site of the town of *DANVERS*. By November 1831, when the Reverend Crissey first came there to preach, there may have been as many as a dozen families residing at Stout's Grove, comprising perhaps 35 or 40 persons.

Here, as at Walnut Grove, the Methodists were not the trail-breakers in religion. That very first year during which the Stouts discovered the big grove, the Reverend Peyton Mitchell, his wife and nine-year-old son, Ebenezer, also discovered it and settled there. They were Scottish Cumberland Presbyterians from Kentucky. The Reverend Mitchell possessed ability in every way equal to that of his colleagues of the cloth, and the only reason he was not as successful as the Reverend Crissey and the other Methodist circuit riders was that he was handicapped because he did not have an effective organization to support him as he traveled the field. In organization the Methodists were supreme, and, consequently, forged ahead.

Squire Robb's "High Water Wedding"

Perhaps best remembered among those who listened to Crissey preach that year of 1831-1832 at Stout's Grove was Matthew Robb, a young pioneer of intellect, energy and character, who settled there in 1827. It was he who evolved into "Squire Robb," local magistrate and oracle of the area for many years.

Illustrative of the man's ingenuity, and typical also of the frontier spirit in Central Illinois during the 1830s, was the famous "High Water Wedding" that Squire Robb performed late one rainy evening.

Darkness had fallen before he was summoned by torchlight to read the marriage vows. Mounting his horse, he rode up Sugar Creek in the rain to meet the couple, whom he found stranded on the opposite bank. Bride and groom were dismayed to discover that the flooded creek was quite impassable. Squire Robb was not dismayed. Commanding that the torches be held aloft, he told the couple to stand at the water's edge, so that he could see them across the creek. The squire then rode into the surging stream up to his horse's belly and, there under the torchlight and drenching rain, shouting across a muddy flood, solemnized the ceremony.

Third Saturday: Not far from Stout's Grove, across another Sugar Creek, was a strong Methodist society, supported jointly by the people of Dry Grove and Twin Grove. The society here provided the Reverend Crissey's final preaching place on the Tazewell Circuit. In the fall of 1831, when the Reverend Crissey first arrived, nearly 20 families and settlers were living near one or the other of these two little groves, separated only by an alley of prairie grass.

Peter McCullough of Kentucky, and his son, William, had arrived there first in 1826. Stephen Webb of Tennessee came a year later. Then, Henry Vansickles, a Pennsylvania farmer, located near Dry Grove in 1828. Others followed rapidly because this settlement, like Stout's Grove, had the advantage of being on a well-traveled road.

After preaching to his people of the two groves in one of the larger cabins there, counseling with the local leaders, reviewing the classes, and performing any official duties needed, Crissey was able to look forward to another Sabbath at Bloomington. The arrival of the morrow meant that he had once more fed his 25 flocks, traversed his more than 250 miles and lifted the name of

130

his Lord to some 500 or more soul-hungry frontier folk. That realization was his chief reward. Indeed, it was virtually his only reward, considering his meager money support. He cherished it, and he considered it sufficient.

After finishing his duties at Dry Grove and Twin Grove, the boy-preacher remounted his horse and turned its muzzle eastward. Inasmuch as the termination of his circuit would find him back in Bloomington, it seems likely that young Crissey, as often as possible, rode the final few miles Saturday evening, enabling him to rest two nights with the Allin family in Bloomington, among warm-hearted friends. His final miles followed the well-traveled Pekin-Urbana-Wabash Trail, appropriately, the same road that had brought him into Bloomington in October 1831.

Because this travelogue following young William Stoddart Crissey around the Tazewell Circuit derives its accuracy wholly from Dr. Leaton's writing, let us conclude this travelogue in Dr. Leaton's own words:

At Dry and Twin Grove was a good society. This was the last appointment on the circuit, the preacher beginning again at Bloomington on the following Sabbath.

The first quarterly meeting of the year was held in Pekin. It was a good meeting. The presiding elder was present. He preached on Sunday from, "Lion hath roared, who will not fear? the Lord hath spoken who can but prophesy?" The subject was admirably adapted to his lion-like voice and manner, and the sermon was one of his most successful attempts.

Two camp meetings were held during the Summer, at both of which were gracious revivals. The first was held by the pastor and local preachers near where Tremont now is. And the second in Randolph Grove close to the Kickapoo. The Presiding Elder was present and most of the official members of the circuit. On Sunday afternoon Mr. Crissey preached. His text was "An enemy hath done this"; and his theme the character and work of the devil . . . .

The year was on the whole a prosperous one. Despite the [Black Hawk] war there was some increase in the membership; and of the $100 quarterage claim of the preacher he received $80.

VIII

"'Tis Mercy All, Immense and Free, for, O My God, It Found Out Me."

—from the 1830 "Collection of Methodist Hymns."

Conceding that Methodism's system of organization was superbly adapted to conquer the American frontier, that advantage alone cannot explain its phenomenal success. What motivated the circuit riders and the church members inhabiting the Atlantic Seaboard who supported them by prayers and money?

Behind Methodism's conquest of the American West there was something more powerful than efficient organization. That mysterious propulsion came from sources not mundane but inexplicable, irresistible, supernal. The mystery of it was eloquently elucidated many years ago by these paragraphs, excerpted from a rare little volume published at London in 1911, *The Love of Jesus*. Sir Henry S. Lunn of Trinity College, Dublin, was its author. He called it ""A Manual of Prayer, . . ." addressed to the "People Called Methodists:"

What was the secret of that flame of love for humanity which revealed itself in early Methodism, incidentally leading to the emancipation of the West Indian slaves and the birth in England of the spirit of Social Reform, and which, according to Lecky the historian, saved England from the horrors of the French Revolution? It is the secret which is revealed in the lives of all the great saints of the Universal Church. These men have been the divine instruments in those periodic revivals of spiritual life which, from generation to generation, have rekindled the embers of a faltering faith, because of their consciousness of the Love of Jesus towards them, and as a result their personal devotion to the Living Christ. This note, of a love that triumphs over all other considerations, characterizes their lives and their teaching.

St. Paul, as he reviews the earlier objects of his ambition, says, "I count all things but loss for the excellency of the knowledge of Christ Jesus my Lord." To him the great object of all his endeavour is "to know the love of Christ, which passeth knowledge." The whole burden of St. John's message is Love. "Herein is love, not that we loved God, but that He loved us and gave His only Son to be the propitiation for our sins. . . . We love Him because He first loved us."

The marvelous power that motivated the Methodists and enabled them to conquer the American West, in the opinion of Sir Henry Lunn, derived wholly from frontier Methodists' devotion to the Lord Jesus Christ. "The love of Jesus" were the four little words by which Sir Henry Lunn designated the source of that supernatural spiritual energy that clothed the Methodist circuit riders with authority.

There lurks here mystery profound, perhaps even a little awesome. The four little words may to some sound puerile, shallow, prosaic. Paradoxically, they defined something very wonderful, very marvelous — it is scarcely exaggeration to call it miraculous. The love of Jesus preached to pioneer families along the early western frontiers by the Methodist circuit riders often induced a change of thinking in the convert that made him for the rest of his life a different and better person. The "Good News" about the love of Jesus, whenever sincerely embraced, implanted in the converted sinner an ardent devotion to Christ that impelled him to worship Jesus as the Son of God, the Light of the world and his own personal Savior.

Their love of Jesus was the glory of early Methodists, and it made their horse preachers invincible.

Origin of the Methodist Circuit Riders

Bishops Thomas Coke and Francis Asbury in 1784 and Bishop Richard Whatcoat, six years later, realized that the future of American Methodism beckoned their ministers westward toward the wilderness. John Wesley himself had converted 18th Century Britain from his saddle, riding horseback year after year, tens of thousands of miles. Wesley's method, successful in Britain, seemed ideally adapted to preaching the Gospel to the far-flung, widely-separated pioneer families settling the Appalachian frontier.

Thus came into being the now-famous Methodist circuit riders. Methodist leaders in Baltimore and elsewhere were wise men. At once they perceived that their horse preachers could never accomplish their work if left to themselves. The preachers who rode the country and wilderness circuits needed supervision and fellowship from other ministers, preferably older and more experienced. The Presiding Elders, selected because of demonstrated leadership on the circuits, were the answer.

Those Methodist horse preachers of the American frontiers during the 19th Century left behind them a niche in United

States history embellished nowadays with a subtle glow of heroism. Their labors while they rode their preaching circuits were brutally taxing. Scarcely ever was a circuit rider permitted to pastor the same circuit longer than two years. Usually after one year he was hurled from one preaching circuit where the work had been dangerous and exhausting to another circuit, often still more demanding. But they rode, comforted by the realization that they did not ride alone; somewhere not too far away, an older, more experienced preacher, and always a loving understanding man — their Presiding Elder — was watching them, praying for them, and quick to help when needed.

On the early American frontier the Methodist Quarterly Conference was always an important occasion. The size of the area served by any particular Quarterly Conference was determined by the number of church members and the appointments comprising that particular preaching circuit.

Attending every Quarterly Conference was the Presiding Elder, the circuit rider, of course, and all his local preachers, exhorters and class leaders. Also, as many of the Methodists living around the circuit as could travel to the site came. They came joyfully, brimming with enthusiasm, lifted up in the Spirit. They came also because every Quarterly Conference afforded opportunity to renew acquaintance with old friends, to fellowship with other religious folk, to listen to fervid sermons, and often to "pray away their sins."

Not surprisingly, camp meetings almost invariably were conducted on the site and concurrently with the Quarterly Conference. These somewhat spectacular assemblies, of which the Quarterly Conference was only a part, usually began on a Friday evening and adjourned the following Monday morning. The circuit's church business was transacted on Saturday. All day Sunday was devoted, of course, to fervent preaching, praying and singing. Some time during Sunday a "Love Feast" was conducted by the Presiding Elder. This charming and emotionally uplifting experience called forth personal testimonies, confessions and

136

contrition with tearful prayers for repentant sinners. The day ended with celebration of the Lord's Supper and sharing together of the sacraments.

Camp Meetings

From the beginning of the 19th Century, through the 1830s and for a considerable while after that, an unwholesome religious frenzy swept through backwoods settlements in Kentucky, Indiana and Southern Illinois. Brimstone and hellfire rantings by illiterate preachers often worked up extravagant emotional reactions among superstitious frontier folk. Hysteria, "jerks," fainting fits, shouting, rolling, and talking with tongues were frequent during prolonged summer camp meetings. These were held usually in "brush arbors," out of doors, where people assembled in the woods, felled trees and constructed crude open air auditoriums. Thus began the camp meetings that once occupied so prominent a place in American frontier life west of the Appalachians.

Camp meetings in the Central Illinois country during the 1830s and later were conducted with considerable care and thoughtful preparation. Tents were pitched around a hollow square. Along the lower edge a preaching platform was built. Slab seats for the listeners filled the square. On each corner of the square stood log pylons six feet high, covered with earth, on which, during the services after dark, fires were kept burning for illumination. The preacher enjoyed the luxury of a candle to light his Scripture. Burning pine knots, fixed onto trees, frequently were kept burning all night, while guards patrolled the tents to guard against attacks by drunken rowdies.

Methodist camp meetings attracted families, sometimes from as far as 30 miles away. Many families came in wagons, with bedding, utensils and equipment, expecting to stay often a week or longer. Others rode horseback, many walked. Attendance was surprisingly large, considering the sparse population of the frontier. John D. Barnhardt states that, "it is very probable that in Illinois the numbers ran over the 1,000 mark at many camp

Starved for Christian fellowship and to hear God's Word preached, frontier families traveled many miles to attend the Methodist camp meetings.

meetings." A good deal of their popularity derived, of course, not only from their spiritual refreshment, but also from happy social visiting among old friends, which the gatherings made possible.

Illinois' Earliest Camp Meetings

The first Methodist camp meeting in Illinois was held during April 1807 at a rural site three miles south of Edwardsville. Jesse Walker, the indefatigable pioneer of early Illinois Methodism, conducted the meeting. Leaton went on to mention a second camp meeting that same summer held on the circuit at a place called Three Springs, afterwards known as Shiloh. This meeting, held in connection with a Quarterly Conference commenced on Friday morning and continued until the following Monday. The Presiding Elder, William McKendree, was present from the beginning of the meeting. He was accompanied by Abbot Goddard and James Gwin. Some local preachers were also present. Leaton wrote of the Three Springs camp meeting in 1807 as follows:

We arrived on Friday morning on the camp-ground, which was situated in a beautiful grove surrounded by a prairie. A considerable congregation had collected, for the news of the other meeting had gone abroad and produced much excitement. Some were in favor of the work and others were opposed to it.

A certain major had raised a company of lewd fellows of the baser sort, to drive us from the ground. On Saturday, while I was preaching, the major and his company rode into the congregation and halted, which produced considerable confusion and alarm. I stopped preaching for a moment and quite calmly invited them to be off with themselves, and they retired to the spring for a fresh drink of brandy. The major said he had heard of these Methodists before; that they always broke up the peace of the people wherever they went; that they preached against horse-racing, card-playing, and every other kind of amusement. However, they used no violence against us, but determined to camp on the ground and prevent us doing harm.

It was Sabbath morning, and I thought it the most beautiful morning I had ever seen.... At eleven o'clock Brother McKendree administered the holy sacrament; and while he was dwelling upon its origin, nature, and design, some of the major's company were affected, and we had a melting time.

After sacrament, Brother McKendree preached to a large congregation, all the principal men of the country, and all in reach, who could get there, being present. His text was, "Come, let us reason together": and, perhaps, no man ever managed the subject better or with more effect.

His reasoning on the atonement, the great plan of salvation, and the love of God was so clear and strong, and was delivered with such pathos, that the congregation involuntarily arose to their feet and pressed toward him from all parts.

While he was preaching, he very ingeniously adverted to the conduct of the major, and remarked: "We are Americans, and some of us have fought for our liberty, and have come here to teach men the way to heaven." This seemed to strike the major, and he afterwards became very friendly, and has remained so ever since.... This was a great day. The work became general, the place was awful [sic], and many souls were born of God.

By the time Methodist camp meetings arrived on the Tazewell Circuit, they had taken on a definite pattern of procedure. At daybreak, a horn woke everybody. Thirty minutes later it sounded for family prayers. Then came breakfast. About 9 o'clock, tent prayer meetings got under way. Preaching started at 10 o'clock in the "auditorium." Dinner was eaten at noon. In the afternoon there was a second preaching service, with special "after meetings" for the mourners. The busy afternoon session closed at sunset. Following the evening supper under the fire lights and shadows, came the "big, highpower conversion service." Sometimes this would be continued by successive preachers until after midnight, occasionally — if "the Spirit was working strong" — even until daybreak. But ordinarily, family prayers about 9 o'clock closed the day.

On Sundays the Lord's Supper was celebrated, and new converts baptized. Monday morning, the camp meeting adjourned with a processional around the grounds, the preachers in the van. The leaders then took their stations and shook hands with every person as they passed in line, exhorting, reproving or encouraging, as seemed best for each. Vast enthusiasm often was engendered by this farewell sevice.

Did the Methodist Frontier Camp Meetings Accomplish Anything?

Were the camp meetings worthwhile? Professor Barnhardt thought so. He said:

> While the extravagances of these services aroused the opposition of many of the cultured and educated and led many to a wrong emphasis in religious life, yet it cannot successfully be denied that they did great good. Thousands were converted and led into a higher life. Rough and lawless bands were broken up by the conver-

sions of their leaders and members. Not only were the numbers of the churches greatly increased, but the ministry was able to gather recruits from among the converts. Great revivals swept through the country as the result of several meetings.

Professor Barnhardt had this to say about the quality of camp meeting sermons:

The frequency with which these ministers preached made them excellent orators. And the circuit riders as a class were pulpit orators of a high degree, for the nature of the work they had before them.

A fine 20th Century tribute to the quality of Methodist circuit riders' preaching was heard at Lebanon, Illinois, July 11, 1962, contained within an address delivered before the annual meeting of the North Central Jurisdiction Historical Society of McKendree College. Dr. John D. Green of the North-East Ohio Methodist Conference was the speaker:

Some of them were men of eloquence and logical acuteness. They pierced through the dull, vulgar, contaminated hideousness of low and vicious life, and sent streaming in upon it the Light of a Higher World and a better Gospel. . . . It was one of different emphasis, rather than of other doctrines. As a sort of afterglow of Aldersgate, it had the sense of the discovery of God, deliverance by God and delight in God.

Dr. Green concluded with this evaluation of Methodism's music on the frontier:

Methodism's message was inseparable from its music. Indeed, it was expressed, conveyed and preserved by its hymns and songs, which stressed the need to be born again. Sin, death, and hell were frankly mentioned. This message was glad news as well as good news. So Charles Wesley set just about the whole of life to evangelical notes, speaking for, to and of the condition of man. In the 1830 Collection of Methodist Hymns, sixty-six of the numbers began with "O!" Two lines of a Wesley hymn express well this sense of awed wonder:

English Methodists about 1790 singing Charles Wesley's hymns.

"Tis mercy all, immense and free,
For, O my God, it found out me."

American Methodism Was Born at Christmastime

It was on a frosty December morning the day before Christmas in the year 1784. At 10 o'clock in the Lovely Lane Methodist Chapel in Baltimore, down near the waterfront, there had gathered some 60 Methodist preachers and two Methodist Bishops, Francis Asbury and Thomas Coke, who had come from London as spokesman for John Wesley. That Friday and the nine days that followed were destined to mark American history with an epochal happening. The new Methodist Episopal Church in America was being born, a Protestant body that for generations to come would embrace more non-Catholic Christians than any other church.

Its spiritual mother had been the venerable and dignified old Church of England. But a war had been fought that had severed the umbilical cord. After its historic Christmas Conference of 1784, American devotees of John Wesley felt themselves forever divorced from England. Theirs was an interlude of far-reaching changes. One of those changes then fermenting the world bore heavily upon the Bishops and preachers gathered at Baltimore. Indeed, when those intrepid Methodists met on Christmas Eve 1784, they were men quite literally without country. Only a little more than three years before, Lord Cornwallis had surrendered to General Washington. But the new nation-to-be was then in gestation; its Constitution was still being debated at Philadelphia; the United States of America did not yet exist.

Truly, what Bishops Coke and Asbury and their 60 Methodist preachers ventured to undertake that Christmastime was a lionhearted feat of valor which could have been validated only by Powers Celestial. Measured against the populous, prosperous solidly established churches of the Congregationalists, Presbyterians, Episcopalians and the numerous Dutch Reformed parishioners, the handful of Methodists at Baltimore were infants, pygmies, weaklings.

They owned only 60 little chapels in the whole country. Up and down the Atlantic Tidewater colonies Methodists worshipped at intervals at some 800 "preaching places," served by 104 Methodist circuit riders, or "horse preachers" as they were affectionately called. Those were the sum total of Methodist armaments with which they planned to conquer a continent.

But they marched out of Baltimore, January 2, 1785, in the words of one of their historians, "conquering and to conquer" — because they had girded on the breastplate of faith and their hearts were burning with their love of Jesus.

Unafraid, they looked westward into the brooding menace of a dark, primeval forest of giant trees, many of them centuries old, haunted by wild beasts and savages. Beyond the horizon lurked the barrier of what the Indians called "the Endless Mountains," the tangled wilderness of the Appalachians. Beyond the mountains, awaiting their coming —although they could foresee it only by their prophetic visions of the future — lay immense prairies and plains, some day to nurture a great and burgeoning and virtuous nation.

Those Methodists of 200 years ago marched forth from Baltimore's Lovely Lane Chapel resolved to capture and conquer the continent for the Lord, trusting in the benediction pronounced over them by Richard Whatcoat, one of the pioneer founders:

May the Lord follow our endeavors with a
never-ceasing shower of heart reviving love.

145

Miraculously, by faith, the new Methodist Episcopal Church in America did it! It was the Methodist circuit riders who did it. They penetrated that menacing forest, clambered across the "Endless Montains" and marched on across the flatlands. Their unquenchable faith, preached everywhere with fiery eloquence, won the souls of the lonely frontier families. The Methodist horse preachers conquered the American West.

It was the Methodist circuit riders who were always the earliest pioneers for Christ on the American frontier of the 19th Century. It happened so often as to become something of a joke that within days from when the first wood smoke arose from the chimney of a new settler's log cabin, a Methodist horse preacher would ride up and cheerily halloo the house. Within his saddlebags he carried a Bible, from which he read Scripture to the lonely man, wife and children. After prayers with them, he remounted, promising to call back again soon. He had sown the first seeds, which in time would be nurtured with a cluster of other Method-

ists, meeting at intervals with the traveling preacher for worship; eventually they would grow into a society, then into an organized church.

There was something miraculous about the success of those Methodist circuit riders. The frontier families welcomed heartily the traveling preachers and loved them because the horse preachers themselves brought to the frontier people sincere affection, genuine concern about their welfare. The thing about Methodism's circuit riders that won the souls of the families they visited was their utter devotion to the Lord Jesus. Patently, it was the love of Jesus, shared by the circuit riders with the soul-hungry people out on the frontiers, that conquered the American West.

IX

WILLIAM STODDART CRISSEY
1811 - 1888

In the year 1818, at Cincinnati, Ohio, the 7-year-old lad, William Stoddart Crissey, suddenly was stricken by a double tragedy that — by the inscrutable ways of Providence — set in motion influences that ultimately molded the boy into one of God's valiant soldiers. He became an eloquent circuit-riding preacher, a talented pastor to several of the foremost churches in Illinois, and a heroic Army Chaplain who ministered to his troops through some of the bloodiest campaigns of the Civil War. At the end of his long life — 70 years beyond that tragedy — venerated old William Stoddart Crissey still remembered with awe that terrible touch of God's finger that ordained his future life.

That event had been the simultaneous deaths of his mother and father, presumably caused by some deadly epidemic, such as were all too common during the early decades of the 19th Century. Their sudden deaths propelled the lonely and heartbroken boy into the affectionate arms of his uncle, William T. Crissey, a druggist and doctor living in Cincinnati. It had been the persuasions of Dr. Crissey that had weaned young William's parents away from Salisbury, Connecticut (where he had been born April 21, 1811), and had brought them in 1815 by coastal sailing ship to Philadelphia, then by stage across the mountains to Pittsburgh, and from there by steamboat down the Ohio River to Ohio's great river port.

Both his parents had been devout Presbyterians; but his Uncle William and Aunt Margaret in Ohio were equally devout Methodists. And that little happenstance injected into the boy's life something that determined the kind of man he was destined to become. For if William Stoddart Crissey had grown up a Presbyterian, he would never have become one of Illinois' Methodist circuit riders. Perhaps he might have become a doctor like his

148

uncle, or a merchant, or even a river steamboat captain; but it seems highly improbable that he would have become a clergyman. And if that had happened, this modest narrative would have had no reason to be written.

FORMATIVE YEARS

Immediately upon being settled in with his uncle's family, little William found himself escorted by his uncle and aunt each Sunday morning and evening to services at the Old Stone Methodist Episcopal Church. Every Wednesday evening the Crisseys attended the congregational prayer meeting. Here, the lad grew accustomed to seeing his uncle kneel in the church aisle while he addressed long, solemn prayers to the Almighty.

The very first evening in his uncle's home, young William discovered that his uncle invariably ended the evening meal by taking down his big family Bible and reading a chapter from it; after which the devout doctor knelt and prayed. His parents, little William remembered, although sincere Christians, had not been so conspicuously pious. William was a thoughtful boy, and his uncle's devotions left their mark on him. Ensconced within a family circle so intensely religious, it was inevitable that a boy of keen intellect and unusually sensitive perceptions should have imbibed more and more of his uncle's faith, and have felt himself in time irresistibly attracted toward that supreme Figure of Christendom, Jesus Christ.

The Crissey boy's growth in faith was immensely encouraged by his regular attendance at a weekly Methodist Class conducted by Samuel Huston, a Cincinnati man of long membership at Old Stone Methodist Episcopal Church. In this, Huston was imitating the practice originated by the Wesleys, and, with him, as with them, the class indoctrination method achieved lasting results. A considerable number of boys approximately of young William Stoddart's age attended Huston's classes, and all of them together, after experiencing conversion, joined the Methodist Church and pledged before the congregation their allegiance to Jesus Christ.

The Decision that Determined His Life

That solemn consecration, professed publicly in 1821, proved to be the commitment that governed all the remaining years of William Stoddart Crissey's long life.

Young William Stoddart was permitted to enjoy his new church fellowship only two years. His uncle, by 1823, had contracted a bad case of that frontier malady, pandemic among American pioneers — the insatiable yearning to follow the ever-retreating frontier. Thus it happened that in 1823 Dr. Crissey moved his family from Cincinnati, down the river to Louisville, Kentucky, where he re-established his practice. But neither did Louisville long satisfy Dr. Crissey; for two years later he moved his family again, this time across the Ohio River and northward through the dense Indiana timber to the village of Bloomington, Indiana.

Changes of locality, however, did not dampen the boy's ardent religiosity. At Bloomington, Indiana, young William Stoddart soon won the friendship of James Armstrong, a leader in the first Methodist Episcopal church there. As young Crissey moved into his pubescent years, his zeal for his Lord grew apace. Armstrong noticed this, and encouraged William Stoddart to practice more public speaking — anticipating, perhaps, that here before him in the person of teen-age William Stoddart Crissey stood a future Methodist preacher.[1]

---

[1] John Wesley had discovered the value of talented laymen, able to "exhort" (urge earnestly, admonish strongly) congregations of worshippers. In the spread of Methodism across the American West, exhorters played roles of important influence.

Armstrong's advice was sound, for young Crissey, in his 17th year, asked his sponsor to license him to exhort. By that time his voice had changed and he was filling out in stature. He thoroughly enjoyed public speaking, and in 1828 he was an eloquent and effective congregational speaker. Despite his immature years, Armstrong licensed the boy officially as a Methodist exhorter.

The next year, 1829, found the Crisseys to have moved again, this time across the Wabash River into Illinois, where they settled at the village of Paris, in Edgar County, only 10 miles west of the Indiana-Illinois state line. By this time, young William Stoddart Crissey was thoroughly familiar with his church's organization and discipline. The Methodist Annual Conference in September of 1829 at Edwardsville, Illinois, was too far away for him to attend, but his name came before the Conference when his close friend, James Armstrong of Bloomington, Indiana, sponsored him as candidate to begin preaching. Young Crissey was delighted when Armstrong stopped by Paris, Illinois, on his way home and told the 18-year-old youth that the Annual Conference, on Armstrong's strong endorsement, had licensed him officially to preach.

PREACHING MINISTRY

The Methodist Annual Conference in September, 1830, met at nearby Vincennes, Indiana, and William Stoddart Crissey attended as a lay delegate. Although only 19 years old, young Crissey that year was officially ordained as a minister of the Methodist Episcopal Church and became a member in full standing within the Illinois Conference. At once, he was put to work as a circuit-riding preacher, serving the Paoli Circuit in Southern Indiana.

Paoli, Indiana, was a frontier station of the Methodist Church, situated some 70 miles over rough timbered trail east of

Vincennes, and about 50 miles northwest of Louisville, Kentucky. The circuit served 15 "preaching places," all around his parish once every two weeks. Strong in faith and in body, young Crissey exulted in the work. Arduous as were his duties, the enthusiasm of his parishioners persuaded him that his talents were well suited to a clergyman's career. So long as his Lord sustained him, he determined to go on.

As was customary along the Methodist circuits, their pastors changed every year. So it came as no surprise to young Crissey that at the Annual Conference of October 1831 at Indianapolis, when Bishop Robert Richford Roberts read out for him another appointment. He was to return to Illinois and begin ministering to the new Tazewell Circuit near the center of the state. It was a formidable assignment, inasmuch as the Tazewell circuit contained 25 settlements, each to be served once every three weeks. The rider traversed some 250 miles — traveling constantly with never a day of rest, beginning again every third Sunday at the little village of Bloomington, Illinois.

On fire with zeal for his Lord's Gospel, the 20-year-old clergyman accepted Bishop Robert's appointment with gladness. Indeed, he left Indianapolis before the Conference adjourned, in order to begin his new duties without delay. He had heard much about the fiery Peter Cartwright of Illinois, who would be his Presiding Elder. The challenge only added to his eagerness to serve.

As the reader will remember, William Stoddart Crissey's work on the Tazewell Circuit comprises the text of Chapters V, VI and VII; therefore, the interval of his life between October 1831 and September 1832 will not be dealt with here.

In 1830, William Stoddart Crissey's Uncle
Settled Permanently in Decatur

While these things were happening, his uncle, Dr. William T. Crissey, in 1830 had moved his family a fourth time — but this time the place the doctor chose would become his permanent residence. The town was Decatur, Illinois, seat of Macon County, a flourishing little community destined years later to become one of the great Prairie State's best known and most important cities. Twice during the year 1831, Dr. Crissey's nephew visited him at Decatur. "I visited Decatur and Stevens Creek in May, 1831," William Stoddart Crissey recorded years later, "preaching in both places; also in the fall of 1831."

That sermon preached by young Crissey in May 1831 was the first delivered by an ordained clergyman in Decatur. There being, of course, no church edifice available, he preached to his little congregation in the log house of Isaac Miller (located east of what many years later would be the Illinois Central Railroad station). His uncle soon bought a small house in Decatur, later exchanging it for a bigger and better residence, as his practice prospered. Dr. Crissey was the first physician to settle in Macon County and in time achieved a career there of some local distinction. In 1836, Dr. Crissey was elected a member of Decatur's first Board of Trustees and was re-elected in 1839. Until his death in 1850, Dr. Crissey remained the same enthusiastic Methodist he had been when he took orphaned and homeless little 7-year-old William Stoddart Crissey, his nephew, into his home at Cincinnati. Uncle and nephew all their years together cherished toward each other an affection much warmer than the usual avuncular filiation.

On the Jacksonville Circuit, 1832-1833

The Methodist Annual Conference for 1832 met at Jacksonville, Illinois, late in September with Bishop Joshua Soulé[2] presiding. Crissey was present, of course, and heard his bishop read out his next appointment as pastor to the Jacksonville Circuit.

That circuit was considerably less exhausting than the Tazewell Circuit had been. It embraced only Morgan, Cass and Scott Counties, serving 15 settlements, to be covered once every two weeks. Starting at Jacksonville, the larger towns served that year by Crissey were Ashland, Virginia, Bearstown, Winchester, Manchester and Murrayville. Having been settled longer than the Tazewell region, towns were larger, roads better, and overnight accommodations more comfortable.

---

[2] Wholly unforeseen by the youthful circuit rider attending the 1832 Annual Conference at Jacksonville, Illinois, the bishop presiding, Joshua Soulé, whom

Crissey met for the first time that September, was destined soon to become the great dominant figure of American Methodism. Bishop Soulé had been born and educated in Maine, but he was a leader of statesmanship, who loved all Methodists, not only his Yankee brethren but equally the Southerners and those from Western States. Soulé was chairman of the General Conference, held that year in Manhattan's Greene Street Church. Soulé strongly objected when Northern Methodists tried to expel the Southern Bishop, James O. Andrew, because his wife owned slaves. When the sectional dispute became acrimonious and ugly, Joshua Soulé, the Yankee from Maine, left his chair and dramatically led all Southern Methodists out of New York's Greene Street Church, then

Bishop Joshua Soulé of Maine, a giant churchman and statesman of early 19th Century Methodism.

later helped them organize their own separate Methodist Episcopal Church, South. That schism severed the great national American Methodist Episcopal Church; the breach was not closed until the year 1939.

These improvements notwithstanding, Crissey that year did not find his work "comfortable"; indeed, he encountered that year perhaps the most fearful danger he was ever to experience. For the summer of 1833 brought to Morgan County, Illinois, the dreaded plague, Asiatic cholera. The countryside was numbed with dread as scores of people died, both in Jacksonville and on the farms. The disease struck swiftly, for it was ferociously contagious. Sometimes death followed within hours. There was no cure.

In the spring of 1833, Crissey received the help of an assistant pastor, young C. B. U. McCabe, a local preacher who came from the lead mining region of South-Central Missouri. Together, the two youthful ministers rode their horses daily from post to post, aware that all around them lurked the dreadful Asiatic Cholera. Despite the universal panic, or perhaps in part because of it, most of their appointments showed by Conference time "a general advance, and a slight increase in membership," according to Dr. Leaton's summary.

On September 25, 1833, the Methodist Annual Conference met on the camp ground of Union Grove, St. Clair County, not far from East St. Louis. Because of its remoteness from most Methodist work in Illinois, only 17 preachers were present when the Conference started. Even the Bishop was absent, and Peter Cartwright presided as President Pro Tempore. He appointed the Reverend Crissey to serve the Mount Carmel circuit, on the opposite side of the state. He named young William Kerns, a preacher not yet received into the Conference, to share the work.

This was to be the fourth consecutive circuit ridden by young Crissey, and the hardships were beginning to undermine his health. Few Methodist circuit riders possessed the iron constitutions of Francis Asbury or of Peter Cartwright, who boasted that he was God's ordained "sod-breaking plow horse." Cartwright's assignment of William Kerns to help Crissey carry the load around the Mount Carmel Circuit may have been Cartwright's concession to accumulating signs that Crissey's health had been damaged by ordeals sustained during his previous three circuits.

The Annual Methodist Conference of 1833 recognized Crissey's growing stature by electing him to Deacon's Orders — one of the final preparatory steps in Methodism before assigning full responsibilities.

When Kerns and Crissey arrived at Wabash County, Illinois, they found a region conspicuously older and more settled than the regions they had known in Central Illinois. Mount Carmel was a bustling river town sitting on the west bank of the Wabash River about 20 miles downstream from old Vincennes, Indiana. It was a two-weeks' circuit, serving 15 preaching places in Wabash and Edwards Counties, in which Mount Carmel, Albion and Grayville were the three most populous towns.

An Old Book,
Speaking Vicariously for William Stoddart Crissey,
Describes in Detail a Circuit Rider's Ordeals,
Paralleling Crissey's Experiences

Dr. Leaton during his pastorate at the First Methodist Episcopal Church in Decatur became a firm and intimate friend with old William Stoddart Crissey. It is almost a certainty that Leaton compiled his notes about the Tazewell Circuit while visiting with Father Crissey in the little Crissey cottage on West Prairie Avenue.

In appreciation of the invaluable help that Dr. Leaton had received from William Stoddart Crissey, Dr. Leaton autographed a copy of his new history, and presented it to the old circuit rider.

In 1980, by a chain of almost unbelievably fortunate circumstances, that very book, given by Dr. Leaton to my grandfather almost 100 years earlier, came into my possession. A loving and patient scrutiny of the old book discovered an exciting possibility.

All through the old book once owned by William Stoddart Crissey after the year 1884, I encountered pen and ink underlinings written painstakingly and in a hand that trembled slightly. It was obvious that the old circuit rider had inserted those underscores for some reason that he considered important. What reason could it have been, but that he sensed that the text selected for special emphasis related experiences and situations paralleling experiences and situations that he remembered clearly having happened to him, way back in the 1830s while he rode the four Methodist frontier preaching circuits in Indiana and Illinois?

The particular paragraphs here and there that old William Stoddart Crissey painstakingly underlined described certain people, particular places, dramatic experiences, special occasions, all narrated back in 1815 by a young clergyman, John Scripps, who was assisting Jesse Walker, minister to the Methodists of Southern Illinois that year. In my opinion, there can be no reasonable doubt that my Grandfather, as he read Leaton's history with absorbed interest, underscored those precise paragraphs with pen and ink only because of one compelling reason. His reason was that those precise paragraphs reminded him vividly, across the 40 years that had elapsed since he had ridden the Methodist circuits, of identical ordeals that he, too, had suffered as a young horse preacher, patiently riding along those primitive trail ways, faithfully carrying the Lord's Holy Word to spiritually famished families then inhabiting the lonely frontier, surrounded by the giant grasses of the Illinois prairies.

Every word of the text quoted below can be seen today in Leaton's old faded volume, which once belonged to William Stoddart Crissey. The old pen and ink underlinings stand out very clearly. They tell a story, and these excerpts are quoted here because old Father Crissey's inked emphases preserve the language that vicariously the old circuit rider, in all probability, would have written about himself if he had kept a journal during his circuit-riding years.

157

The site of the events narrated below was Southern Illinois, far south of the latitude of St. Louis, Missouri, and never far from the northern banks of the Ohio River, at that point flowing wide, swiftly and deep. The scattered Methodists then peopling the southern extremity of Illinois Territory were designated the Illinois District, comprised within the Tennessee Methodist Conference. The year was 1815. Chief actor of the narratives was the bold and tireless Jesse Walker, but the journal itself was written, methodically and in patient detail, by young John Scripps, Walker's assistant pastor.

Our roads were narrow, winding horse paths, sometimes scarcely perceptible, and frequently for miles no path at all, amid tangled brushwood, over fallen timber, through swamps and low grounds, overflowed or saturated with water for miles together, and consequently muddy, which the breaking up of the Winter and the continued rains gave a continued supply of. . . .

It was a common occurrence, in our journeying, to close our day's ride drenched to the skin by continually descending rains, for which that Spring was remarkable. Our nights were spent, not in two but in one room log-cabins, each generally constituting our evening meeting-house, kitchen, nursery, parlor, dining and bed room, — all within the dimensions of sixteen feet square, and not unfrequently a loom occupying one-fourth of it, together with spinning-wheels and other apparatus for manufacturing their apparel. . . .

Our needs were not of select, but of just such aliment as our hospitable entertainers could provide (for hospitable, in the highest sense of the word, they were); corn-cakes, fried bacon, sometimes butter, with mild or herb-tea, or some substitute for coffee.

We have sometimes sat in the large fire-place occupying the entire end of a log cabin, and plucked from out the smoke of the chimney above us pieces of dried and smoked venison, or jerk, the only provision the place could afford us, and the only food the inmates had to sustain themselves, till they could obtain it by the cultivation of the soil. Our horses fared worse, in muddy pens, or tied up to saplings or corners of the cabin, regaled with the refuse of Winter's fodder. . . .

Our lodgings were on beds of various qualities, generally feather-beds, but not unfrequently fodder, chaff, shucks, straw, and sometimes only deer-skins, but always the best the house afforded, either spread on the rough puncheon floor before the fire (from which we must rise early to make room for breakfast operations), or on a patched-up platform attached to the wall, which not unfrequently would fall down, sometimes in the night, with its triplicate burden of three in a bed. Such incidents would occasion a little mirth among us, but we would soon fix up and be asleep again. . . .

The weather in Winter was in general intensely cold; nor were the means then in the country of procuring habiliments adequate to the season. The prairies, where the cold north-easter raged with unchecked fury, were settled only on their margins; and, at whatever time of day we entered on one, however extensive, we could have no comfortable hope of seeing a fire, or shelter from the most pitiless storm, till we had crossed it.

On one occasion we entered a twelve-mile prairie at about four o'clock in the evening, with our upper garments completely saturated — the effects of an afternoon's hard rain. At about five o'clock the wind changed and the residue of our way we traveled in a sleet, or rather, a storm of ice, while the darkness of the night compelled us to yield the reins to our horses; and, on our arrival at the house we were obliged to require assistance to help us off our horses, as our clothes were so inflexible with ice that we could scarcely move in them, and could not, without help, have dismounted.

It is not unreasonable to surmise that old William Stoddart Crissey's memory, as he underscored the concluding paragraph immediately above, reverted to those winter rides on the Tazewell Circuit, which he suffered through every second Friday of the circuit. That was the most punishing trip of the entire 250-mile three-week circuit; it was 20 miles long, crossing one of Illinois' most vast prairies; from four to six hours the rider plodded straight north all the way, often in the teeth of freezing wind, sleet or snow. That dreaded lap of his circuit began at Ollendorf's Mill and concluded at Old Mackinaw Town.

The illness which eventually compelled the Reverend William Stoddart Crissey to resign from the ministry was tuberculosis of the lungs. This was the unanimous opinion of the three Bloomington physicians who analyzed the data about Crissey's breakdown of health. The prolonged exposure and exhaustion endured by young Crissey on the Tazewell Circuit in the winter of 1831-1832, they believed, probably caused his lungs to become diseased.

Crissey's First Resident Pastorates Notably Successful

On the first day of October, 1834, the Annual Conference joined the two young circuit riders by convening at Mount Carmel. Bishop Roberts presided. The 1834 Conference terminated Crissey's internship as a youthful "apprentice preacher" learning how to manage an established church, by appointing him resident pastor to the First Methodist Episcopal Church at Eugene, Illinois, near Danville, which was included with the Eugene parish. Crissey's year at Eugene-Danville was notably successful. Leaton commented on it, thus:

... he was sent to Eugene, and in 1835 to Danville. The latter charge had been included in the former which was divided at the conference of 1835. Mr. Crissey's residence was at Danville during both years. During his first year he commenced the building of a church at Danville, and completed it the next year. It was, for those days, a great undertaking, and the whole country for twenty miles around was canvassed for means to build it. At the last quarterly-meeting a camp-meeting was held, a few miles from Danville, at which there were about one hundred and twenty conversions and accessions to the Church, and about twenty-five professed to be entirely sanctified.

Significantly, at the beginning of Crissey's second year at Danville, Bishop Roberts, during the Annual Conference at Springfield, Illinois, appointed the young Reverend David Coulson, a native of Tennessee, who had been transferred to the Illinois Conference in 1834, to assist him. Weighed against Crissey's subsequent declining health, this may have indicated some apprehension on Bishop Roberts' part.

If so, the fear had dissipated by October 1836; for Bishop Roberts, during the Annual Conference that opened October 5 at Rushville, Illinois, named William Stoddart Crissey pastor of the faraway and strategically-important Milwaukee (Wisconsin) Station, superintended from the Chicago District, under Presiding Elder M. S. Taylor.

By 1837 apparently fully recovered in health, the Reverend Crissey heard himself appointed by Bishop Soulé, during the Annual Conference at Jacksonville, September 27th -October 5th, to the important pastorate at Joliet. Leaton said of Crissey's two years at Joliet:

These were very successful years. Many souls were won to Christ, and general advancement was made.

161

A church that had been begun before at Plainfield was completed, and another at Joliet. In the Winter of 1838 Mr. Crissey formed the first class at Lockport. Mr. Beggs, who was his colleague on this charge, says of him: "He was a good preacher, a faithful pastor, and possessed a good business tact. He was an indefatigable laborer, attending to all matters both small and great." So faithful was he in attending to all his disciplinary duties that, it is said, while on his circuit he read, at all the appointments, Mr. Wesley's sermons on Dress and Evil Speaking, and the General Rules.[3]

Throughout his second year at Joliet, Crissey was supported by the Reverend Ashbury Chenoweth, whom Leaton described as "a young man of fair mind, clear headed, fine looking, fastidious about his personal appearance, and a fair preacher." S. R. Beggs also assisted the two young clergymen during their year together at Joliet.

Hardships Suffered on the Circuits Undermine Crissey's Health

The appointment of Beggs to assist Crissey at Joliet indicated again Crissey's failing strength. Although young in years,

---

[3] Leaton's report here, be it noted, is only hearsay, but apparently Leaton considered it true that young Crissey read "at all appointments" John Wesley's famous sermons on the three subjects mentioned. If so, he must have taxed his parishioners' patience! Wesley's sermon "On Dress" (No. 93 in the collection published at New York in 1850) contained 5,400 words, and would have consumed about one hour's reading time. Leaton's mentions of two additional sermons perhaps tripled that time, consuming about three hours of solid reading. It seems probable that Crissey parceled out Wesley's sermons to his congregations at intervals throughout the Conference year, in comfortable half-hour segments.

he felt compelled to ask the next Annual Conference of 1839, held at Bloomington, Illinois, to permit him to cease pastoral duties temporarily, by granting him a superannuated relation. Reluctantly, Bishop T. A. Morris, acceded to Crissey's request, whereupon the 28-year-old clergyman, ill in body but with his heart still on fire for the Lord, returned to his uncle's home at Decatur.

Crissey's three years of convalescence at Decatur were not uneventful. He had married in 1838, and, for the first time in his life, he experienced the happiness of domestic quietness in company with his bride, Maria Catherine.[4]

Crissey's designation by his Annual Conferences of 1836, 1837 and again in 1838 to be responsible "for Sunday School Reports" indicated clearly that he possessed marked talents for teaching. His anxious concern at his every appointment that Methodist Sunday Schools function efficiently demonstrated Crissey's opinion that better schools were then the country's most urgent need.

He had not been living at Decatur very long before his concern about education motivated him to undertake the establishment at Decatur of a college. Within the town in 1840 stood a conspicuous knoll, beautifully timbered and undeveloped. Crissey envisioned it as an ideal college campus. Enlisting the financial support of his uncle, by then Decatur's best-known and most prosperous physician, the temporarily retired clergyman was able to buy the hill.

In 1840 Crissey had the hilltop and sides laid out for development, and then offered the site to the town for use as a college campus, on condition that college buildings would be constructed

---

[4] It is not an unreasonable assumption here to think that the new Mrs. William Stoddart Crissey had objected gently against the rootlessness of her itinerant husband's work, and that her objections had been heard. In any event, after 1839, William Stoddart Crissey maintained his permanent home at Decatur, even though his residence there was interrupted during the Conference Year of 1843-1844 by his pastorate at Springfield, Illinois.

within 10 years. Regrettably, Crissey's vision was 60 years ahead of its time.[5] In 1840, Decatur taxpayers were not much interested in financing a new college, so the project lagged. Discouraged, finally Crissey willed the land to the Methodist Missionary Society. But in 1888 when William Stoddart Crissey died, no such society existed, and the land reverted to his children. Among elderly Decatur residents nowadays the place is still called College Hill.[6]

In September 1841, Crissey attended the Annual Conference at Jacksonville, journeying from Decatur to Jacksonville by cross-country stagecoaches. Halfway through the Conference, Crissey found himself too sick to continue, so asked Bishop Morris to allow him to leave. Immediately, Bishop Morris had a motion introduced from the floor that "William Stoddart Crissey be given the Conference's leave of absence for the remainder of the session." Sadly, Crissey packed his carpetbag and climbed into the next stage northbound.

The year that followed Crissey's disappointment at Jacksonville worked some kind of a miracle on his health. For in mid-August 1842, when the Annual Conference convened at Winchester, Illinois, the Reverend William Stoddart Crissey was one of the first members of the Conference to report to Peter Akers, President Pro Tempore. With enthusiasm — almost exuberance! — Crissey told Akers his health was recovered, and that he wanted to return to full-time duty.

Bishop Roberts, aware that Crissey had but recently recovered from prolonged and dangerous illness, and that he had married in 1838, and was then living at Decatur with his bride, appointed Crissey to the newly reorganized Decatur Circuit, enabling Crissey to spend most Sundays at his home. Prior to 1842,

---

[5] A Methodist college was established at Bloomington in 1850, but Decatur's Millikin University was not established until 1901.

[6] During the 1880s the Decatur construction firm of Chambers, Bering and Quinlan built two mansions on the hill. In 1913, A. E. Staley bought one of the mansions. About 1915 the other was purchased by C. E. England.

the Decatur Circuit had been the most arduous in Illinois; more than 300 miles in circumference, serving 30 preaching places, requiring four weeks to traverse. Gradually, its length and burdens had been reduced, until in 1842, the Decatur Circuit's eight preaching places were confined chiefly within Macon County.

Crissey's Most Successful Year in the Ministry

The secretary of the Annual Conference for 1842, when writing up his minutes, opened one of his paragraphs with five bland words, "Bro. Crissey was returned effective," that presaged a sensational year of work on the Decatur Circuit performed by William Stoddart Crissey. That Crissey theretofore had been something less than "effective" was known to the Bishop, the presiding Elders and every preacher-member of the Conference, for "Bro. Crissey" had been on superannuated leave of absence several years because of lung trouble. But how remarkably "effective" Crissey was in 1842-1843 is documented by various records, all corroborative.

Crissey's new exuberance in mid-August 1842, which he felt to be strong health fully restored, deceived him and led him to over-exert himself. Two years later his health would fail again. But his year on the Decatur Circuit in 1842 and 1843 proved to be by far the most successful of his entire ministry.

One duty at Decatur he particularly enjoyed, namely, that of debating with preachers representing the aggressive new sect then invading Illinois from the South, the Disciples of Christ.[7] Crissey soon displayed marked skill in these encounters, as was recorded by the Conference Secretary:

---

[7] Usually nicknamed derisively by the Methodists "Campbellites," after their founder, the frontier evangelist Alexander Campbell.

These were the days of controversy. The persistent efforts of the Campbellites to urge their heresy and their unblushing attempts at proselytism from all other denominations rendered it necessary for our preachers to come out boldly in defense of the truth and in opposition to their destructive heresy. On the Decatur circuit there was much controversy on baptism and baptismal regeneration and also on unconditional final perseverance. Dr. Akers preached lengthily on these subjects, and the preacher on charge, W. S. Crissey, preached on one occasion on baptism. Indeed all the Presiding Elders and many of the preachers felt that they would be false to their ordination vows if they failed to instruct their congregations in regard to the destructive influence of the Campbellite heresy and the danger of the Calvinistic portion of the Cumberland Presbyterian creed.

The Secretary's minutes recorded also a second instance of Crissey's Herculean labors that year:

At Decatur under the labors of W. S. Crissey, a meeting was commenced at the old frame church on the third of February and continued for six weeks. Though the population of the town at that time was only about five hundred, there were nearly a hundred conversions as the result of the meeting, and about seventy connected themselves with the Methodist Church. Another result was the organization of a Baptist Church a few weeks later under the ministry of Elder Hodge.

Many years later, the *Decatur Review* published further dramatic details about William Stoddart Crissey's powerful evangelism, in a column-long article featuring him, based on interviews with his daughter, Margaret, and his son, Truman Crissey, then his only surviving descendants. Excerpted from the newspaper's article, its reporter stated:

One of the early settlers of Decatur who had much to do with the early history of the city was Rev. William S. Crissey, and it was especially in the religious life of the community that he did some remarkable work. It was through his efforts that the First Methodist church building was finished. . . . Mr. Crissey not only was instrumental in getting Methodism started in Decatur, but in a revival meeting which he held he inspired the organization of the Baptist church.

Many interesting incidents occurred during the service of this pioneer preacher. One story is told of a revival meeting, which led to the conversion of Dr. J. T. B. Stapp, who later gave such a generous contribution toward the construction of a new Methodist church that the building was named, after him. Stapp's chapel, afterwards known as the Grace Methodist church, is now the Eldorado Temple of the Masons.

It happened one evening during the revival meeting above mentioned that Dr. Stapp and other young men were playing cards. Stapp remarked to another of the young men, J. R. Gorlin, "Let's go over and see what they are doing at that meeting."

"I don't care about going," was the reply.

It was, however, decided to go, but the young men said they would sit in a back seat so they could slip out if they got tired.

As a result of that meeting both men became members of the church, and when the building later known as Stapp's chapel was erected, Dr. Stapp gave about $8,000 toward its cost.[8]

The 1843 Annual Conference met at Quincy. Many of his colleagues at Quincy congratulated Crissey for his strong work in Decatur. His health still being apparently sound, he had no hesitation about accepting the Bishop's appointment to serve the strategic Springfield Station.[9] While pastor at Springfield, Crissey conducted a successful "Protracted meeting," or revival. Leaton commented, "a number of souls were clearly converted." He achieved something else, too, of lasting importance to the Springfield Station congregation: he brought his unusual skill in Church finances to bear on the congregation's long-arrears debt. It was paid off.

While Crissey's two successful years at Decatur and Springfield earned him high praise throughout the Conference, the unusually hard work wore him out. Before the 1844 Annual Conference assembled, Crissey was acutely aware that his old cough and chronic exhaustion held him captive once again. He attended the Conference at Nashville, Illinois, in September, but he felt compelled, though embarrassed, to request Bishop Morris to once again grant him superannuated relationship. With reluctance mixed with real fear for Crissey's survival, Bishop Morris granted William Stoddart Crissey temporary retirement from duty.

---

[8] Dr. Stapp's 1842 contribution toward the new church building, translated into purchasing values of the 1980s might approximate $75,000.

[9] The church that Crissey served during 1843-1844 at Illinois' State capital was progenitor to what in the 20th Century came to be one of the largest congregations of Methodists in the Middle West. Until recently razed, the cream-colored limestone edifice at Fifth and Capitol Streets, downtown Springfield, was cherished as "The Old Stone Church on the Corner." Its cornerstone had been laid in 1884, the fourth church edifice on that site. The log building Crissey preached in was the second Methodist home serving the state capital.

Thus, early in September 1844, the young clergyman, only 33, packed his carpetbag and, somewhat apprehensive
about his future, climbed aboard a stagecoach, northbound toward
distant Decatur, where he yearned for the tender nursing care of
his wife and the company of his babies.

The End of His Career as an Active Methodist Clergyman Ministering to His Own Church

Mercifully, he did not realize it at the time — for he hoped,
prayed and believed that he would be used by his Lord for many
more years of strenuous service — but the stagecoach that
September day in 1844 carried William Stoddart Crissey forever
beyond further active ministerial duties within his beloved Methodist Church. Never again would he shepherd a church congregation of his own.

Had the brevity of Crissey's ministerial career destroyed
it? Or had he, despite his illness, achieved some things of permanent value?

No historian of Illinois Methodism knew William Stoddart Crissey as well as did the famous Dr. James Leaton, Conference Historian in 1883 (whose three volumes are quoted many
times in this work). The two men were close friends. Leaton lived
at Decatur for some time in the 1870s, during which period he
visited the old one-time circuit rider frequently in the Crissey
home. Leaton described and evaluated many preachers — always
conservatively. Of William Stoddart Crissey, Leaton wrote, "Mr.
Crissey remained in the Conference, filling some of its most
important appointments, until 1849, when he located. He was in
his prime one of the strong preachers of the conference."

Dr. Leaton in volume one of his history of Illinois
Methodism published a biography of William Stoddart Crissey of
some 825 words. Leaton wrote:

Mr. Crissey . . . was a good preacher, somewhat given to metaphysical discussion, but acceptable and popular. He was scrupulous in observing all the requirements of the Discipline, fasting every Friday, visiting among the people, and regularly meeting the classes. In this duty he was particular in inquiring of the members in regard to their attention to family and secret prayer, and their abstinence from intoxicating drinks. He was a faithful administrator of discipline; and while blessed with many gracious revivals of religion, his forte seemed to be the purification and building up of the Church.

Leaton's mention of Crissey's "fasting every Friday" documents the remarkable depth and sincerity of Crissey's loyalty to John Wesley's tenets. Beyond doubt, Crissey possessed a volume of Wesley's sermons, and studied them often. He was well aware, therefore, that the Methodist Conference in England once chose 52 of their great founder's sermons and appointed them as "necessary reading of all candidates for the Wesleyan Methodist ministry, and forming part of the official doctrinal standards of Methodism." Crissey took that discipline very seriously. Within John Wesley's famous 27th sermon, "Method of Fasting," Crissey would have pondered this powerful passage:

Let every season, either of public or private fasting, be a season of exercising all those holy affections which are implied in a broken and contrite heart.   Let it be a season of devout mourning, of godly sorrow for sin. . . . Yea, and let our sorrowing after a godly sort work in us the same inward and outward repentance, the same entire change of heart, renewed after the image of God, in righteousness and true holiness; and the same change of life, till we are holy as He is holy, in all manner of conversation.

Let it work in us the same *carefulness* to be found in Him, without spot and blameless; the same *clearing of ourselves,* by our lives rather than words, by our abstaining from all appearance of evil; the same *indignation,* vehement abhorrence of every sin; the same *fear* of our own deceitful hearts; the desire to be in all things conformed to the holy and acceptable will of God; the same *zeal* for whatever may be a means of His glory, and of our growth in the knowledge of our Lord Jesus Christ; and the same *revenge* against Satan and all his works, against all filthiness both of flesh and spirit.

And with fasting let us always join fervent prayer, pouring out our whole souls before God, confessing our sins with all their aggravations, humbling ourselves under His mighty hand, laying open before Him all our wants, all our guiltiness and helplessness. This is a season for enlarging our prayers, both in behalf of ourselves and of our brethren.

His Illness Worsens

Significantly, the minutes of the Annual Conference at Springfield in September 1845, contain the ominous notation, "William Stoddart Crissey absent for being sick." A year later when the 1846 Annual Conference met at Paris, Illinois, again he was absent because of illness. And in 1847 it was the same. The dreaded consumptive disease that was trying to kill him refused to leave.[10]

In 1848 during the Annual Conference at Belleville, Illinois, Peter Cartwright, the truculent, old, long-time circuit rider, who in 1831-1832 had supervised young William Stoddart Crissey on the Tazewell Circuit, forced through a Conference decision against Crissey which, in my opinion, seems not unreasonably to have been motivated by something very close to cruelty.

To understand Cartwright's action, a word needs to be said first about Cartwright's prejudice against all Easterners, particularly those better schooled than he. Peter Cartwright was 26 years older than Crissey. Born in Virginia in 1785, he had emigrated with his parents to Kentucky when a small boy of five. All during his life he held higher education in contempt, and enjoyed ridiculing the "oyster-eaters" of the Atlantic Seaboard.

William Stoddart Crissey thus began his ministry in Illinois, already suspect by Cartwright because he was a native New Englander, aggravated by his sound theological training at Cincinnati. Crissey's 10 months on the Tazewell Circuit passed without serious disagreement with his Presiding Elder, although it did not take the younger man long to perceive that old Peter did not approve of his Eastern birth or his Cincinnati learning.

The two continued to meet each other at Annual Conferences, of course, but there was little cordial friendliness between them. Cartwright had observed Crissey's repeated absence from Annual Conferences caused by sickness. Toward illness,

---

in primitive cabins, irregular eating habits and poorly-balanced diet, fly-infested food and myriads of malaria-carrying mosquitoes all summer long — it was their consensus that Crissey contracted tuberculosis, in the 19th Century always called "consumption". They thought it probable that the disease began invading his lungs as early as his first summer in Illinois when he rode the Tazewell Circuit. After 1850, living at Decatur, freed from his exhausting ministerial work and under the watchful eye of his wife, symptoms of the disease began to retreat. By August, 1863, when Crissey enlisted in the 115th Regiment of Illinois Volunteers as Chaplain, Army doctors found no trace of tuberculosis. He was commissioned, and followed his troops through two years of rugged compaigning. After Crissey returned home in 1865, he lived actively in good health at Decatur for another 23 years.

Cartwright felt no sympathy, because he himself all his life enjoyed indestructible health. Given these circumstances, it is conceivable how old Peter in 1848, suddenly remembering Crissey's "effete" Eastern origins, decided that Crissey was malingering.

But Cartwright's animosity toward Crissey in September 1848 must surely have stemmed from emotions deeper than prejudice. Could it have been a tinge of jealousy?

Despite Cartwright's self-abasement, frequently professed in his autobiography, contemporaries who knew him best did not consider Peter Cartwright a modest man. His labors on Methodist frontiers in Kentucky, Tennessee and Illinois had been prodigious, but never had he pastored congregations in the larger towns.

Cartwright, like every other Presiding Elder in the Illinois Conference, had watched Crissey's spectacular successes at Decatur in 1842-1843, followed by his effective work at Springfield the following year. It would not have been alien to his temperament if Cartwright, hearing Crissey praised widely for his accomplishments during the 1844 Annual Conference, had begrudged the younger man's acclaim for superior feats in congregations larger than any he had ever served. The contrast may have offended him. If so, he kept his feeling to himself until September 1848.

One month before the 1848 Conference, Crissey wrote a letter from his sickbed at Decatur to his presiding Elder, the Reverend John S. Barger at Bloomington, stating that continuing ill health would make it impossible for him to accept a pastoral appointment. Barger, as well as the Bishop and every Presiding Elder and preacher in the Conference, was reluctant to release Crissey. They all knew that his well-known pulpit eloquence was needed. His enthusiastic evangelism that had converted hundreds of sinners was needed. His leadership in Sunday School work was needed. His spectacular skill in rebuilding ailing church finances was needed.

Urgently as they needed him, however, every man attending the Conference that September knew that "Brother Crissey has been awfully sick." They knew why he did not answer to his name on the roll call. Bishop Morris and the entire Conference of preachers were shocked, therefore, when Cartwright took the floor and, in his usual fog-horn voice and bull-dozing temperament, called attention to Crissey's many absences, insinuated that Crissey was shirking duty, and demanded that he be appointed to serve the Methodist Church at Rushville, Illinois.

Peter Cartwright's Malice

Cartwright then added churlish words, which can be excused only if one remembers charitably that old Peter Cartwright in social sensitivity was something of a backwoods barbarian. Annoyed at his colleagues when he observed that they were embarrassed by his crudity, Cartwright added egregious insult by "explaining" that Crissey must be sent to Rushville "in order to punish people there." These remarkable words, quoted from the minutes, sound like words uttered by an irresponsible old man in a fit of temper.

It was a preposterous "justification," inasmuch as the Reverend William Stoddart Crissey was one of the ablest preachers, administrators, fund-raisers and educators in the entire Illinois Conference, and universally well liked. Cartwright's final insult was indefensible. However, so loud was his voice, so pugnacious his manner, so powerful his determination, so overwhelming his self righteousness, that Bishop Morris reluctantly consented to appoint Crissey to the Rushville Church.

The appointment was read out and the Conference Secretary instructed to notify the Reverend Crissey at Decatur. When Crissey received the letter, he was both puzzled and grieved. In September 1848, he was still a very sick man. He feared that if he undertook full time duties at Rushville, before the 1849 Annual

Conference would assemble, his wife would be a widow and his children orphans. He simply ignored the Bishop's summons. Several weeks lapsed before everybody concerned realized that Crissey would not appear at Rushville. Some embarrassment ensued until the Presiding Elder of that District hurriedly transferred the Reverend J. C. Pinkard from the Columbia, Illinois, church to the vacant Rushville pulpit.

Inevitably, of course, since Crissey possessed many friends among the preachers in the Conference, some of whom soon visited him at Decatur, it was not long until he learned of Peter Cartwright's behavior at Belleville. It shocked him and saddened him. But it did not embitter him; William Stoddart Crissey loved the Lord Jesus too much to forget Jesus' injunction about forgiving injuries and loving enemies.

Nonetheless, the events at Belleville, Illinois, in September 1848, signaled the end of Crissey's career as an active minister within the Methodist Episcopal Church. The 1849 Annual Conference at Quincy, presided over by Bishop E. S. Janes, granted to William Stoddart Crissey "a location," which term in Methodism meant that he was permanently removed from the ecclesiastical succession. He was only 37 years old.

INTERLUDE BEFORE WAR

Crissey's constitution, basically, was sound and durable. His forebears in New England had been tough, long-lived Yankees. Within the quiet comfort of his own cottage at Decatur, convalescing under the day-by-day loving care of his wife and watched over solicitously by his old uncle, Dr. William T. Crissey, his strength began to gain, his health to mend.

As his precocious advancement in church-related responsibilities at Cincinnati had foretold when he was a boy, William Stoddart Crissey possessed a superior mind. He read everything he could find to read, and formed sensible opinions about issues then current, both in church matters and in civic and political matters. After 1830, however, his day-after-day pursuit of his circuit and later his church appointments allowed him little time to study current events. His prolonged convalescence, he discovered gratefully, rewarded him at least with plenty of time for extensive reading.[11]

In Mid-America, the late 1840s and the early 1850s were volatile and pregnant years. One day in 1850 while walking in downtown Decatur, Crissey encountered face-to-face the far-away California hysteria. Edmund Packard, a friend of his, had suddenly caught the gold-rush virus, and was in a fever to be off for the Far West. Packard owned ten acres of undeveloped town lots. These he regarded only as encumbrance, delaying his departure. Meeting Crissey on the street, Packard pleaded with the Methodist clergyman to buy his land — "at any price!" Half in jest, Crissey offered to trade Packard his gold pocket watch and chain for the land. Whereupon, to Crissey's amusement and astonishment, Packard seized the watch and chain, and was gone![12]

The late 1840s were the years also of the Mexican War, and war news filled the air and the newspapers. Crissey was a Whig, the national political party committed to conservative policies, vehemently against slavery. In 1884, James K. Polk, a Democrat, had been elected President; under Polk, Mexico had been invaded and a war fought. Crissey's party, the Whigs, opposed the war; Crissey opposed it.

The Presidential election of 1848 saw his candidate, Zachary Taylor, a Whig, elected. The issue most hotly debated during Taylor's administration of 1849-1853 was the extension

---

[11] Many years later, Crissey's daughter, interviewed by the Decatur Review, described her father as "an eloquent, effective speaker, highly gifted in prayer, and said to be the best read man in Macon County."

[12] On his way to the railroad station to catch the next train westbound, Packard was later reported by a witness to have bragged about his swap, insisting that he had gotten "the best of the bargain."

of slavery into the territories newly conquered from Mexico. Like most Illinoisans of his time inhabiting the middle and northern counties, Crissey hated slavery. Being the articulate speaker that he was, Crissey's voice was heard often in Macon County after 1850, flaying the terrible sin of buying and selling Negroes, "fellow human creatures, God's children." It was a topic to which his ardent spirit easily warmed.

Crissey's Leadership in Education
Attracts Public Attention

Crissey's long-time and ever-enthusiastic interest in better schools motivated him as early as 1847, despite his frail health, to accept election by Macon County voters as their County School Commissioner. Year after year, Crissey was returned to the office, until 1861. His active participation in civic affairs did not stop there. In 1851, Decatur's voters elected Crissey President of the town's Board of Trustees. His acceptance indicates that his health by that time was much improved.

Convinced that he would soon be in good health again, there must have been many times after 1851, when William Stoddart Crissey deplored the premature termination of his career as a preacher, evangelist, Church builder. He had demonstrated outstanding ability to perform those duties. His Church needed him. But there was no place for him. The frustration was hard to bear, but it never embittered him. He mitigated the frustration by preaching often in Decatur Churches and in other pulpits in Central Illinois where he was frequently invited as guest. His reputation for eloquence continued to be long remembered among Illinois Methodists of the mid-19th Century.

His devotion to his own local church in Decatur was constant, his participation in its work, active. Between 1850 and 1863, Crissey served as its Sunday School Superintendent. Every autumn he attended the Methodist Annual Conference, taking part in floor discussions, although no longer an active member of the clergy. The Annual Conference in 1851 appointed Crissey a member of a special committee "to sell lots in Decatur given by the late Dr. Crissey."

By summer 1854, Illinoisans everywhere were heatedly arguing the recent repeal of the Missouri Compromise, because its repeal seemed to invite the extension of slavery into all new Western territories. Worse still, Illinois' own Senator Stephen A. Douglas was believed in Decatur to be the blackest villain of all because he had sponsored the repeal. After May 22, 1854, when the hated Kansas-Nebraska Bill passed Congress, straw-stuffed effigies of Douglas often were seen burning by night on Illinois courthouse squares. In all Macon County, no man at that time was heard speaking more eloquently against the Kansas-Nebraska Bill than the Reverend William Stoddart Crissey.

Crissey's powerful voice, his vehemence against en-slavement of black men, and also his long-demonstrated leadership in behalf of improved education generally, were being noted by Macon County political leaders within the "Anti-Nebraska Party," as it was beginning to be called.[13]

Two years later, Crissey's gathering fame as a political orator plus his distinguished leadership in improving Macon County public schools eventuated in his being chosen by Macon County Anti-Nebraska delegates to the Bloomington Convention,[14] as their "favorite son" nominee at Bloomington for the office of Illinois State Superintendent of Public Instruction.

---

[13] The term "Republican" did not become popular in Illinois until well after the 1856 Presidential campaign, because Senator Douglas had rendered the name distasteful by constantly referring to members of the new Illinois party as "Black Republicans."

[14] The convention at Bloomington on May 29, 1856, brought together delegations representing the five anti-slavery political parties of Illinois committed to merge into one new party supporting a fusion ticket of anti-slavery nominees at the November 1856 election.

So it came about that the Reverend William Stoddart Crissey, in the 45th year of his life, for a few days seemed poised on the threshold of elevation to one of Illinois' most prestigious elective offices. If William Stoddart Crissey had been the nominee at Bloomington on May 29th, he would have been elected the following November, when the new Illinois anti-slavery coalition party swept the election.

Alas! it was not to be, for the Bloomington Convention quickly chose as its nominee for that important office William H. Powell of Peoria, who came to Bloomington clothed with a brilliant reputation as perhaps Illinois' ablest school man.

Crissey Becomes Acquainted with Abraham Lincoln

Crissey's train trip from Decatur to Bloomington on Wednesday, May 28th, did, however, enable him to meet a fellow Illinoisan from Springfield, one Abraham Lincoln, who had boarded the train at Danville. Lincoln was a former Congressman, a successful circuit-riding lawyer, well-liked in Macon County. Crissey's and Lincoln's paths had not crossed before they met on the Illinois Central Railroad train en route to Bloomington.

For Crissey, the happening at Bloomington, Thursday, May 29, 1856, that impressed him most was not his defeat for nominee to the office of State Superintendent of Public Instruction; it was the prodigious — the almost incredibly powerful! — oration delivered at the end of the convention by Abraham Lincoln.[15]

---

[15] Lincoln's stupendous address at Bloomington, Illinois, May 29, 1856, was so overwhelming that all news reporters and editors present forgot to take notes. Lincoln spoke without manuscript, and when he refused to write out what he had said, it came to be known as "Lincoln's Lost Speech." The speech retrieved Lincoln from oblivion and opened to him the pathway that in 1860 led to Lincoln's election to the Presidency.

The next day, Friday, May 30th, returning by train to Decatur, the Macon County men could talk of nothing but Abraham
Lincoln's spectacular oration the evening before. (Lincoln was
not with them, having returned to Springfield.) The spell of it lay
upon William Stoddart Crissey for weeks afterward, for he
himself was a platform speaker of much experience. What he had
listened to at Bloomington far surpassed any speech he had ever
heard. He readily agreed with other men in the Macon County
delegation that a hero of the new Illinois Republican Party had
been born at Bloomington that Thursday evening of May 29,
1856. Thereafter, Crissey continued to watch Lincoln's political
progress closely, as the erstwhile circuit-riding lawyer from
Springfield debated Stephen A. Douglas across Illinois in 1858,
as he achieved the Republican Presidential nomination at Chicago
in 1860, as he was elected in November that year, and finally as
he journeyed to Washington, D.C., as President-Elect Abraham
Lincoln.[16]

A ware that Lincoln had come to the Bloomington Convention a cast-off office seeker, a failure and thoroughly dis-
credited, Crissey, a reflective and knowledgeable man, must have
pondered thoughtfully the "miracle" of Lincoln's meteoric rise to
the nation's most powerful office within the brief span of four-
and-one-half years. That one 90-minute oration had transformed
gangling, ugly Abraham Lincoln from a nobody to a national hero.
Crissey remembered that speech vividly; and even after four-and-
one-half years, memory of it caused his nerves to tingle. It would
have been in his manner of thinking to have attributed the

---

[16] In February 1861 Crissey was to meet Lincoln again, for he was among the
throng of well-wishers at the Decatur railroad station to greet the President-
elect as he stopped off briefly on his way to Washington. Lincoln had requested
that his train pause at Decatur. He alighted from his special car and strolled the
platform, shaking hands. Emboldened by memory that he and Lincoln had
ridden the same train, May 28, 1856, to Bloomington, and that he had listened
to the fabulous oration, Crissey elbowed his way to Lincoln's side, and
introduced himself. Instantly, Lincoln recognized him and chatted with him
jovially for a moment.

"miracle" to the Great Jehovah described by Job as He "Who doeth great things and unsearchable."

Ten months after Crissey became acquainted with Abraham Lincoln at the Bloomington Convention, tragedy touched his family circle at Decatur when his 16-year-old son, Franklin, died. The boy's father read the Methodist funeral ritual, then at the graveside sprinkled the traditional clods over the coffin, symbolizing the corpse's "return to the earth from whence it came."

Crissey Endeavors to Build a Fine Hotel in Downtown Decatur

About the year 1859, Crissey bought the choice business lot on the northeast corner of the Old City Square, and began energetically to build there what he hoped to make Decatur's finest hotel. Plans were drawn for a three-story hotel housing some 50 or more upstairs rooms, with dining room, kitchen, parlors and lobby on the street level.

Unfortunately, the fast-approaching war between the states had inflated costs disastrously. Only the north and south walls were completed, when Crissey ordered work stopped in 1860 for lack of funds. The failure of his project acutely embarrassed him, but he was never a man to burden others with his private troubles.

Sometime before 1863, Crissey sold the land and the partially-finished building to Decatur businessman Franklin Priest, who completed the hotel, giving it his own name. It long operated as Decatur's favorite downtown hotel, passing through several owners and changes of name: the New Deming after 1880; the Arcade Hotel in 1892; in 1900 the Decatur Hotel. In 1904, it burned, but was rebuilt. When it burned again in 1915, it was not rebuilt as a hotel, although parts of its original structure survived and were being used until well after 1930.

Long before Fort Sumter was fired upon, Crissey was a powerful spokesman against those who threatened to divide the

Federal Union and an equally eloquent foe of Negro slavery. By the year 1861, he was 50 years old, and the stubborn disease that had ruined his pulpit career in the 1830s and 1840s had been thrown off. Once again he was a virile man of abundant energy, deep emotions and disciplined mind, universally esteemed by everybody in Decatur for his unfailing kindness toward every person and animal in town. Nonetheless, gentle as Crissey was in person, the cannonading of Fort Sumter, which, he realized, irretrievably plunged the nation into bloody war of brother against brother, did not daunt his valiant spirit. Dreadful and appalling as civil war would be, he felt that if the curse of Negro slavery could be extirpated from the nation only by blood, so be it. Being a daily Bible reader and thoroughly familiar with Scripture, Crissey must have pondered often those mysterious and awesome words in the New Testament's Letter to the Hebrews: "Almost all things are by the law purged with blood; and without shedding of blood is no remission."

Answering President Lincoln's call for volunteers, the first man from the Crissey family circle to don a blue Union Army uniform and march away to war, was 22-year-old Samuel, a robust, red-haired, six-foot giant. For some weeks, Samuel Crissey had been busy closing his store in Decatur. On June 2, 1861, he rode the train over to Springfield and found conveyance out to Camp Butler, where he promptly enlisted. He was at once commissioned First Lieutenant commanding Company I in the 68th Regiment of Illinois Volunteers.

Ten weeks later, William Ernest, eldest of the Crissey boys, rode the train over to Springfield, where he also volunteered. With other new recruits, he was sent by rail down to Camp Sherman in Mississippi, where he was mustered in as a private in Company G of the 116th Regiment of Illinois Volunteer Infantry. One year later, Private W. E. Crissey on July 20, was promoted from Commissary Sergeant to Adjutant, and transferred to the Non-Commissioned Regimental Staff by order of Governor Yates at Springfield.

ARMY CHAPLAIN

Letters from the battlefields written by his two sons deeply stirred the father. But it was the cumulative defeats and frustration of the Union troops in 1861, 1862 and into the summer of 1863 prior to Gettysburg that finally convinced 52-year-old William Stoddart Crissey that he, too, must answer the call to the colors. However, his age and his professional training predicated for him duties in the Army wholly different from those of his two soldier sons.

As early as September 1862, Governor Richard Yates of Illinois had begun recruiting another regiment of soldiers — the 115th Illinois Volunteer Infantry, drawn from the central counties. On September 23, 1862, the Reverend Arthur Bradshaw of Decatur had been commissioned its Chaplain. When Bradshaw resigned three months later, the commission was offered to the Reverend Richard Holding, also of Decatur; but when Bradshaw told him of the hardships, Holding declined the commission. In the early months of 1863, while the regiment was being filled, news of these matters came to Crissey's ears. He telegraphed Governor Yates his willingness to be the new regiment's Spiritual Mentor on the battlefields. The Governor replied by mailing Crissey's commission to him from Springfield.

By August 1863, the 115th had been filled, and was camped at Tullahoma, Tennessee, where it had been vigorously training for some time. Crissey, carpetbag in hand, bade his family good-bye and boarded a train for St. Louis. From there he traveled by rail on into Rebel Country, two days later overtaking his fellow Illinoisans, deep in the heart of Dixie. August 19, 1863, at Tullahoma, Tennessee, William Stoddart Crissey was inducted into the 115th Illinois volunteer Infantry as regimental Chaplain.

Chaplain Crissey had by no means led a sheltered life, of course; he had borne many hardships from riding his circuits and had witnessed innumerable heartbreaks among his parishioners. Yet he entered the Army quite unprepared to face the fearsome juggernaut of war soon to roar down upon him.

Chaplain Crissey had been in camp less than one month when he and his men suddenly were hurried by forced marches across the Cumberland Mountains and on to Rossville, Georgia, five miles south of Chattanooga. On the 19th of September, Chaplain Crissey's ears heard for their first time the awesome uproar of battle: the thunder of artillery, the crackle of rifle fire, the screams of wounded horses, the yells and curses of fighting men. The next day his soldiers found themselves hurled straight into the bloody fight at Chickamauga Creek, one of the fiercest battles of the Civil War. Attacking the Union troops were seasoned Confederates under Generals Bragg, Hood, Longstreet and Forrest. Trying to hold them off were Union troops — some of them new and raw, as were the Illinois 115th Volunteers — under Generals Grant, Thomas and Rosecrans.

Later, a Confederate observer wrote how "the dead were piled upon each other in ricks, like cord wood, to make passage for advancing columns. The sluggish Chickamauga Creek ran red with human blood." General Grant's description admitted that at the end of the two-day battle, "not more than one-fourth of the shattered Army of the Cumberland who went into battle at the opening were there. Thomas' losses had been dreadful....Granger's hat had been torn by a fragment of shell; Steedman had been wounded; Whitaker had been wounded; and four of his five staff officers killed or mortally wounded. Of two brigades numbering 3,500, one-fifth had been killed or wounded in twenty minutes."

The Illinois 115th marched into the cauldron of fire on September 20, the second and bloodiest day of the great battle. At once, they were engaged in fighting so fierce that "half the entire command was cut down," according to an 1886 publication by the Illinois Adjutant General.

Chickamauga was a costly defeat for the Union. Federal General George H. Thomas had exerted almost superhuman effort to stop the Southerners. His heroic stand earned him the name, "Rock of Chickamauga." Overwhelmed at last, Thomas' troops, including Chaplain Crissey and survivors from the Illinois 115th, retreated into Chattanooga, 25 miles north.

At Chattanooga, the beleaguered Federals rested for two months. After the Union defeat at Chickamauga, Grant was made supreme commander in the West, while Sherman succeeded to command of the U.S. Army of the Tennessee and joined the forces at Chattanooga.

Late in November, the Illinois 115th was fighting again. On November 23 the Federals captured Orchard Knob east of Chattanooga; the next day they assaulted Confederates dug in on Lookout Mountain; and on November 25 they stormed and captured Missionary Ridge, east of Chattanooga.

Chaplain Crissey Learns the Cost of War

The Illinois 115th's initiation into battle had been appallingly bloody. Its action at Chickamauga and Chattanooga killed, wounded or captured almost 250 enlisted men and 10 commissioned officers. To Chaplain Crissey, an ordained Christian minister dedicated to the peace of Jesus' Gospel, it was a traumatic shock. But he was too busy to permit its horror to depress him. Night and day he labored with his men, reading burial rites over the dead, praying for the wounded, writing innumerable letters dictated to him by the dying. The letters were to the men's families, many of whom were in faraway Decatur, Illinois, and some of whom he remembered as friends back home. That whole autumn episode of 1863 in Georgia and Tennessee was to Chaplain Crissey a daily horror that, to his dying day far in the future, he was never able to erase.

The bruising losses suffered by the 115th at Chickamauga and Chattanooga necessitated reorganizing the regiment and merging it into the Army of the Cumberland under Major General Thomas. But by February 1864, Chaplain Crissey's regiment was rested, and ready to fight again. Presently, they marched over to Cleveland, Tennessee, where they camped until May 3rd, when they moved off down the valley into Georgia.

Chaplain Crissey and his soldier boys from Central Illinois were beginning that day what historians in later years would remember as the most spectacular march of the American Civil War: General Sherman's ruthless advance upon Atlanta. Thus, Chaplain Crissey found himself a part of Sherman's famous "Grand Army." Day after day he rode his fine horse alongside the columns, watching the foot soldiers slog forward, row after row, file after file. Sometimes he chatted with them. Now and then he

On facing page: Chaplain Crissey preaching to the troops -- officers and soldiers of the 115th Regiment of Illinois Infantry Volunteers (almost all of whom were Macon County men) -- on a Sunday morning in May, 1864. The site was on the line of march of Sherman's Army in northwest Georgia, approaching Atlanta.

recognized a young man he had known back in Decatur, and when he did, the Chaplain saluted and smiled. Always, the soldier smiled back gratefully.

He observed the soldiers when they broke ranks to steal chickens and pigs from Georgia farms. This conduct, and much more, revolted Chaplain Crissey's sensibilities. He winced whenever he sighted a handsome country mansion burning, for he knew that it had been set on fire by Union troopers. Silently, he prayed often about such sinful behavior of men fighting a war. But he refrained from rebuking his men. He possessed the authority to rebuke them, but his fine sense of discretion told him that they needed his love more than his reprimand. It was his duty to love the men (and the Rebels, too), to share Christ's Gospel with them in worship services conducted out of doors on the field, and to comfort them, for many were scarcely more than boys, far from home, and perhaps soon to die. It was his duty, he was convinced, to personify God's love, to heal and help, to never hate or hurt. He realized that his niche in the Army was a paradox, for he rode alone among a horde of soldiers eager to kill and steal and burn and destroy.

Sometimes while he was praying at night in his tent, there came moments when Chaplain Crissey feared that the Almighty had hurled down upon America this ghastly war as divine vengeance against the nation's wickedness. The possibility made him shudder as he prayed more fervently for mercy. Invariably, though, his irrepressible faith would bring him back again to hope and thankfulness.

He gave thanks to God especially for his presence among the soldiers. The finger of the Lord, he believed, may have pointed him to these battlefields. Unquestionably, if he had continued preaching in Illinois pulpits, it would have been unlikely that he would be ministering now to these young men in blue, far from home, afraid, lonely. They needed him so much more urgently than the civilians back in Illinois! Reverent reflections such as these convinced Chaplain Crissey that the Lord had been guiding him all along, getting him ready to carry the Gospel out onto these bloody fields of battle. He began to feel surer of himself than at any time since his preaching work in the Methodist Church had been terminated those many years ago.

By the middle of May, the 115th Regiment was attacking the Confederates in upper Georgia, defeating them, but losing 30 men and one officer. By summer, Chaplain Crissey's regiment was assaulting the great Southern rail center of Atlanta, Georgia. The 115th Regiment was in the fight when Atlanta surrendered. The Atlanta campaign cost the Illinois 115th more than 100 men and officers. These constantly accumulating casualties imposed on Chaplain Crissey heavy work — more exhausting than anything he had endured on the circuits, and incomparably more brutal, more harrowing, more painful. But the dreadful ordeal did not break him, as it did many chaplains.

In October 1864, the daring Confederate General John B. Hood of Texas suddenly threw his Army on Sherman's rear, and began marching toward Chattanooga. Opposing Hood, the 115th suffered a costly defeat when its Company D stubbornly defended a blockhouse at Buzzard's Roost Gap, Georgia, holding off the Texans for 10 hours, but finally surrendering. One third of the company, also according to the Illinois Adjutant General's report of 1886, was killed or wounded, and the remainder were captured.

Leaving Atlanta in ruins, General Sherman pointed his Grand Army eastward to the sea. The 4th Army Corps, to which the Illinois 115th belonged, was detached and ordered back toward Tennessee to intercept the Rebels. During November and December 1864, Chaplain Crissey followed his regiment as it engaged and destroyed the Confederate Army commanded by General Hood, again sustaining substantial losses.

Crissey Finds Himself Chaplain
Within the Famous "Iron Brigade"

By Christmas 1864 the 2nd Illinois Brigade, of which the 115th Regiment was part, had acquired a good deal of military glory. Long before, when Colonel J. H. Moore of the 115th took command of the war-scarred 2nd Brigade, that unit had become accustomed to hearing itself designated throughout the U.S. Army Department of the Cumberland, as "The Iron Brigade." It was an appellation of honor cherished ever afterward not only by Chaplain Crissey, but by every infantryman and officer in the Brigade.

Having broken Hood's army and driven its remnants across the Tennessee River, the 4th U.S. Army Corps, which embraced the Illinois 115th, moved over into Alabama, where the troops went into winter quarters near Huntsville. By the middle of March 1865, Chaplain Crissey and his regiment were marching across Eastern Tennessee, heading for Lynchburg, Virginia, from whence they expected to hurry on eastward to assist in the capture of Richmond. At that juncture, on Sunday, April 9, 1865, the Army telegraph clicked out the thrilling announcement that the Confederate Commander-in-Chief, General Robert E. Lee, had surrendered to Union General Ulysses S. Grant at a tiny Virginia crossroads named Appomattox.

The very next day, the Illinois 115th reversed its fast march and started back toward Nashville at a more leisurely pace. There it went into field quarters at Camp Harker. Infantrymen and officers relaxed. But for the regimental Chaplain there was no respite. In the field hospitals lay scores of wounded men and some officers from the 115th. Crissey called on each man, comforted him, often wrote letters, and aided him in all ways possible. The cannons were silent now, the fighting was over, but the agony lingered on.

Sunday, June 11, 1865 at Camp Harker, Chaplain Crissey and all his comrades in uniform were mustered out of the Union Army. The next day they entrained for the North. Four days later, on Friday, June 16, the train bearing the Macon County men arrived at Decatur, where they were welcomed hysterically with brass bands, red-white-and-blue bunting, flags and speeches.

On the train platform awaiting Chaplain Crissey as he stepped down from the train was his eldest son, Adjutant William Ernest Crissey, in uniform. The father was not surprised to see his son, for his wife had written him that William Ernest had been mustered out the previous January 30th. Their other soldier-son, First Lieutenant Samuel Crissey, commanding Company I in the Illinois 68th Regiment, was still in the Army, and would not reach Decatur until one month later. After shaking hands with the Adjutant, Chaplain Crissey immediately embraced his wife and daughter, finally shaking hands with young Truman.

June 23rd, Chaplain Crissey at Camp Butler received his honorable discharge and collected his officer's pay. It seemed for a moment that, for him, the war was over. It was not to be; for years to come his activities would be works of mercy whose needs derived from the old battlefields. The killing had ended, but the suffering and dying continued for a long time.

POST WAR

Folk in Decatur, Illinois, like all other Americans, pampered their soldiers back from the war and called them all "heroes." On the downtown streets of Decatur during the late 1860s, none was more honored than "Chaplain Crissey." This was due to no small extent to the stories told about his work of mercy on the field by the returned veterans of the 115th. All of the veterans loved him. Each time an ex-soldier met him anywhere, the former Chaplain received a smart salute, which was unfailingly returned with a smile. That extra deference lasted for many years.

While in uniform, Chaplain Crissey had earned the respect and friendships of two Decatur men, both commissioned officers: James H. Moore, who had joined the 115th Regiment as Colonel a few weeks after Crissey's arrival, and Woodford W. Peddecord, regimental Adjutant, who had joined a month after Moore. In recognition of the 115th's valor on the battlefields, Colonel Moore, on May 15, 1865, had been promoted to the rank of Brevet Brigadier General. All three officers had returned to Decatur on the same train. Thereafter, for years, whenever Crissey met either his former General or Adjutant, he was smartly saluted and warmly greeted.

Gradually, after 1865, the streets of Decatur, again like the streets of every town and city in America, both North and South, began to be populated with legless veterans, some hobbling on wooden pegs, some on crutches; and there were even more armless men, with their empty coat sleeves pinned to their shoulders. Among these walking amputees, and also among the bed-ridden invalids in their homes, the former Army Chaplain found himself constantly engaged: swapping war stories, comforting those who were in despair because of their mutilation, reading Scripture to the bed-fast, praying with the dying.

Crissey Helps Build a New Church in Decatur

Love for the Methodist Church was never far from Crissey's thoughts; he gave higher priorities only to his devotion to his Lord and to his family. He had been out of uniform scarcely one year before he plunged energetically into helping his pastor, the Reverend Levi Pitner, plan an important revival within Decatur's First Methodist Episcopal Church. He himself, of course, had

192

conducted a good many successful revivals while on the circuits and also while pastor at Eugene-Danville, Milwaukee, Joliet-Lockport, Decatur and Springfield. Pastor Pitner found Chaplain Crissey's enthusiastic and experienced support invaluable.

The 1866-1867 Methodist revival focused upon erecting a larger church edifice. The protracted meetings generated sufficient spiritual momentum to project the new edifice and to raise enough money to begin digging foundations, laying stones and bricks. In 1868 the handsome new house of worship was finished. It stood at the corner of Water and William Streets near the center of Decatur. Its outside dimensions were 84 feet by 120 feet, containing a sanctuary, 60 by 67 feet.

It cost $65,000 — in 1868 a staggering outlay, equivalent in money values of 100 years later to perhaps $500,000. By the year 1871, all debts were paid, and on Sunday, January 14, 1872, the new Church was formally dedicated by the distinguished Methodist bishop T. M. Eddy of Baltimore. When Bishop Eddy paid special tribute to "Chaplain Crissey" as a prime mover in the achievement, nobody in the big congregation questioned the rightness of the Bishop's praise.

Heartbreak struck Crissey's own home in 1869, when, on September 14, his wife, Maria Catherine, was taken from him by death. She was 55 years old. A fine double lot atop an eminence in Decatur's handsome, hilly and timbered Greenwood Cemetery was purchased by the sons. Because the loss was so intimate, the grief so intense, a brother clergyman read the funeral service for Maria C. Crissey. Accompanying the bereaved father at the graveside were his three sons and daughter.

Near Christmastime, 1873, the Crisseys were again visited by death, when Mattie Amo Crissey, wife of Samuel B. Crissey, died at the early age of 23. The Victorian era was a time when persons were not ashamed to publicize their religious faith, and the epitaphs on the Crissey monument at Greenwood Cemetery so testify. Beneath young Franklin's inscription are carved

193

the words, "Asleep in Jesus." Beneath the name and dates of Maria C. Crissey, wife of William Stoddart Crissey, buried in 1869, appear these words from Solomon: "She rests from her labors, and her works follow her." Mattie Amo's epitaph concludes with this couplet:

Not dead but living above
Waiting to welcome us home.

My first inspection, in 1948, of the 18-foot marble shaft marking the Crissey graves revealed interesting aspects of the Crissey's later years. The well-situated double burial lot and the tall expensive center shaft of marble testified to the family's affluence during the years after the Civil War and well into the late 1870s.

But one could not avoid noticing something on the base of the big monument that was pathetic. Its most conspicuous panel obviously had been reserved for William Stoddart Crissey. But in 1948 it was bare and empty, even though the old hero for whom it had been reserved had died 60 years before. Upon seeing that large empty space and considering what it implied, I felt a pang of pity.

Plainly, the Crisseys, by 1888, had fallen into financial stringencies so severe that they could not afford to employ a stone carver; hence, William Stoddart Crissey's panel on the front of the big Crissey monument had remained empty for 60 years, and his grave was unmarked. In the 1970s my brother, Virgil S. Crissey of Grand Junction, Colorado, and I at long last added the missing epitaph and a headstone.

The beloved former Army Chaplain and one-time Methodist circuit rider never lost his keen interest in politics. Although a strong Republican by party faith, and an admirer of President U. S. Grant, whom he remembered seeing in action on Lookout Mountain, Tennessee, the gross corruption of Grant's administrations made him wonder whether the nation's hideous bloodbath had, in the end, achieved any moral improvement in the nation worth dying for. Grant's debacle discouraged old William Stoddart Crissey, and puzzled him. But not enough to make him abandon his beloved Republican Party.

"Father Crissey:" Venerated and Beloved

By the mid-1870s everybody in Decatur who knew him (and almost everybody did!) spoke of him and addressed him as "Father Crissey" — an appellation of homage and affection that he accepted modestly. He retained remarkable health. As late as 1880, when he was 69 years old, William Stoddart Crissey possessed a clear mind and excellent command of language, as was demonstrated that year by the long article he wrote for the *Macon County Centennial History*.

Father Crissey entitled his article, "The Methodist Episcopal Church," and started it way back in 1829 with the Illinois Annual Conference held that year at Edwardsville, Illinois. After accurately detailing many names and dates, he concentrated on the history of the Methodist Church in Macon County. When he came to that part of his article that dealt with his parish during 1842 and 1843, he wrote:

> The Decatur circuit for many years was very large — three hundred miles around it; it was gradually curtailed, till in 1842 it was mostly confined to the county, with eight and ten regular appointments, Decatur having every other Sabbath, and Long Creek and some other place the other Sabbath. The other places were all visited during the week.

Obviously, at that point, he was writing from memory about things on the Decatur Circuit that he himself had experienced. Presently, referring to himself in the third person, he told of the successful revival he had conducted while ministering to the Decatur Circuit. He wrote:

> Of the several revivals, the one special for Decatur, with its few hundred population, was during the year of the Rev. W. S. Crissey's labors — a protracted meeting, beginning February 3rd, and continuing six weeks. Some seventy professed conversion, and about the same number were added to the church.

If the Decatur Circuit in 1842 embraced "eight or ten regular appointments, with Decatur having every other Sabbath," as Crissey described it in 1880, obviously it imposed on its pastor a heavy schedule of work, with several of the preaching points yoked together on the same days. Young S. Stephen Foster, a student in 1963 at Illinois Wesleyan University, Bloomington, majoring in history, in his dissertation, "From Pioneer Preaching Point to Urban Parishes," admitted himself perplexed by the apparent impossibility of William Stoddart Crissey serving that overly-busy Decatur Circuit in 1842, yet simultaneously conducting that highly-successful six-weeks revival. Foster concluded that the explanation "can only be surmised."

Remembering the remarkably efficient framework of organization evolved by the Methodist pastoral system serving its frontier circuits, the solution seems not too difficult to discover. It is almost a certainty that Crissey resolved the conflict thus: at every preaching point he had a local preacher trained to carry on the religious work while the circuit-riding ordained pastor was elsewhere. (On the Tazewell Circuit, the reader will remember, young Reverend Crissey visited each of his appointments only once every three weeks.) During his six weeks' revival at Decatur in 1842, it is sensible to assume that Crissey allocated his rural meetings to his local preachers, perhaps visiting them once or twice during his six-weeks' absence. Acknowledging higher priority due the Decatur Church, this temporary arrangement would have been accepted amicably by the smaller congregations.

The paragraph with which Father Crissey closed that section of his article in the *Macon County Centennial History* testified to his bigness of heart toward members of competing denominations. Revered old Father Crissey considered all who loved the Lord Jesus his brothers, and he rejoiced in their blessings as heartily as if they had been Methodists. The famous Peter Cartwright (his Presiding Elder in 1831-1832 while he rode the Tazewell Circuit) would never have written these kindly words about the Baptists:

> A bright star, as the fruit of this meeting, were the families and persons converted of Baptist parentage, who aided all through the meeting; and, after its close, wisely followed early proclivities in calling to their aid Elder H.W Dodge, of Springfield, for membership; and in due time the organization of the Baptist Church, thus born in a revival. May it ever so continue. Amen.

EPILOGUE

That the long-time-ago circuit rider retained during his older years a keen mind and insatiable curiosity was demonstrated publicly in Decatur as late as June, 1908, when the city's daily newspaper published a top-headlined article about a human skull, discovered by boys ransacking the vacant Crissey house at 429 West Prairie Avenue. The mysterious skull titillated the reporter's imagination as he wrote, June 21, 1908:

> A frightened lad in the old, empty Crissey house at 429 Prairie Avenue, Saturday afternoon picked up a moldy skull from the bottom of a heavy chest which he had found in one of the dark closets on the upper floor. His

197

terror was soon overcome, however, and with the other boys he played with the skull a while. Then, not liking the smell, he nailed it up in the box and put it back in the closet.

In one of the rooms on the second floor, the ceiling slopes downward and a partition built up made one of the old fashioned closets. The door of this closet was fastened with a nail and the boys exploring the house were alert the instant it was discovered.

"Bet there's something awful inside," said one as the door was being wrenched off. Far in one of the corners was a box. It was nailed. One lad pried off the top and found the skull. Immediately the news flashed through the neighborhood. The skull presented a mystery but not a horror, for no one knowing the Crisseys thought there was anything wrong.

When the reporter interviewed Truman Crissey, son of William Stoddart Crissey, the mystery was quickly dissipated. The son explained that his father in his late years had become much interested in phrenology, the technique of classifying human beings by differentiating shapes of their skulls. His father, said the son, was a thorough student of whatever he investigated; and had bought the human skull to further his theories.

"The old skull belonged to my father," the reporter quoted Truman Crissey as saying. "He used it in his lectures. He died twenty years ago, and undoubtedly left the skull in the box, just where the boys discovered it. We often wondered what had become of it. Thinking that the attic closet was empty, we never thoroughly examined it. No, there is nothing sinister or scandalous about father's old skull. I am glad to have it back again."

This amusing and somewhat bizarre incident is mentioned here, not because of any inherent historical importance, but only because it documents William Stoddart Crissey's keen intellect, unimpaired faculties and continuing public activities, well into his old age.

About three years after being mustered out of the Army, William Ernest Crissey, the eldest son, moved to Missouri, where he settled at Windsor, a village in the west-central part of the state. At nearby Calhoun, Missouri, February 4, 1882, he was married to Miss Dora Greene, previously of Tennessee.[17]

The young widower, Samuel B. Crissey, with his son, Maurice, born at Decatur in 1871, continued living in the Crissey cottage while he engaged in business until about 1885, when he moved to St. Louis, where he settled permanently. His son, Maurice, then a high school student, accompanied his father to St. Louis.

The Crissey house at 429 West Prairie Avenue, where the boys found the old skull, had been built in 1848 by William Stoddart Crissey. Accommodations must have been somewhat congested, with five Crisseys in it for so many years; but the Crisseys were ever a happy brood. The family patriarch, of course, was the gray-haired venerated Civil War hero and long-time-ago Methodist circuit rider. The youngest member of his family was his grandson, Maurice. There were three other adults: Truman, youngest son, born in 1843; his brother, Samuel; and Margaret E., the only daughter, born in 1840.

Margaret, after her mother's death in 1869, assumed full charge of the cottage, and continued to be the homemaker for more than 50 years. She never married and neither did her younger brother, Truman. In her latter years, Margaret Crissey came to be known throughout Central Illinois as a zealous crusader on behalf of temperance. She was President of both the Macon County and Decatur chapters of the Woman's Christian Temperance Union and its state organizer. The *Decatur Review* said of her, June 30, 1928, at the time of her death:

> During her active life, Margaret E. Crissey was one of the best known women in Central Illinois. She

---

[17] Of their four children, I am their youngest, and the only survivor. -- E.C.

unquestionably was known by sight to more people in Macon County than any other person, and most of the people knew her personally. She was quiet and gentle in her manner toward all things except the liquor traffic, against which she waged unrelenting warfare.

Doubtless, Old Father Crissey
Sometimes Pondered These Questions

It is not out of character to the man to believe that old William Stoddart Crissey in the 1880s, on those occasions when he found himself at home alone, quietly reminiscing in his favorite rocking chair, wondered sometimes whether his Heavenly Father judged his life work well-spent or ill.

Those successive failures during his early years must have bothered him. His preaching ministry had been cut short by consumption when he believed he had been on the very threshold of his most important work. In 1840, he had failed to establish a college in Decatur. In 1856 he had failed to be elected the Illinois State Superintendent of Public Instruction, only narrowly missing nomination at Bloomington (remembering that every candidate on the Anti-Nebraska ticket that fall had been elected). Further, when he remembered his failure in 1860 to complete the building of his hotel in downtown Decatur, he suffered acute embarrassment. All failures!

But the grand old Christian possessed an unconquerable soul. Ever since William Stoddart Crissey consecrated his life to the Lord Jesus when he was a boy back in Cincinnati, his outlook on life had remained unalterably hopeful. Now that he was an old man, his faith that his Saviour would never fail him continued as strong as it had been when he was a teen-age circuit-riding preacher.

Over-balancing the failures, there had been splendid victories. His preaching on the circuits and in the resident pulpits had

200

won hundreds of souls to Christ. And he had endured those hardships around the circuits cheerfully and patiently, obedient to Saint Paul's stern admonition: "I beseech you therefore, brethren, by the mercies of God, that ye present your bodies a living sacrifice, holy, acceptable unto God, which is your reasonable service."[18] He had truly presented his body a living sacrifice through torturing it year after year, buffeting the dangerous ordeals of the circuits. Those sufferings endured on the circuits, quite literally, had cost him his health — "a living sacrifice acceptable unto God." And, like the Great Apostle to the Gentiles, the old circuit rider deemed the price he had paid nothing more than his "reasonable service."

Inexorable, his memory then must have traveled on to his war years. Horrible as were some of those memories, there had been glory in them. He would have thought about the hundreds of maimed and dying soldiers with whom he had prayed on the blood-soaked battlefields of Chickamauga, Chattanooga, Atlanta and on the Tennessee River, where his regiment had helped pulverize General Hood's Confederates. Visions of the host of invalided men lying in the field hospitals whom he had comforted would have floated across his mind. How grateful they had been. He must have thought about the innumerable pathetic letters he had written beside the cots of dying soldiers. At that point, the eyes of the old War Chaplain probably misted over, for his was a very tender heart, and he knew well the tears that had flowed when his letters were read. He would have remembered, too, the quiet reverence of the out-of-doors worship services he had conducted so many times. But, saddest of all, had been the burials — the endless burials! — of countless corpses shoveled under the yellow southern earth, while he read their funeral rites, officers and men standing silently, heads uncovered.

Ah, merciful God! the tragedy of it all! Faithfully, he had labored very hard to alleviate a little of the heartbreak. And he

---

[18]*Romans* 12: 1

201

had. It would be less than truthful to deny that he had been a good Chaplain. His officers and men had told him so. His Chaplaincy, he hoped, had redeemed his previous failures. He felt assured now that an all-wise Providence had molded him, preserved him, in order that he should, in God's good time, serve as one of the Lord's Soldiers of Mercy. Yes, he would have concluded, his Chaplaincy had redeemed his failures. The old man at that point no doubt breathed a little prayer of thanks, smiled and dozed.

"CROSSING THE BAR"

—Alfred, Lord Tennyson

Thou shalt come to thy grave in full age,
Like as a shock of corn cometh in his full season.

—*Job* v: 26

In 1888, after a short illness at his home, the grand old man died. Because he had occupied so prominent a place in community awareness, his passing was noticed and mourned by hundreds of Macon County folk, most poignantly, of course, by his former comrades in arms — grayed, crippled and aging infantrymen who once had marched beside Chaplain Crissey as he rode his handsome horse alongside the column — many years ago in faraway Georgia, Tennessee and Alabama. With military honors, William Stoddart Crissey's remains were buried in Greenwood Cemetery beside the graves of his wife and daughter-in-law.

For 84 years revered old Father Crissey quietly slept his long sleep on his hilltop in Greenwood Cemetery, Decatur, while an oak tree nearby, decade after decade, grew ever taller and spread its branches ever farther over his grave. By the year 1972, six other Crisseys were sleeping beside him.

That year, 1972, the quiet of the Crissey hilltop was broken by a colorful hour of pageantry — a kind of long-delayed epilogue — that paid homage to William Stoddart Crissey's career. The ceremony came in May on a beautiful Sunday afternoon. The occasion was the dedication of a bronze plaque, newly bolted to the stone base of the Crissey family's tall marble shaft in Decatur's Greenwood Cemetery.

Officials of the Macon County Historical Society presided. The Stephen Decatur chapter of the Daughters of the American Revolution placed a memorial wreath, as did the Ladies of the Grand Army of the Republic, the Woman's Dunham Relief Corps, the Macon County Heritage Committee and the Decatur Civil War Round Table. Television and newspaper cameras recorded the event.

Dr. Laren Spear, pastor of St. Paul's United Methodist Church, in Decatur, eulogized the long-time-ago Methodist frontier preacher and Civil War Chaplain, ending by reading this stanza from Mary Carolyn Davies' little poem, "The Circuit Rider":

> God rode out of His ancient quest,
>> Healing, saving, commanding.
> Here in the savage unknown West —
>> Settlement, cabin, landing —
> Well they knew the steady beat
> In the stillness of God's horses' feet.

When the red canopy concealing the plaque was pulled away by its donor, Elwell Crissey of Bloomington, Illinois, grandson of the man buried there, it was seen to read:

1811
WILLIAM STODDART CRISSEY
1888

Frontier Circuit Rider
Crusader Against Negro Slavery
First Methodist Preacher in Macon County
Builder of Strong Churches in Illinois
Macon County Commissioner of Schools
President, Decatur Village Board of Trustees
Civil War Army Chaplain
Friend of Abraham Lincoln

The ceremonies ended when musket shots were fired over the grave by two young men, one wearing the blue uniform of the Union, the other the gray of the Confederacy.

It seems not inappropriate to conclude this little history of William Stoddart Crissey by quoting here a brief encomium from the *Book of Psalms*, once addressed by a Singer of Ancient Israel to some good man whom he reverently admired. Thousands of years ago and from half a world away come these kindly words of eulogy written by an unknown Hebrew poet. They might well describe also this good man whom we have been considering:

His work was honorable and glorious.

SOURCES AND RESEARCH

Chapter I.

For more than 100 centuries before the first European gazed upon them in awe and astonishment, prodigious tallgrass prairies flourished magnificently across a relatively narrow belt of country near the middle of the North American continent. Nowhere else on earth did such tall grasses grow. Beginning in the 17th Century, the fame of the giant grasses then clothing most of Central Illinois had reached geographers and travelers all over Europe and the Americas. It is surprising, therefore, that so little was written about the great Illinois prairies. Descriptions left by the seven eyewitnesses quoted in Chapter I remain the best sources extant. To their writings must be added the monograph by Douglas McManis prepared for the University of Chicago and published in 1961, which delineates the timbered and prairie regions of Illinois in 1839 and 1841.

During several trips to Springfield, where I interviewed the Illinois State Museum's distinguished botanists, I explored late 20th Century ecological literature about Illinois' ancient tallgrass prairies but found them to be inappropriate to the historical nature of this account. The one exception to my sweeping exclusion of modern sources is John Madson's rewarding study, *Where the Sky Began, Land of the Tallgrass Prairie*, (Houghton Mifflin, Boston, 1982). Madson's charming and authoritative work is quoted at some length in Chapter I.

Chapter II.

The inexorable push westward during the 19th Century by Methodists and their conquest of the trans-Appalachian frontier were dramatically told by Luccock and Hutchinson in *The Story of Methodism* (New York, 1926). Ezra Squier Tipple's excellent book, *Francis Asbury: the prophet of the long road (Methodist Book Concern, New York, 1916),* supplied ample details about Bishop Asbury.

Dr. James Leaton's *History of Methodism in Illinois from 1793 to 1832* (Cincinnati, 1883) chronicles his thorough research into Jesse Walker's career. This great work, which published only its first volume, provided a treasure-trove of details about early Illinois Methodism. Most of Peter Cartwright's story is paraphrased and quoted from his own famous autobiography.

Chapter III.

In order to recreate the environment, climatic phenomena and the family living conditions of his parishioners as they existed when my Grandfather traveled across the prairies, I selected a few books from the considerable library of those describing pioneer and frontier life in Illinois during the early 19th Century.

The most graphic descriptions of the Big Snow were recounted in Charles Chapman's *History of Tazewell County,* (Chicago 1879). The several histories of the five counties traversed by young Crissey on the Tazewell preaching circuit in 1831 and 1832 revealed many interesting details.

As for McLean County, especially important, of course, was Professor Etzard Duis' *Good Old Times in McLean County* (Bloomington, 1874). Henry Clay Tate's recent history, *The Way It Was In McLean County 1972-1822* (McLean County '72 Association, Bloomington, 1972) contributes a vivid description of the ferocious green-headed blood-sucking flies that tormented frontier people and beasts inhabiting Central Illinois so long as the tall-grass prairies survived.

Other material was derived from that excellent history of the McLean County Funk Dynasty, *Funk of Funk's Grove* (Pantagraph, Bloomington, 1952), written in the late 1940s and early 1950s by Dr. Helen Cavanagh, professor of history at Illinois State University.

Chapter IV.

Obviously, the most prolific and, indeed, indispensable source of details portraying the Reverend Crissey's day-by-day experiences as he ministered to Illinois frontier families was Leaton's unique "travelogue" — the discovery of which inspired this book.

Chapman's history of Tazewell County was a rich source of firsthand descriptions of the Asiatic cholera plague in the summer of 1833. Additional materials were drawn from the histories of DeWitt, Logan and Woodford Counties (see below). Data about the Indians came from the four histories of Logan County.

For McLean County, no richer source of soundly documented eyewitness material exists than Duis' unique "Old Times," previously mentioned. Volume I of Leaton's history of Illinois Methodism again proved a treasure.

Chapter V

This and the next two chapters are the backbone of this book: the rudiments that justify its being written, as was explained in the Introduction. Dr. Leaton's lengthy and closely detailed day-by-day description escorting the young Reverend Crissey around his 250-mile-long horseback journeys (which Dr. Leaton printed separately, and did not include in his three-volume history), provides the road map for these chapters. Leaton's (Crissey's) description of the old circuit was so meticulously accurate that this author had no trouble locating every one of Crissey's 25 preaching places.

His first 100 miles traversed only McLean County, and served nine preaching places. Identifying the people at each station who comprised his congregations necessitated close reading of nine township histories in Charles Merriman's *History of*

McLean County (Chicago, 1879). Merriman's massive research filled 1,064 pages, more than 300 pages of which narrate in detail the histories of each of McLean County's 30 townships.

After locating on a county map the townships containing his appointments, I separated out the settlers who had arrived prior to November 1831. Those names constituted a census of each of Crissey's congregations, inasmuch as the visit once every three weeks of the Methodist circuit riding preacher brought together virtually every adult within riding distance.

Professor Merriman's text about Bloomington Township was the source for information about the people Crissey preached to on the first Sunday of the circuit. Towanda Township comprised his congregation on his first Mondays, and the tiny congregation of his first Tuesdays were people living within Money Creek Township. On his first Wednesdays the Reverend Crissey met one of his largest congregations in the big Patton cabin in Lexington Township. His first Thursdays carried him almost the length of McLean County, to the group of Methodists comprising the big Cheney family and neighbors; they were named by Merriman in his history of Cheney's Grove Township. Crissey's first Friday congregation was found in the history of Old Town Township and his first Saturday congregation, encountered the final day of his beginning week at Conoway's Grove, is described in the history of Empire Township.

I derived invaluable assistance from Warner and Beers' exciting *Atlas of McLean County and the State of Illinois* (Chicago, 1874). Extensive investigative research is exemplified in the large scale maps of each of McLean County's 30 townships. Every farm and its owner is identified as are all settlements and roads, every watercourse and the outlines of the original groves. The cartography is exquisite. The maps printed in tinted colors are beautiful. I spent many hours in Bloomington's old Withers Public Library poring over this old atlas, tracing Grandfather Crissey's journeys.

Chapter VI.

On every second Sunday of the circuit, the small group of Methodists inhabiting the region around Randolph Grove in southern McLean County, on the west bank of Kickapoo Creek, assembled in the most spacious cabin of the settlement for Crissey's last Sunday service in McLean County. Leaton praised them as one of the circuit's strongest societies, and Merriman's history of Randolph Township mentioned them all.

His Monday congregation at Funk's Grove was small, but it bore the name of the famous Funk Family, a dynasty destined to leave important traces on Illinois history. Merriman's description of Funk's Grove Township supplied materials about the Funks, but I found Dr. Cavanagh's history of Isaac Funk's family even more helpful.

Tuesdays of the second week of the circuit carried him into DeWitt County. Interesting anecdotes about the eccentric Sylvania Shurtleff were gleaned from Waynesville township histories in *W. R. Brink's History of DeWitt County, Illinois* (Philadelphia, 1882), and from Charles Chapman's *Portrait and Biographical Album of DeWitt and Piatt Counties, Illinois,* (Chicago, 1891).

The identities of Crissey's Wednesday congregations were gleaned from the three township histories, Atlanta, Elkhart and Hurlbut; the sources were Donnelley Publishers' *History of Logan County, Past and Present* (Chicago, 1878) and Inter-State Publishing Company's *History of Logan County, Illinois* (Chicago, 1886).

Ollendorf's Mill was the Reverend Crissey's second Thursday appointment. The site of the Ollendorf's grist mill straddled the boundaries between Eminence and East Lincoln Townships. The histories of those townships, published in the two Logan County histories (see above), disclosed the identities of young Crissey's parishioners at Ollendorf's Mill—with plentiful amusing yarns about Robert Musick, "Man-Without-Toe."

Crissey's first preaching appointment for his second Fridays was Old Mackinaw Town, a long horseback ride northward into Tazewell County. Another appointment the same day saw him at an important settlement on Dillon Creek, close to Elm Grove and Pleasant Grove.

The names of Crissey's congregation at Old Mackinaw Town were gleaned from Chapman's histories of Mackinaw Township and Deer Creek Township, while the second and larger congregation was identified in his Elm Grove and Tremont Township histories.

Chapman's histories of Sand Prairie and Dillon Townships name the settlers at Sand Prairie, the small settlement that Crissey preached to on his second Saturdays.

Chapter VII.

The Reverend Crissey's third Sundays found him in Pekin, seat of Tazewell County, and by far the largest and most important charge on his circuit. Chapman's county history devotes much text to Pekin in the 1830s, from which it was easy to separate out the parishioners by their dates of arrival.

On his third Monday mornings, the young horse preacher rode to a small Methodist settlement named Wesley City in honor of the great founder of its church. Its history is recounted in Chapman's item, Groveland Township.

The following morning, Crissey moved on to Holland's Grove and Wrenn's Grove. The identities of his congregation living in these neighboring groves are found in Chapman's text under Washington Township.

On the mornings of the Reverend Crissey's third Wednesdays, he encountered the little village of Walnut Grove, surrounded by a magnificent forest of thousands of towering black walnut trees. His people there are named in the histories of Olio and Cruger Townships, described in B. J. Radford's *History of Woodford County* (Peoria, 1877) and also in the county history published by William LeBaron Jr., *The Past and Present of Woodford County, Illinois* (Chicago, 1878).

Riding eastward, the young clergyman spent his third Thursdays in a wilderness inhabited only by a few settlers living near a grist mill. The names of the worshipers at Willis' Mill were found in the Palestine Township section of Radford's Woodford County history. Leaving the Panther Creek wilderness the next morning, Crissey entered the northwestern corner of McLean County to find Stout's Grove, a fairly large Methodist society whose members' names and identities were carefully recorded by Merriman in his history of McLean County's Danvers Township.

On his final Saturday on the Tazewell Circuit that conference year, young Crissey ministered to a strong Methodist society of families living in two small stands of timber, Dry Grove and Twin Grove. Merriman names these people in his history of Dry Grove Township. Because it was only a few miles farther, Crissey usually jogged on into Bloomington, where he knew friends awaited him in old James Allin's big house.

Chapter VIII

The fabric of this chaper is provided by the scholarly study of John D. Barnhardt Jr. At the publication of his brilliant monograph, "The Rise of the Methodist Episcopal Church in Illinois from the Beginning to the Year 1832" *(Journal of the Illinois State Historical Society*, April 1919), Methodism in Illinois recognized him as its ablest historian.

A good evaluation of the quality of the sermons that Methodist circuit riders preached during the early 19th Century was found in the minutes of the 1962 North Central Jurisdictional Historical Society.

I mined rich nuggets from chapters XIV, XV and XVI of Luccock's and Hutchinson's superb *The Story of Methodism* , cited elsewhere. Volume I of Leaton's history, cited frequently, and the resources of the Historical Library of the Illinois United Methodist Conference at Bloomington contributed significantly.

Details of Methodism's Christmas Conference and the westward thrust of the circuit riders come from Volume I of *The Encyclopedia of World Methodism* (United Methodist Publishing House, Nashville, 1974) edited by Bishop Nolan B. Harrison.

Chapter IX

The historical research by which this life story of William Stoddart Crissey was retrieved extended over an embarrassingly long time. During the span of that quarter century I explored many sources: old newspapers, old books, county histories, United States Army archives and, naturally, the minutes of the Annual Conferences of the Methodist Episcopal Churches in Central Illinois.

All, in different ways, were helpful. But one source was essential. Dr. James Leaton's *History of Methodism in Illinois, from 1793 to 1832* provided meticulously accurate source materials — unique and indispensable — out of which this life story evolved. The manuscript copies of his unpublished second and third volumes were read in the Historical Library of the Illinois United Methodist Conference, adjacent to the campus of Illinois Wesleyan University at Bloomington.

In that same library I found and analyzed the minutes of the Annual Conferences of the Methodist Episcopal Church in Central Illinois for the years 1832 through 1848. Chaplain Crissey's military record during the years 1863, 1864 and 1865 were exhumed from the official United States Army records of the Civil War preserved in the Illinois State Historical Library at Springfield.

I found that the Crissey family occupies conspicuous places in the histories of Macon County, Illinois and that the Reverend Crissey is mentioned several times in the McLean County histories.

ACKNOWLEDGMENTS

Illinois' Prodigious Tallgrass Prairies

Dr. Alfred Koelling, Curator of Botany for the Illinois State Museum at Springfield, was generous with his time in analyzing the plant and animal inhabitants of Illinois' ancient prairies.

For his praise of my unprecedented historic evaluation of Illinois' unique tallgrass prairies, and for his encouragement, I am indebted to my long-time friend, Ivan Huber Light of Shirley, Illinois, an astute student of Illinois history.

Living at Godfrey, Illinois, a small town on the Mississippi River near Alton, are John Madson and his wife, Dycie, two artists and devotees of Illinois' tallgrass prairies. Madson, a nature writer and conservationist of national repute, probably knows more about those majestic tall grasses which once clothed Illinois than any person alive. Their 1982 book, *Where the Sky Began: Land of the Tallgrass Prairie,* illustrated by his artist wife, Dycie, provides excerpts that embellish and enrich my Chapter I. I am grateful to the Madsons for their generous permission to quote at some length from their joint book.

The Illinois Frontier in the 1830s

For his clear-sighted criticisms of my early drafts of Chapter II I am indebted to Dr. Harold L. Fair, Associate Book Editor of the United Methodist Publishing House at Nashville.

For his criticisms and encouragement I am indebted to one of Illinois' most respected historians, Dr. Mark Plummer, former Chair of the Department of History, Illinois State University, Normal.

213

The Tazewell Preaching Circuit

The inspiration for this book came from Dr. James Leaton's detailed description of Grandfather Crissey's travels around the Tazewell preaching circuit in 1831 and 1832, and Volume One of his *History of Methodism in Illinois* became indispensable as my work progressed.

For information about Grandfather's routes of travel, I consulted frequently with William Brigham (1874-1959), for many years McLean County's much-beloved Superintendent of Schools and a neighbor of mine. His exhaustive knowledge of rural McLean County immeasurably enriched Chapters V, VI and VII.

The Artists

The painting on the front cover is the work of the late Clayton A. Nicles of Denver, Colorado.

For the dramatic frontispiece of the "Circuit Rider" equestrian statue standing on the Oregon State Capitol campus at Salem, I am indebted to Addie Dyal, Oregoniana Consultant for the Oregon State Library, who commissioned new photographs for this book. Her photograph was skillfully retouched by Quen Carpenter of Plano, Illinois, to remove shrubbery that obscured part of the statue.

Professor Richard Hentz of the Illinois State University Art Department painted the picture in Chapter IX, illustrating Chaplain Crissey preaching to his troops in Georgia. He also painted "Cholera Gravestones" on page 79.

The remarkable and unique map of McLean County, Illinois, in 1830 is the work of Dr. Shamim Naim, cartographer and visiting professor at Illinois State University.

The many line drawing illustrations scattered through Chapters II, III, IV and VIII were excerpted from Luccock's and

Hutchinson's *The Story of Methodism* and from Halford E. Luccock's delightful booklet, *Endless Line of Splendor*. The respective illustrators are Harold Speakman and Lynd Ward, two artists whose imaginative drawings aid in evoking a clear picture of Illinois prairie life.

The painting of a Christian minister preaching to covered wagon travelers in the West in the mid-19th Century adds strength to the conclusion of Chapter VIII. For permission to reproduce it I am indebted to the John Hancock Mutual Life Insurance Company of Boston, whose Director of Advertising, Patricia Bond, graciously had the painting newly photographed.

Illinois Methodism in the 1830s and Its Circuit Riders

I am indebted to Dr. Donald L. Lowe, Administrative Assistant to Bishop White at Springfield, for his help in guiding my coverage of the topics on which frontier circuit riders preached, and for his insights that allowed me to avoid certain pitfalls.

In pursuit of hard-to-find old Illinois Methodist reference materials, Dr. Joe Kraus, former Chair of Libraries at Illinois State University, Normal, demonstrated in my behalf his impressive mastery of library science.

I am indebted also to Illinois United States Senator Paul Simon for enlisting the Library of Congress in pursuit of what seemed once a key reference verifying Methodist doctrines.

The Book

I am grateful to my long-time friend, Dr. Lloyd Bertholf, formerly President of Illinois Wesleyan University, for his sound and correct counsel when I confronted delicate choices which needed to be decided with tact and wisdom.

The publication of this book is the work of my son, Dr. Brian Laird Crissey, of Tigard, Oregon, without whose support

215

my manuscript would have vanished into limbo. I deeply appreciate also the astute editorial insights provided for this book by Gretchen Lingle of McMinnville, Oregon.

William Stoddart Crissey

Many of the bricks which enabled me to reconstruct Grandfather Crissey's career I dug out of the several excellent histories of Macon County, Illinois, named in "Sources and Research." The librarians at the Decatur Public Library were diligent in aiding my research. So, too, were the archivists at the Decatur *News-Herald* where I found many informative clippings about Crissey family activities in Macon County.

The indispensable data expanding Chaplain Crissey's service in the Civil War were ferreted out for me by James C. Patrick, one of Decatur's most learned scholars on Illinois' role in the Civil War.

At Bloomington, the late Thelma Van Ness Breen, esteemed librarian of Bloomington's old Withers Public Library, accorded me endless courtesies. I also am indebted to Lois Wood, Mrs. Breen's highly competent assistant at the Withers Library. Whenever I asked Lois Wood for help, she never failed me.

In the library of the United Methodist Conference offices near the Illinois Wesleyan University campus in Bloomington, archivist Catherine Knight gave me invaluable help in perusing the old volumes of the Illinois Methodist Annual Conference minutes.

Completion of this work would have been impossible without the tireless and constant support of my loving wife, Densie, whose skills in many areas I have found unsurpassed.

E. C.

Index

Adams, Jane, 118-119, 121
Adams, John G., 120, 121
Akers, Peter, 164, 166
Allin, James, 49, 86, 87, 88, 131, 211
Andrew, Bishop James O., 154
Annual Conference of Methodist Episcopal Church in Illinois, 195, 212
  Belleville (1848), 172
  Bloomington (1839), 163
  Edwardsville (1829), 195
  Jacksonville (1832), 77, 154
  Jacksonville (1837), 161
  Jacksonville (1841), 164
  Mount Carmel (1834), 160
  Nashville (1844), 168
  Paris (1846), 171
  Quincy (1843), 168
  Rushville (1836), 161
  Springfield (1835), 161
  Springfield (1845), 171
  Union Grove (1833), 155
  Winchester (1842), 164, 165
Armstrong, James, 150-151
Army of the Cumberland, 186
Asbury, Bishop Francis, 32, 33-36, 135, 206
  at Christmas Conference (1784), 144
  as circuit rider, 34, 155
  self-ordination as Bishop, 33
Asiatic cholera, 77-79, 155, 207
Atlanta, Georgia, 189
Atlanta Township, Illinois, 209
Atlas of McLean County and the State of Illinois, 208
Atteberry, William P., 126

Bailey, David, 118
Baltimore. *See* Christmas Conference (1784); Methodist General Conference
Baptist Church, 166, 167, 197
Barger, John S., 173
Barnard, M.N., 90
Barnett, Rachel. *See* Conaway, Rachel Barnett
Barnhardt, John D. Jr., 138, 141-142, 211
Barr, John, 105
Bartholomew, Joseph, 89
Battle of Chickamauga. *See* Chickamauga Creek, battle of
Beggs, Rev. Stephen R., 124, 128
  as W.S. Crissey's colleague at Joliet, 162
  as W.S. Crissey's predecessor on Tazewell Circuit, 87, 112-113
Belly timber, 54-56
Bethard, Elza, 122
Big Grove, 103, 104-105
Big Painter Woods, 125
Big Snow, 46-49, 206
Bishop, John, 94
Black, Isaac, 126
Black Hawk. *See* Chief Black Hawk
Black Hawk War (1832), 72, 76, 92, 120-121
Blooming Grove, 49, 55, 56, 87, 93
Bloomington, Illinois, 49, 55, 56, 86-87, 208
  speech by Abraham Lincoln in, 179-181
  as start and end of Tazewell Circuit, 86, 131, 211
Bloomington Circuit, 77

Bogardus, John, 115
Bowman, Ezekiel, 110
Bracken, Matthew, 126
Bradshaw, Rev. Arthur, 183
Brink, W.R., 209
Brittin, Jane. *See* Hendrix, Jane
  Brittin
Brock, Mrs. William, 103
Brock, William, 101
Brown, William, 118
Broyhill, James, 116
Broyhill, William, 116
Brumhead, Isaac, 90
Brumhead, Joseph, 90
Buckles' Grove, 94

Camlin, Thomas, 122
Camp meetings, 136-137
  in Illinois, 137-139
  origins of, 137, 139-140
  on Tazewell Circuit, 77, 141-142
Canaday, John, 88
Cartwright, Peter, 2, 41-45, 155
  autobiography of, 41-42, 44-45,
    206
  orders W.S. Crissey to Rushville,
    172-175
  as Presiding Elder of Tazewell
    Circuit, 69, 77, 152
Cavanagh, Helen, 206, 209
Chambers, Bering and Quinlan, 164
Chapman, Charles, 48, 206, 207,
    209, 210
Chapman, James, 115-116
Cheney, Ann. *See* Dawson, Ann
  Cheney
Cheney, Jonathan, 91
Cheney's Grove, 91, 208
Chenoweth, Rev. Ashbury, 162
Chickamauga Creek, battle of, 184-
    185

Chief Black Hawk, 73, 74-75, 92,
    116
  at Stillman's Run, 116, 120-121
Cholera, 77-79, 155, 207
Christmas Conference (1784), 30,
    144-145, 212
Christmas of 1831, 95-97, 99-100
Church of England, 30, 144
Circuit Rider (poem), 203
Circuit riders
  importance of, 58, 146
  life of, 46, 66-71, 86-132
  origin of, 135-136
  pay of, 66, 131, 132
Civil War, W.S. Crissey in, 182-
    192, 216
Clearwater, Reuben, 95
Clothing of pioneers, 56-57
Coffee, scarcity of, 54-55
Coke, Bishop Thomas, 135, 144
College Hill (Decatur), 164
Collot, Victory, 25-26
Conaway, Aquilla, 95
Conaway, James Harvey, 94-95, 96
Conaway, Rachel Barnett, 95
Conaway's Grove, 94-96, 208
Conferences. *See* Annual Confer-
    ence of Methodist Episcopal
    Church in Illinois;
    Christmas Conference;
    Illinois Conference;
    Methodist General Conference;
    Methodist Qtrly Conference;
    Tennessee Conference;
    Western Conference
Cooper's Island, 117
Coulson, Rev. David, 161
Covered wagons, 19, 20
Crissey, Dora Greene, 199
Crissey, Margaret, 76, 166-167,
    199-200

Crissey, Maria Catherine, 163, 193, 194

Crissey, Mattie Amo, 193, 194

Crissey, Maurice, 193

Crissey, Samuel, 182-183, 191, 193

Crissey, Truman, 167, 193

Crissey, William Ernest, 183, 191, 199

Crissey, William Stoddart:
  accepts appointment to Spring-field Station, 168
  acquaintance with Abraham Lincoln, 179-181
  appointed Chaplain of 115th Illinois Volunteer Infantry, 183
  appointed pastor of Milwaukee (Wisconsin) Station, 161
  appointed to Decatur Circuit, 164
  appointed to Jacksonville Circuit, 154
  appointed to Mount Carmel Circuit, 155
  appointed to Paoli Circuit, 151
  appointed to pastorate at Eugene-Danville, 160-161
  appointed to pastorate at Joliet, 161
  appointed to Tazewell Circuit, 152
  as Army Chaplain, 184-192
  birth of, 148
  as circuit rider, 46, 66-69, 86-132
  as County School Commissioner, 177
  death of, 202
  death of parents, 148-149
  death of son, Franklin, 181
  death of wife, 193
  in Decatur, viii-ix, xi-xii, xv, 163-169, 177-179, 181, 192-195, 199, 202-204
  effort to establish college at Decatur, 163-164

Crissey, William Stoddart:
  elected to Deacon's Orders, 156
  and end of Civil War, 190-192
  failures of, 200
  fasting of, 170-171
  as foe of slavery, 182
  friendship with Dr. James Leaton, viii-x, 156-157, 169-170
  grave of, 194
  growth in faith of, 149-150
  health of, 160, 162-163, 164, 168-169, 171-175, 182
  ignores appointment to Rushville Church, 174-175
  and John Wesley sermons, 162
  joins Methodist Church, 150
  at Joliet, 161-162
  licensed as Methodist exhorter, 151
  licensed as Methodist preacher, 151
  marriage of, 163, 164
  move to Bloomington, Indiana, 150
  nominee for Illinois State Super-intendent of Public Instruction, 178-179
  on Paoli Circuit, 151-152
  payment as circuit rider, 131, 132
  plans for hotel, 181
  politics of, 176-177, 178-179
  preaches first sermon in Bloom-ington, 88
  preaches in Decatur, Illinois, 153
  as President of Decatur Board of Trustees, 177
  Sunday School appointments of, 163
  on Tazewell Circuit, 69-71, 86-132
  tribute to, 203
  and tuberculosis, 160

Crissey, William Stoddart:
    victories of, 200-202
    view of prairie, 1-2, 26-27
    wife of, 163, 164, 193, 194
Crissey, William T., 148
    moves family to Decatur, Illinois,
        153
    raises William Stoddart Crissey,
        148-151
Cromwell, Anna Eliza, 118
Cromwell, Nathan, 118
Cruger Township, 210
Cunningham, Robert, 91
Curtiss, Daniel S., 14-16

Danvers Township, 211
Danville, Illinois, 160-161
Davidson, Caleb, 126
Davidson, William, 126
Davies, Mary Carolyn, 203
Davis, Hezehiah, 115
Dawson, Ann Cheney, 92
Dawson, John Wells, 92-93
Decatur, Illinois, 167-168. *See also*
        Crissey, William Stoddart, in
        Decatur;
        First Methodist Episcopal
        Church, Decatur, Illinois
    becomes home of William T.
        Crissey, 153
    College Hill, 164
Decatur Circuit, 164-166, 195-196
Decatur Review, 166-168
Deer Creek, 107, 210
Delaware Indians, 32, 92
DeWitt County, 30, 69, 103-105,
        207, 209
Dickens, Charles, impressions of
        Illinois prairie, 17-18
Dickens, Rev.J.H., 81
Dillon Creek, 115, 116, 210
Diseases of pioneers, 59-63

Douglas, Senator Stephen A., 178,
    180
Dowdy, Eliza, 126
Dowdy, John, 126
Downing, James, 106
Downing, John, 106
Downing, Robert, 106
Downing, Ruth, 106
Downs, Illinois, 98
Downs, Lawson, 95, 96
Dry Grove, 130-131, 211
Duis Etzard, 90, 206, 207
Dunham, William W., 105

Eads, Brother, 116, 122
East Lincoln Township, 209
Eddy, Bishop T.M., 193
Eggleston, Edward, 42
Eldorado Temple, 167
Elkhart, Illinois, 108-109, 209
Elkhart Grove, 107
Elm Grove, 115, 210
Eminence Township, 209
Empire Township, 208
Encyclopedia of World Methodism,
    212
England, C.E., 164
Eureka College, 126
Evans, William, 93
Ewing, Christopher C., 73-74, 111
Ewing, Elizabeth, 111
Ewing, John, 111
Exhorters, 150

Farmer's Creek, 123
Fasting, 170-171
Father Crissey, viii, 195. *See also*
        Crissey, William Stoddart
Father Dickens. *See* Dickens, Rev.
        J.H.
Fireplaces, 50-51
First Methodist Episcopal Church,
        Decatur, Illinois, 156, 192-193

First Methodist Episcopal Church, Eugene, Illinois, 160
Flesher, Conrad, 90
Fletcher, Eli, 107
Fletcher, Marian, 107
Flies, green-headed biting, 62
Fling, Richard, 89
Flower, George, 4-7
Fond du Lac, 122
Food of pioneers, 54-56
Ford Crossing, 89, 91
Forests, 2-4. *See also* Prairies
Fort Clark, 91, 102, 121-122. *See also* Peoria; Peoria, Illinois
Foster, S. Stephen, 196
Fox Indians, 73, 74, 120
Francis Asbury: *The Prophet of the Long Road*, 206
Frankeberger, Jesse, 94
Frontier life. *See* Pioneers
Funk, Absalom, 101
Funk, Adam, 101, 102, 103
Funk, Cassandra Sharp, 102
Funk, Dorothy. *See* Stubblefield, Dorothy Funk
Funk, Isaac, 101, 102, 209
    home of, 49-51, 53
Funk, Jacob, 101-102
Funk, Jesse, 102
Funk, Sarah. *See* Stubblefield, Sarah Funk
Funk of Funk's Grove, 206
Funk's Grove, 100-103, 206, 209
    first Methodist Church at, 103
Furniture of pioneers, 52-54

Gerhard, Frederick, 8-9, 11-14, 16, 22, 23-24
Gibson, Cyrus J., 122
Gildersleeve, James Turner, 63
Goddard, Abbot, 139
Good Old Times in McLean County, 206, 207

Gorlin, J.R., 167
Grace Methodist Church, Decatur, 167
Grand Army of Gen. Sherman, 186
Grand Prairie of Illinois, 22, 23
Green, Dr. John D., 142-143
Greene, Dora. *See* Crissey, Dora Greene
Greenman & Dunham store, 104
Greenman, Esek, 61
Greenman, Jeremiah, 94
Gridley, Asabel, 87
Grist mills, 54, 104, 108, 127. *See also* Ollendorf's Mill
Grove as place name, 21, 71
Groveland Township, 210
Gwin, James, 139

Haines, William, 118
Hall, Basil, 9-10
Hall, Zadok, 124
Haner, John, 90
Harness, Jacob, 89
Harrison, Bishop Nolan B., 212
Havighurst, Dr. Robert, 21-22
Hawley, Gideon, 116
Heath, William, 123-124
Hendrix, Jane Brittin, 92
Hendrix, John, 92-93
Henline Fort, 91
Heyworth, Illinois, 98
History of DeWitt County, Illinois, 209
History of Logan County, Illinois, 209
History of Logan County, Past and Present, 209
History of McLean County, 207-208
History of Methodism in Illinois from 1793 to 1832, ix, xiv, 206, 212
History of Tazewell County, 206

History of the English Settlement in Edwards County Illinois, 4-7
History of Woodford County, 211
Hittle family, 115
Hodge, Elder, 166
Hodge, William, 98
Holding, Rev. Richard, 183
Holland, William, 123
Holland's Grove, 123, 210
Hopkins, Ezekiel, 110
Hopkins, Joseph, 90
Horse preachers. *See* Circuit riders
Houses of pioneers, 49-51
Hurlburt Township, 209
Huston, Samuel, 149
Hutchinson, Paul, 34-36, 44, 205, 211

Illinois As It Is, 8-9, 11-14, 16
Illinois Conference, 41, 77, 212. *See also* Annual Conference of Methodist Episcopal Church in Illinois
Illinois District of Tennessee Conference, 158
Illinois Methodism, 31-32, 206
    Bardhardt as historian of, 211
Illinois prairies. *See* Prairies
Illinois State Department of Conservation, 20-21
Illinois State Museum, 205, 213
Illness in frontier life, 59-63. *See also* Crissey, William Stoddart, health of
Imlay, Gilbert, 5
Indiana, 41. *See also* Paoli Circuit
Indians, 71-76. *See also* Chief Black Hawk
Iron Brigade, 190
Isham, George, 105
Itaska, 108

Jacksonville Circuit, 80-81
    Crissey tranferred to, 77
Jacoby, Henry, 95, 96
Jefferson, Thomas, as host to George Flower, 4
Jones, John B., 105

Kerns, William, 155
Kickapoo Creek, 83, 98, 103, 104, 105, 209
Kickapoo Indians, 32, 73-74, 92, 111

Lackland, David, 116
Lane, Tillman, 105
Lantis, Daniel, 109
Latham, Richard, 108-109
Latham Settlement, 107
Lawndale, Illinois, 110
Leaton, Dr. James, xiii, xiv, 40-41, 86, 131-132, 139-140
    friendship with W.S. Crissey, viii-x, 156-157, 169-170
    as writer of Methodist history, xiv, xvi, 156-157, 169-170, 206, 209, 212
LeBaron, William, Jr., 211
Lexington, Illinois, 89, 208
Lillard, Joseph, 29
Lincoln J, 3-4
Lincoln, Abraham, 179-181
Lincoln's Lost Speech, 179, 180
Livestock of pioneers, 55-56
Log houses, 49-51
Logan County, 30, 69, 106-112, 207, 209
Loneliness of pioneers, 57-59
Long, William, 106
Love of Jesus, 133-134
Lovely Lane Methodist Chapel, Baltimore, 143-145
Lowert, David, 106

Luccock, Halford E., 34-36, 44, 205, 211
Lunn, Henry S., 133-134

Mackinaw Grove, 114. *See also* Old Mackinaw Town
Mackinaw River, 75, 83, 116, 125
Macon County Centennial History, 195-197, 212
Madson, John, 16-17, 22, 24-25, 205, 213
Man-Without-Toe, 111, 210
Marvel, Prettyman, 104, 105
Marvel, Rebecca, 105
Matches,Introduction of, 54
Maxwell, William, 93-94
McCabe, C.B.U., 155
McClun, John Edward, 63
McClure, Robert, 63
McClure, Samuel, 106
McCullough, Peter, 130
McCullough, William, 130
McGraw, John J., 105
McGraw, William, 106
McKendree, William, 35, 40, 139, 140
McLean County, 30, 69, 83, 86-103, 128-131
    history of, 62-63, 206, 207
    map of, 84-85, 214
McManis, Douglas, 205
Merriman, Charles, 94, 207-208, 209, 211
Methodism:
    in America, 30, 143-145
    in Illinois, 31-32, 206, 211
    origin of horse preachers, 135-136
Methodist Episcopal Church, South, 154
Methodist Episcopal Church in America, 29-30. *See also* Conferences

Methodist Episcopal Church in America:
    founding of, 143-145
    Francis Asbury appointed General Superintendent of, 33
    schism with Methodist Episcopal Church, South, 154
Methodist General Conference, 35
    creates Illinois Conference, 41
Methodist Missionary Society, 164
Methodist Quarterly Conference, 136-137
Miller, Henry, 86-87
Miller, Isaac, 153
Mills. *See* Grist mills
Milwaukee (Wisconsin) Station, 161
Missouri Conference, 32, 41
Mitchell, Ebenezer, 129
Mitchell, Rev. Peyton, 102, 129
Moats, Henry, 89
Moberly, Mordecai, 115
Money Creek, 49, 88-89, 208
Moore, Campbell, 126
Moore, Charles, 126
Moore, Colonel James H., 190, 192
Moore, Jacob, 109
Moore, John A., 126, 127, 128
Morgan, J.C., 115
Morgan County, Asiatic cholera in, 78-79, 155
Morris, Bishop Thomas Asbury, 38-40, 163, 164, 168, 174
Morrow, James, 106
Mount Carmel, 156
Mount Pulaski, 106
Musick, Robert, 109, 110, 111, 210

North, Rufus, 115
Northwest Territory, 30

Oatman, Rev., 126
Ogden, Benjamin, 90

223

Old Mackinaw Town, 55, 56, 112, 114-116, 210
Old State Road, 129
Old Stone Methodist Episcopal Church, Cincinnati, 149
Old Town, 93-94, 208
Olio Township, 210
Ollendorf, Benjamin, 110
Ollendorf, Christopher, 110
Ollendorf, Elizabeth, 110
Ollendorf, Joseph, 110
Ollendorf's Mill, 73, 92, 110-111, 209
Ollendorf's Woods, 110
Onstatt, Abraham, 105

Packard, Edmund, 176
Palestine Township, 211
Pantagraph J, 62-63
Panther Creek, 125, 127, 211
Panther Grove, 128
Paoli Circuit, 2, 151-152
Paris, Illinois, 1, 2, 151
Passenger pigeons, 52, 63-65
Past and Present of Woodford County, Illinois, 211
Patton, John, 49, 90, 208
Patton's Creek, 90
Paulding, James Kirke, 19
Peddecord, Woodford W., 192
Pekin, Illinois, 49, 55, 56, 116, 117-119, 121, 210
Pekin Circuit, 77
Pendleton, Preston, 106-107
Peoples, John, 101
Peoples, Robert, 101, 103
Peoria, Illinois, 119. *See also* Fort Clark
Perkins, Major Isaac, 116, 120
Pinkard, J.C., 175
Pioneers:
  clothing of, 56-57
  food of, 54-56

Pioneers:
  furniture of, 52-54
  houses of, 49-51
  illness among, 59-63, 77-79, 155
  livestock of, 55-56
  loneliness of, 57-59
  utensils of, 52-54
Pitner, Rev. Levi, 192-193
Place name:
  Grove as, 21, 71
  Sugar as, 83
Plague. *See* Asiatic cholera
Pleasant Grove, 115, 210
Portrait and Biographical Album of DeWitt and Piatt Counties, Illinois, 209
Pottawatomi Indians, 32, 72-73, 92, 104
Powell, William H., 179
Prairie Creek, 100, 103
Prairie Plants of Illinois, 20-21
Prairie Schooners, 19, 20
Prairie State designation, 22-23, 70
Prairies:
  Crissey's view of, 27-28, 113
  Dickens impression of, 17-18
  fire on, 14-17
  first sightings of, 7-8
  Flower's description of, 5-7
  Gerhard's description of, 11-14
  Hall's description of, 9-11
  Imlay's description of, 5
  from Ollendorf's Mill to Old Mackinaw Town, 112-114
  Paulding's description of, 19
  vegetation on, 20-27
  wildlife on, 51-52
Priest, Franklin, 181
Prophet of the Long Road, 36, 206

Radford, B.J., 210-211
Radford, W.W., 52

Ramkin, Daniel, 116
Randolph, Brooks, 106
Randolph, Gardner, 95, 98
Randolph, James, 106
Randolph, William Patton, 106
Randolph, Willoughby, 106
Randolph Grove (McLean County), 77, 98, 99, 102, 209
Randolph neighborhood (Logan County), 106, 107
Reed, John, 110
Reese, James, 116
Reynolds, John, 38
Richardson, Aaron, 126, 128
Richardson, James M., 126, 128
Robb, Matthew, 129-130
Roberts, Bishop Robert Richford, 152, 160, 164
Rock of Chickamauga, 185
Romance of North America, 20-21
Roosevelt, Theodore, 2-3
Royal, William, 103
Rutledge, Thomas Officer, 98
Sac Indians, 73, 120
Salt, scarcity of, 55
Salt Creek, 92, 105-106, 107
Sams, Alfred, 106
Sams, Edmund, 106
Sand Prairie, 116, 210
Sangamon Circuit, 41
Sangamon County, 107
Sangamon District of Illinois Conference, 69
Sangamon River, 83, 91
Schertz, Joseph, 122
Schorger, Arlie, 64
Scott, James, 105
Scottish Cumberland Presbyterians, 129
Scripps, John, 157, 158-160
Settlers. *See* Pioneers
Sharp, Cassandra. *See* Funk, Cassandra Sharp

Sherman, General, 186, 189
Shugart, Edom, 104
Shugart, Zion, 104
Shugart Mill, 104
Shurtleff, Sylvania, 104, 209
Smith, David, 89
Smith's Grove, 88-89
Snell, Elizabeth, 118
Snell, John S., 119
Snell, Thomas, 118, 119
Snell Schoolhouse, 119
Soulé, Bishop Joshua, 77, 154, 161
Spawr, Jacob, 89
Spawr, Valentine, 89
Spear, Dr. Laren, 203
Springfield, Illinois, 55, 56, 168
Staley, A.E., 164
Stapp, Dr. J.T.B., 167
Steers, John, 89
Stephenson, Nathaniel Wright, 3-4
Sterling, William, 116
Stillman's Run, 120
Story of Methodism, 34-36, 44, 205, 211
Stout, David, 129
Stout, Ephram, 129
Stout, Ephram Jr., 129
Stout's Grove, 128, 128-129, 211
Stretch, Jess, 90
Stringfeld, Alfred, 98
Stringfeld, Severe, 98
Stubblefield, Absalom, 102
Stubblefield, Dorothy Funk, 101, 102
Stubblefield, John, 103
Stubblefield, Robert, 101, 102, 103
Stubblefield, Sarah Funk, 102
Sugar as place name, 83
Sugar Creek, 101, 103, 110
Sugar Grove, 106, 107
Tallgrass prairies. *See* Prairies, vegetation on
Tate, Henry Clay, 62-63, 206

225

Taylor, Elder M.S., 161
Tazewell Circuit, 2, 30, 69-71, 86-132
 division of, 77
 outermost point on, 116

Tazewell County, 69, 114-119, 121-124, 206, 207
Tecumseh (Indian chief), 72-73
Tennessee Conference, 32, 158
 Francis Asbury at, 33, 34-35
Tharp, Jacob, 117-118, 119
Tharp, Jonathan, 117-118
Tharp, Northcott, 117-118
Thomas, General George H., 185
Tipple, Ezra Squier, 36, 205-206
Topographical Description of the Western Territory of North America, 5
Toverca, Thomas, 95, 96
Towanda, Illinois, 88, 208
Tremont, Illinois, 77, 114, 210
Trimmer, David, 86
Trimmer, John, 89
Trout, Michael, 116
Turley, Charles, 109
Twin Grove, 130-131, 211

United Brethren, 90-91
University of Chicago, 205
Utensils of pioneers, 52-54

Van Buskirk family, 89
Vandeventer, Abram, 106
Vandeventer, John, 106
Vansickles, Henry, 130
Vegetation. *See* Prairies, vegetation on

Wabash County, 156
Walden, Jesse, 89
Walker, Jesse, 37-41, 158, 206
 conducts first Illinois camp meeting, 139

Walker, Jesse:
 at Holland's Grove, 123
Wallis, Charles L., 41-42
Walnut Creek, 124
Walnut Grove, 124, 125-127, 210-211
Walnut Grove Academy, 126
Warner and Beers. See Atlas of McLean County and the State of Illinois
Warrick, Montgomery, 106
Washington Township, 210
Watterson, Dr. Arthur, 26
Way It Was in McLean County, 206
Waynesville, Illinois, 103
Wearing apparel of pioneers, 56-57
Webb, Stephen, 130
Wesley, Charles, 143
Wesley, John, 150
 as circuit rider, 135
 dispatches Francis Asbury to colonies, 33
 and fasting, 170-171
 sermons of, 162
Wesley City, 55, 122, 210
Western Conference, 29, 31, 40
Western Portraiture, 14-16
Whatcoat, Richard, 135, 145
Where the Sky Began: Land of the Tallgrass Prairie, 16-17, 22, 205, 213
Wildlife, 51-52
Willis, Francis M., 127, 128, 211
Willis Mill, 127, 211
Wilson, Jacob L., 122
Winning of the West, 2-3
Woodford County, 30, 69, 124-128, 207, 210-211
Wrenn's Grove, 123, 210

Young, Benjamin, 29
Young, Margaret, 52